Praise for *The God of Intimacy and Action*

"An important call to ground our evangelism and social action in a powerful personal relationship with the living God nurtured by regularly seeking the presence of God in our lives. A helpful book on an urgent topic."
—Ronald J. Sider, president, Evangelicals for Social Action

"Wow! What a helpful book! If you, with me, sometimes find that your walk with God is shallow and your service for God ineffective, this book could change your life. This is a book you will value and return to over and over again. When you do, thank me for recommending it to you."
—Steve Brown, professor, Reformed Theological Seminary, Orlando, Florida; author; and teacher on the syndicated radio program *Key Life*

"This is a book that combines action and contemplation so that we can become like Christ and change the world. By combining their love for social justice with a compelling vision of the Christian life, Campolo and Darling offer a wonderful resource for our life with God. I really enjoyed this book and have benefited from it."
—Dr. Gayle D. Beebe, president, Westmont College, Santa Barbara, California

"This book combines years of experience in Christian social activism with a profound spirituality that holds the key to longevity and vitality in ministry. It is a must-read for anyone who wants to be empowered to 'preach good news to the poor, proclaim release to the captives, and recovery of sight to the blind' in a world that so desperately needs it."
—Dr. Brenda Salter McNeil, president, Salter McNeil & Associates, LLC; and coauthor, *The Heart of Racial Justice: How Soul Change Leads to Social Change*

THE GOD OF
Intimacy
AND ACTION

THE GOD OF *Intimacy* AND ACTION

Reconnecting Ancient Spiritual Practices,
Evangelism, and Justice

Tony Campolo and Mary Albert Darling

JOSSEY-BASS
A Wiley Imprint
www.josseybass.com

Published by Jossey-Bass

A Wiley Imprint

989 Market Street, San Francisco, CA 94103-1741   www.josseybass.com

Wiley Bicentennial logo: Richard J. Pacifico

Readers should be aware that Internet Web sites offered as citations and/or sources for further information may have changed or disappeared between the time this was written and when it is read.

Credits are on page 231.

Jossey-Bass books and products are available through most bookstores. To contact Jossey-Bass directly call our Customer Care Department within the U.S. at 800-956-7739, outside the U.S. at 317-572-3986, or fax 317-572-4002.

Jossey-Bass also publishes its books in a variety of electronic formats. Some content that appears in print may not be available in electronic books.

Library of Congress Cataloging-in-Publication Data
Campolo, Anthony.
  The God of intimacy and action: reconnecting ancient spiritual
practices, evangelism, and justice / Tony Campolo and Mary Albert Darling.—1st ed.
    p. cm.
  Includes bibliographical references and index.
  ISBN 978-0-7879-8741-1 (cloth)
  ISBN 978-0-4703-4521-4 (paperback)
  1. Mysticism. 2. Spiritual life—Christianity. I. Darling, Mary Albert.
II. Title.
  BV5082.3.C36 2007
  248.2'2—dc22   2007010268

Printed in the United States of America
FIRST EDITION
HB Printing   10 9 8 7 6 5 4 3 2 1
PB Printing   10 9 8 7 6 5 4 3 2 1

CONTENTS

PART THREE
Taking Intimacy with God into the World
Mary Albert Darling and Tony Campolo

To David and Michael Darling

I pray that you, being rooted and established in love,
may have power, together with all the saints,
to grasp how wide and long and high
and deep is the love of Christ,
and to know this love that surpasses knowledge—
that you may be filled to the measure of all the fullness of God.

—Ephesians 3:17–19 (NIV)

———————

Yahweh our God proclaims:
I put water in the desert of your souls
. . . that you might drink deeply and know Me,
. . . that your thirst for Love may be satisfied and flourish,
. . . that you be filled with abundance and grace to share,
. . . that My Life may take root in you
and spring forth in peace and justice,
. . . that you be empowered to further My Kingdom
and to announce My praise.

—Marcy Keefe-Slager, "Water in the Desert" (based on Isaiah 43:20–21)

ACKNOWLEDGMENTS

WE ARE GRATEFUL to more people than we can name without whose influence and help this book would not have been written. The convictions in it come from years of wanting a deeper and more authentic faith, and wrestling with what that kind of faith looks like—on the inside as well as the outside. Conversations with others, including the numerous "regular" saints and mystics whom we know personally, as well as supersaints we have gotten to know from our readings, have helped shape who we are and what we have tried to articulate in this book.

We want to thank several people by name, taking the risk that we are not mentioning many others who had a significant role in the making of this book, whether or not they realize it. We are especially grateful to:

Sheryl Fullerton, for her impressive editorial instincts, ongoing support, and wise guidance.

Andrew Winckles, for his excellence as our research assistant, and for his willingness to continue to provide exceptional help long after he was supposed to be done.

Mary's sister Judy Hunt, sister-in-law Barbara Darling Smith, husband Terry, and friend Paula Hopper, for each giving many hours of their time helping us to clarify and refine our thoughts.

Oreon Trickey, Paul Nemecek, Robert Moore-Jumonville, Pat Ballard, Becky Hollow, and Lisa Olson, for also reading various parts of the manuscript and offering valuable advice, as well as gracious corrections. Please give them all credit for what you think is expressed well, and if something is not, that probably means we didn't take their advice.

Sarah Blaisdell, for her proofreading and formatting, as well as her helpful ideas for content changes; and James Warren, Tony's executive assistant, for his overall assistance.

Beverly Nemecek, Father Bernie Owens, the Manresa Spiritual Direction class, and Richard Foster: the idea for writing this book came from the ways they have each deeply affected Mary's life.

Spring Arbor University, for granting Mary a sabbatical to work on the book, and to her colleagues Charles White, for helping us both better understand John Wesley's commitment to social reform, and Robert Woods, for his constant encouragement.

We also want to name some people not already mentioned who have significantly influenced our understanding of, and commitment to, what it means to walk with Jesus. Whether it was through their role modeling, insights, challenges, or willingness to try new spiritual practices to live more deeply for Jesus, they have helped us shape and refine not only the ideas in this book, but who we are.

Mary thanks dear friends Deb and Roger, Becky and Royl, Janice, Gloria, Marci, Michaella, Sharon, Marty, Kimberly, Devo, Rob, Dianna, Joan, Wayne, Carla, and Damon; former Spring Arbor University students, especially Bobbie, Jacki, Jaime, Caitlin, Dave and Shelby, Dustin, and Sarah; and her Spiritual Directors' group.

Tony thanks his son Bart, as well as his Tuesday morning breakfast group that gathers in the backroom of Joe's: David Black, Allan Beverly, Rick Eisenstaedt, John Galloway, and James Sweet.

Finally, and most of all, we express our deep gratitude to our families, especially Peggy Campolo and Terry Darling, for being so supportive and patient during this project. We love you.

AN INTRODUCTION TO
MYSTICAL CHRISTIANITY

THE GUIDEBOOK FOR ITALY suggested that a good side trip from Florence would be a visit to the small mountain municipality of Assisi—the one-time home of Francis, the twelfth-century saint known for taking the teachings of Jesus literally as his rule of life. The description of Assisi made the place seem interesting, so my wife and I decided to go there.

I was not prepared for how that small, ancient, walled city in the hills of Umbria would affect me. It was not just the simplicity of the tiny chapel of San Damiano, where Francis first heard the voice of Jesus tell him to rebuild his ruined church, that hushed my noisy mind and heart. Nor was it the solemnity of the cave where Francis and his closest followers were entombed that stirred my soul. Rather, it was a sense that wherever I walked in that peaceful town, I was on holy ground.

Beginning with that visit, I became obsessed with the little saint who called himself "God's fool." Everything about Francis intrigued me. Here was a man who had an intimate and immediate sense of God—a mystic of the highest order. What I learned, however, was that his spirituality did not lead him out of the world, as it would have for other orders of monks, but rather engaged him with the world in ways that would make him a ceaseless evangelist for his Lord, a constant servant of the poor, and a lover of God's creation. It is fair to say that in many ways Francis became my model for a Christian who combined the lifestyle of an evangelist with the commitments of an advocate for the lost and oppressed of the Earth.

That insight about Saint Francis is what motivated me to partner with Mary Albert Darling in writing this book. She, too, had sensed Francis's mystical presence in her own visit to Assisi with her husband and two sons. Plus, Mary had already been a student of the kind of mystical Christianity that generated and sustained the activism of Francis. The spiritual practices of Francis and other Catholic saints and mystics that Mary has been learning about for years opened me up to a wealth of spiritual resources that I, as a Protestant, had not always considered. Francis, as well as other saints such as Ignatius of Loyola, showed me a wellspring from which a stream of living waters flows that can nurture both evangelism and justice. It is from this wellspring that Mary and I want to share.

I have always been both an evangelist and a social activist, but I had a great deal to learn from Mary, who, though Protestant, had spent much time reading and experiencing what Catholic saints can teach us. She helped me weave mystical spirituality, evangelism, and a broad sense of justice together into a seamless garment of a "holistic Christianity." In our conversations we came to realize that mystical Christianity provides the nexus that holds evangelism and justice together and keeps them both dynamic and vital.

In the course of our conversations and readings, we came to recognize that some of the best expressions of this holistic Christianity can be found not only in Catholic saints, but in Protestants too, especially John Wesley, the founder of Methodism. The desire to share what we have been learning from these saints of the church, both Catholic and Protestant, provided the incentive to write this book together. Although Mary and I have each written different sections, we hope that the scope of our collaboration in every chapter is apparent to the reader.

In Part One of the book, I provide a brief survey of how this mystical spirituality has fostered the church in living out its dual mission of evangelism and justice.

In Part Two, Mary tells how she was awakened to this holistic gospel and suggests specific ways to nurture and fuel one's spirituality. She addresses those of us who know that there is something more to Christian living than right beliefs and right behavior. Part Two speaks to those who want to experience the love and acceptance of God; be empowered by the indwelling presence and dynamism of the Holy Spirit; and sense a personal intimacy and unity with Christ that will compel the sharing of the good news in word and in action.

In Part Three, Mary offers in Chapter Ten strong warnings about committing to only part of Jesus' gospel. In Chapter Eleven, I describe some current examples of how the kind of mystical spirituality we are talking about inspires and empowers not only individuals, but communities, to the holistic gospel of Jesus Christ. In the Postscript, I indicate why this is the kind of Christianity our hearts long to experience.

THE GOD OF
Intimacy
AND ACTION

PART ONE

KNOWING GOD INTIMATELY

WHERE CHRISTIAN MYSTICISM CAN TAKE US

Tony Campolo

WHAT MYSTICAL CHRISTIANITY IS ALL ABOUT

*The Christian of the future will be a mystic,
or he or she will not exist at all.*

—Karl Rahner, *The Practice of Faith* (1983)

THIS BOOK IS ABOUT spirituality. It is about how ordinary people can mystically experience God in the depths of their beings and the ways in which such experiences transform them. When we were drawing up plans to write this book, Mary was concerned that the words *mystic* and *mystical* would present difficulties for some readers. She worried that some might think that we were into a kind of New Age religiosity, even though she knew from her studies and personal experience that certain forms of mysticism have always been, and still are, a vital part of Christianity. We finally decided to use the term "mystical Christianity" to distinguish the kind of spirituality we are advocating from other forms known in the Christian community. For instance, using the word *mystical* makes it clear that the Christian spirituality that we are discussing here is not to be confused with the kind used as a synonym for personal piety, which too often comes with destructive legalism, or scholastic Christianity, which can reduce faith to theological propositions. Both of these kinds of spirituality can lead to a loveless religion, which the Apostle Paul strongly warned against when he wrote, "If I speak in the tongues of mortals and of angels, but do not have love, I am a noisy gong or a clanging cymbal" (I Corinthians 13:1).

This book is about tapping into the love and reality that go beyond what rules and reason alone can apprehend. We want to show how daily moments marked by mystical revelations of God's love reveal the limits of propositional truth. As Paul wrote to the church in Corinth, "This is what we speak, not in words taught us by human wisdom but in words taught by the Spirit, expressing spiritual truths in spiritual words. The man without the Spirit does not accept the things that come from the Spirit of God, for they are foolishness to him, and he cannot understand them, because they are spiritually discerned" (I Corinthians 2:12–14).

When we use the word *mystical* we are referring to experiences that involve being filled with this same Spirit. This is Christian mysticism. William James, in his book *The Varieties of Religious Experience,*[1] helps us see a variety of ways in which the Holy Spirit works in our lives, even though James was not writing specifically from a Christian perspective. For James, mystical experiences transcend rational description, can defy verbal expression, and, although at times short-lived, can provide a special sense of intimate "knowing" that has a profound effect on those who have them. A mystic, therefore, is one who experiences God in transrational and nonempirical ways. This kind of transcendent intimacy with God is what is involved in "getting to know Jesus" and being "born again."

Types of Mystical Experiences

Although there are many types of mystical experiences, I explore five of them that are particularly relevant to increasing our intimacy with God: new insights, I-thou relationships, heightened awareness, conversion experiences, and breakthrough experiences. Most of us will readily admit, upon reflection, that we have experienced at least some of these.

New Insights

First, there is a kind of mystical experience that breaks into the consciousness when something you have experienced before is suddenly, with no conscious effort, perceived in a new and more profound way. This can be such a common experience that most people are reluctant to even call it mystical. Something akin to this may happen to a Christian who, while reading scripture under the influence of the Holy Spirit, suddenly gains a new and profound insight or truth. You are apt to hear the person say, "I've read that passage a hundred times, but I never before understood what I understand now." It is as though there has been a revelation from

God, and the reader cannot help but feel a special excitement upon discovering this new and deeper meaning of that scriptural passage.

Most of us have had such moments of insight when we see familiar things in completely new ways. This is something of what Jesus predicted when he told his disciples, "When the Spirit of truth comes, he will guide you into all the truth; for he will not speak on his own, but will speak whatever he hears, and he will declare to you the things that are to come" (John 16:13).

We hope that the spiritual practices that Mary lays out in Part Two of this book will make those who commit to them more ready for and susceptible to such moments of revelation. One of our prime goals is to enable you to find richer meanings in your reading of scripture and to gain an enhanced capacity for listening to what God is trying to say to you as you read.

I-Thou Relationships

The second kind of mystical experience involves a special subjective connectedness with another being. Martin Buber, a twentieth-century Austrian Jewish philosopher, translator, and educator, in his classic book *I and Thou*,[2] helps us understand something of what happens during such mystical encounters. Although Buber wrote mainly about such interactions with humans, he also believed that these encounters can occur with nonhumans as well. Buber distinguishes between knowing objectively *about* another being and *knowing* that being. For example, when we know *about* someone we might have pertinent information regarding that person, but that data fails to connect us with that person's essential self. Buber called this an "I-it" relationship.

Beyond these I-it relationships, in which other people or animals are viewed as objects or "things out there in the world," there are mystical encounters that Buber calls "I-thou" relationships, in which we connect with others in such a way that we feel a oneness of mind and heart. These I-thou experiences prove to be so profound that each individual feels he or she knows the deepest thoughts and emotions of the other. In such encounters there is a spiritual unity so intense that it seems that each knows the other as if he or she *is* the other. These are holy moments and are, in part, what the Apostle Paul was trying to explain to us when, in his great love chapter, he wrote, "For now we see in a mirror, dimly, but then we will see face to face. Now I know only in part; then I will know fully, even as I have been fully known" (I Corinthians 13:12).

Jesus had the capacity for these I-thou encounters *par excellence*. The Bible tells us that "he himself knew what was in everyone" (John 2:25).

Whenever we imagine how Jesus interacted with people, it would help if we tried to understand them in terms of these I-thou encounters.

Heightened Awareness

The third kind of mystical spirituality is that in which the Christian senses a "hyperawareness" of the glorious presence of God in the everyday experiences of life. The spiritually alive person enjoys the ordinary things in life in a most extraordinary manner. All of us can experience Christ in more mystically transforming ways by starting with the ordinary—it is as simple as that. Through these inklings of mysticism, we begin to see our lives and the world with a new awareness.

In Thornton Wilder's play *Our Town,* the main character, Emily, discovers the joy of being fully alive too late. After she dies, she pleads to be allowed to return and look in on one day of her life, one last time. She picks her twelfth birthday. During the play, Emily becomes dismayed as she recognizes how little the people she loves comprehend the joys of life or experience them with any depth of awareness. She cries out to be taken away, so that she does not have to witness how little her family and friends pay attention to the preciousness of life. Listen to Emily's words:

> Goodbye, Grover's Corners. . . . Goodbye to clocks ticking . . . and Mama's sunflowers—and food and coffee—and new-ironed dresses and hot baths—and sleeping and waking up! Oh earth, you're too wonderful for anyone to realize you! Do any human beings ever realize life while they live it—every, every minute?[3]

One of the marks of mystical Christianity is a growing awareness of the wonders of our everyday, ordinary experiences, which leads to a greater sense of how precious the ordinary really is. As writer and minister Frederick Buechner once said, "There is no event so common place but that God is present within it, always hidden, always leaving you room to recognize Him or not to recognize Him."[4]

I hope that everyone can have those mystical times when, endowed by the Holy Spirit, the world comes alive in ways that thrill the soul. The grass appears greener, the sun shines brighter, the flowers exhibit new and magnificent luster, and the whole Earth radiates beauty that is almost intoxicating. As Paul told us in Romans 8:10, those of us who were experiencing a deadness to life are suddenly "made alive." We experience life in a new way in these moments, and we experience it "more abundantly" (John 10:10 KJV).

A "heightened awareness" type of mystical spirituality not only changes the way we perceive the world, it also infuses the ordinary experiences of everyday life with a mysterious thrill and a divinely inspired meaning. This is the kind of spirituality that is movingly taught in the writings of Brother Lawrence. This seventeenth-century Catholic saint showed us ways to "practice the presence of God," so that even while completing his mundane chores in the kitchen of his monastery he consciously moved his heart and mind toward God. We too need to cul-

> *One of the marks of mystical Christianity is a growing awareness of the wonders of our everyday, ordinary experiences.*

tivate mystical moments such as these so as to better see the holy in the everyday places of our lives, as Brother Lawrence did—even in the pots and pans. He prayed, "Lord of all pots and pans and things . . . make me a saint by getting meals and washing up the plates!"[5] For Brother Lawrence, his time of daily chores did not differ from his time of prayer. He said he could "possess God in as great tranquility"[6] in the midst of the bustle and clatter of the kitchen as he could when he was on his knees, alone with God. That is because he took great pains to do each task purely for the love of God, praying throughout his day for the strength to do this. Whenever his mind wandered, he brought it back to God "always as *with me* as well as *in me.*"[7] Brother Lawrence eventually came to a state where he could say, "It would be difficult for me not to think of God as it was at first to accustom myself to it."[8] He had learned to live with his mind "stayed on Thee" (Isaiah 26:3 KJV).This glorying in the ordinary is a kind of mysticism that can make our lives into heaven on earth.

There is an ancient saying: "Before enlightenment—chop wood, carry water. After enlightenment—chop wood, carry water." Those who become spiritually alive in the ordinary may go on doing the same things they did before, but they will do them with an entirely new frame of mind and heart. Everything will be changed. In scripture we are told, "Whatever you do, work at it with all your heart, as working for the Lord, not for men" (Colossians 3:23 NIV). Putting ourselves into *every* task, as the scripture tells us, requires that we be invaded by the Holy Spirit in such a way as to energize us and give us passion in all that we do.

All three of these kinds of mystical spirituality are available to anyone who is open to an invasion of the self by the Holy Spirit. There is no need, as an old hymn suggests, to have some supernatural dream or some prophet's ecstasy. Anyone who prays to God for redemption through the life, death, and resurrection of Jesus Christ can have these experiences. They can then be cultivated through spiritual practices and prayerful supplications such as those described in Part Two of this book.

These spiritual disciplines can make us ready to daily receive the infilling of the Spirit of Christ that gives us life. We are instructed in scripture to "watch and pray" (Mark 13:33) and to "wait patiently" (Romans 8:25) because the Spirit "blows where it chooses, and you hear the sound of it, but you do not know where it comes from or where it goes" (John 3:8). We know that we cannot control the Holy Spirit, but we also know that we can prepare our hearts and minds so that "at the midnight hour" when the Holy One comes, we will be like the wise virgins in Jesus' parable, and will be ready to receive the Holy Spirit and be married into an intimacy (Matthew 25:1–13) that will transform us and empower us to help transform the world. It is to that end that we write this book.

Conversion Experiences

The fourth kind of mystical experience that is regularly reported is often associated with sudden and transforming conversions. There are those who, on special occasions, hear and respond to the gospel and report being overwhelmed by God in dramatic ways. William James reports such conversions in *Varieties of Religious Experience*. One woman who was converted in this manner said:

> I was taken to a camp-meeting, mother and religious friends seeking and praying for my conversion. My emotional nature was stirred to its depths; confessions of depravity and pleading with God for salvation from sin made me oblivious of all surroundings. I pled for mercy, and had a vivid realization of forgiveness and renewal of my nature. When rising from my knees I exclaimed, "Old things have passed away, all things have become new." It was like entering another world, a new state of existence. Natural objects were glorified, my spiritual vision was so clarified that I saw beauty in every material object in the universe, the woods were vocal with heavenly music; my soul exulted in the love of God, and I wanted everybody to share my joy.[9]

While other testimonies are less dramatic, all of them, as William James says, denote experiences whereby "a self hitherto divided, consciously

wrong, inferior and unhappy, becomes unified as consciously right, superior and happy, in consequence of its firmer hold upon religious realities."[10] All segments of the evangelical community affirm the validity of
such conversion experiences. The evangelist Billy Graham has, through
his preaching crusades, made conversions of this kind an almost norma-
tive part of American religion.

Breakthrough Experiences

There is still another kind of mysticism exemplified by those whom Mary
and I call the "supersaints," people who have been caught up into some
mystical unity with God and who have enjoyed a kind of heavenly
"breakthrough" experience that can only be called miraculous.

Moses was such a supersaint. When Moses encountered God on Mount
Sinai, he experienced something spiritual that other godly persons will
never enjoy in this life. The scripture tells us of this experience in Exodus
34:4–5: "So Moses cut two tablets of stone like the former ones; and he
rose early in the morning and went up on Mount Sinai, as the LORD had
commanded him, and took in his hand the two tablets of stone. The
LORD descended in the cloud and stood with him there, and proclaimed
the name, 'The LORD.'" The experience was so awesome for Moses that
he removed his sandals because he sensed that he was standing on holy
ground. This was not just an ordinary place and an ordinary experience;
it was God breaking into Moses' world in a miraculous manner.

Consider also the experiences of the Apostle Paul. While he never met
Jesus while Jesus walked the earth, Paul nevertheless claims that he was
once personally taught by Jesus after being taken up into heaven to meet
with him. Paul wrote in his second letter to the Corinthians 12:1–4, "It is
necessary to boast; nothing is to be gained by it, but I will go on to visions
and revelations of the Lord. I know a person in Christ who fourteen years
ago was caught up to the third heaven—whether in the body or out of the
body I do not know; God knows. And I know that such a person—
whether in the body or out of the body I do not know; God knows—was
caught up into Paradise and heard things that are not to be told, that no
mortal is permitted to repeat."

Since Bible times there have been other supersaints who have had
breakthrough mystical experiences with God that, while they do not have
the same authority as the supersaints in the Bible, still challenge us and
give us, if we are candid, a certain sense of uneasiness. This latter group
of supersaints includes Catholics and Protestants alike. Among the
Catholics, we list Saints Francis of Assisi, Ignatius of Loyola, Augustine

of Hippo, Teresa of Avila, and Catherine of Siena. Each of these, along with many others, had experiences that the German scholar Rudolph Otto calls the "*mysterium tremendum.*"[11] These are experiences wherein God breaks into the lives of Christians at certain times so that they experience an ecstatic unity with God that transcends what most will ever know this side of heaven.

Saint Augustine described one such mystical ecstasy this way:

> And I . . . beheld with the eye of my soul (such as it was), above the same eye of my soul, above my mind, the Light Unchangeable. Not this ordinary light, which all flesh may look upon, nor as it were a greater of the same kind, as though the brightness of this should be manifold brighter, and with its greatness take up all space. . . . He that knows the Truth, knows what that Light is; and he that knows It, knows eternity. Love knoweth it. O Truth Who art Eternity! And Love Who art Truth! And Eternity Who art Love! Thou art my God, to Thee do I sigh night and day. Thee when I first knew, thou liftedst me up, that I might see there was what I might see, and that I was not yet such as to see. And thou didst beat back the weakness of my sight, streaming forth Thy beams of light upon me most strongly, and I trembled with love and awe.[12]

On the Protestant side, although leaders like John Wesley, the founder of Methodism, learned much from the Catholic mystics, there has been a shying away from their ecstasies among mainline Protestants. Nevertheless, there are testimonies that should not be ignored. Consider this one from John Bunyan, author of the seventeenth-century classic *The Pilgrim's Progress:*

> The glory of these words was then so weighty on me that I was . . . ready to swoon as I sat; yet not with grief and trouble, but with solid joy and peace. . . . This made a strange seizure on my spirit; it brought light with it, and commanded a silence in my heart of all those tumultuous thoughts that before did use, like masterless hell-hounds, to roar and bellow and make a hideous noise within me. It showed me that . . . Jesus Christ had not quite forsaken and cast off my soul. . . . Now could I see myself in Heaven and Earth at once; in Heaven by my Christ, by my Head, by my Righteousness and Life, though on Earth my body or person. . . . Christ was a precious Christ to my soul that night; I could scarce lie in my bed for joy and peace and triumph through Christ.[13]

Christians do not have to be supersaints to have breakthrough mystical experiences. Mary's mom, for example, told her about an experience she had on the day Mary's dad died. Her mom was called to the emergency room, having just learned that her husband had collapsed suddenly on the golf course. Although paramedics worked on his heart for 45 minutes, they were unable to revive him. When Mary's mom walked into the emergency room, she saw a ball of light between her and her husband. She could not see her husband without looking through that light. No one else saw the ball of light, but she knew it was the light of Christ. Mary believes that God gave her mother miraculous assurance of Christ's presence at that moment. This was no psychological illusion; her mother *knew* it was a mystical revelation.

We may readily accept biblical examples of these kinds of mystical experiences and yet have trouble with them in today's world. We need to honestly ask ourselves why we might criticize, ignore, or shy away from our own and others' mystical experiences with Christ. Is it because even in our postmodern times we still make scientific reasoning the foundation for all other experiences? Or could it even be that we are somewhat envious of others' experiences? If we discount these feelings and experiences and events, then we do not have to wonder why we do not have them too. These are important questions to ask, so that we can discern any blocking of the Spirit in our lives and do not hinder the Spirit's work in others' lives.

I admit that when others' mystical experiences have been described to me, my skeptical side can at times kick in. That's okay, because we are told in I John 4:1 to "test the Spirits" to see if they are from God. We must pay serious attention to mystical happenings, and discern, in the context of biblical understanding in Christian community, whether or not we believe they are of God. Discernment is crucial to mystical spirituality. Without it, anything goes. On the other hand, we must learn to doubt our doubts if we are going to be open to the work of the Spirit in our lives. Throughout the book we talk about a variety of ways to discern what may or may not be of God.

While certain kinds of mystical experiences may be foreign to many of us ordinary saints, mystical experiences, especially those of supersaints, can teach the rest of us a great deal about God and spiritual growth. The ways that these people lived their everyday lives and the spiritual disciplines that they employed can show the rest of us some vital ways to intensify our love for God and for others. Mary and I draw from their teachings and their daily devotional lives—especially the spirituality of

Saint Ignatius—in our exploration of what it means for us ordinary saints to try to live out our lives in love of and service to God and others. We do our best to show how nurturing intimacy with Christ, by following the practical guidance of these supersaints, can do two things: first, create within us a passionate evangelistic drive to bring others into transforming relationships with Christ, and, second, generate an intense commitment to work for justice.

We are *not* saying here that the kind of spiritual practices we are proposing are the only way to encounter God. God meets us and we meet God in all kinds of ways, including rituals such as communion, listening to sermons, studying scripture and other readings, and, as mentioned, experiencing unexpected awareness of God in people and places throughout our days. But we *are* saying that encounters with God, without an intentional plan for consistent growth in intimacy with Christ, will not, as a rule, produce people who are transformed into Christ's likeness. We need to be involved in regular spiritual practices that will develop and deepen our intimacy with Jesus so that we can be more like him in who we are and in what we do.

Cultivating the Good Soil of Our Spiritual Lives

Many Protestant Christians, in particular evangelical Christians, have abandoned numerous spiritual practices that the ancient Catholic mystics prescribed because they say, in line with John Wesley's critique, that any methodology used as a way to try to reach God is a form of "salvation by works" as opposed to salvation by grace alone. The evangelical Protestant faith tradition strongly emphasizes that salvation results from God reaching down to us rather than us reaching up toward God. "Salvation," declare evangelicals, "does not come from what we do, but is a gift of God, according to Ephesians 2:8–9: 'For by grace you have been saved through faith, and this is not your own doing; it is the gift of God—not the result of works, so that no one may boast.'" To many evangelical Protestants, being connected to God through *human* efforts diminishes the truth that our salvation is by grace. There is nothing that we can do to make us recipients of the blessings that they believe can only come through the grace of God.

Perhaps the resolution to this seeming impasse between intentional spiritual practices and grace can be found in Jesus' parable of the sower in Matthew 13:3–9:

> Listen! A sower went out to sow. And as he sowed, some seeds fell on the path, and the birds of the air came and ate them up. Other seeds fell

on rocky ground, where they did not have much soil, and they sprang up quickly, since they had no depth of soil. But when the sun rose, they were scorched; and since they had no root, they withered away. Other seeds fell among thorns, and the thorns grew up and choked them. Other seeds fell on good soil and brought forth grain, some a hundred-fold, some sixty, some thirty. Let anyone with ears listen!

In this parable, Jesus makes it clear that seeds are the blessings of God, which by grace are scattered on various kinds of soil. Most seeds, as he later explains in this chapter of Matthew, fall on soil that is, for one reason or another, incapable of receiving these seeds and producing plants that bear fruit. Jesus compares the nonproductive soil to people God blesses who prove unable to receive these blessings and then produce blessings for themselves and for others. There are those who never really understand what the blessings are about and are easily victims of "the wicked one." Others might have some experiences with God but never develop enough depth through spiritual disciplines to enable their faith to survive the hard times or the persecution that Christians often have to endure. Still others, said Jesus, are like those who fail to enjoy the benefits of God's grace because they are seduced into the materialistic and consumerist values of the dominant culture, which keep them from the kind of self-surrender that spirituality requires. However, Jesus ends his explanation of the parable (Matthew 13:18–23) by making it clear that there are those who, like good soil, can receive what God wants to give all of us and make their lives blessings to themselves and all whose lives they touch.

What is important about this parable, for our discussion, is our belief that while the spiritual blessings of some—if not all—of the kinds of mystical experiences that we describe are available to any who really want them, only those individuals who are prepared to receive these blessings will consistently be transformed by them. What we hope to do in this book is explain how to be those prepared people.

The key to this preparation lies in the definition of Christian mysticism that comes from author and speaker Emilie Griffin, in her book *Wonderful and Dark Is This Road: Discovering the Mystic Path.* She views mysticism as "a deep and sustained intimacy with a loving God, sometimes marked and dramatic in its emotionality, more often anonymous and invisible to the casual observer."[14] Because intimacy is at the heart of what it means to be a Christian mystic, it is important to understand this word in a biblical context. Its Latin root is *intimare,* meaning "to make known," and *intimus,* "innermost." The Hebrew word for "know" is *ya da,* which means to know intimately. Intimacy is relational, in the sense of getting to know someone's character and essence. Paul said in Philippians 3:10–11,

"I want to know Christ and the power of his resurrection and the sharing of his sufferings by becoming like him in his death, if somehow I may attain the resurrection from the dead." This kind of intimate knowing cannot come from reason alone; it comes from being deeply connected to Christ through mystical experiences.

In mystical Christianity we go beyond what our rational minds can comprehend. As Blaise Pascal, a French mathematician, physicist, and religious philosopher of the seventeenth century, once said, "The heart has reasons which reason can not know."[15] What we are talking about in this book is a kind of spirituality through which the Spirit of God, the Holy Spirit, is mystically alive in us, empowering us to do the work of God. It is this kind of intimacy that Jesus hoped we might have with him and with one another when in Gethsemane he prayed "that they may all be one. As you, Father, are in me and I am in you, may they also be in us, so that the world may believe that you have sent me" (John 17:21). Jesus desired that we all might have the kind of turning to him, or "conversion," that leads to mystical intimacy and unity with God and with one another.

> *Intimacy is at the heart of what it means to be a Christian mystic.*

The ultimate goal for the ancient mystics was union between the mystic and God. Mary and I contend that the goal is a unity with God that involves a connectedness with those around us—especially the poor and oppressed. Ultimately this means eliminating the barriers between ourselves and God and the barriers between us and the rest of creation. This, we say, is the kind of unity with God that Jesus expressed in the "Greatest Commandment" (Matthew 22:37 NIV). After telling us that we are to love God with heart, soul, and mind, he goes on to say, "The second commandment is like it"—in other words, the same thing—to "love your neighbor as yourself." Loving God, Jesus tells us, involves loving our neighbor. In I John 4:20 we are told, "For anyone who does not love his brother, whom he has seen, cannot love God, whom he has not seen." This is because the God we want to love mystically waits to be encountered in our neighbor (see Matthew 25:37–40).

Connecting Mystical Intimacy to Transformation

Emilie Griffin, in her discussion of mystical intimacy, does not disconnect intimacy from our work in the world. She writes, "The unitive life is an intimacy with God which continues in the day-to-day course of our existence. Mysticism transforms," she says, "but does not take us out of the human condition."[16] Virtually all Christians agree that conversion to Christ means that we are to be transformed people (Romans 12:2), but they do not necessarily agree on what that transformation involves. Most would say that sharing their faith with others (in the sense of traditional evangelism) and serving others (in the sense of social action) are two essential tasks of the church. Many individuals and churches, however, have emphasized only one of these responsibilities of conversion at the expense of the other and have not even considered the responsibility we might have to care for other aspects of God's creation. To make a sweeping generalization, mainline churches have tended to emphasize the social concerns of the gospel while evangelical congregations have focused on winning converts. However, many individuals, as well as churches, are realizing that something is missing.

Many Christians are questioning whether evangelicals care enough about trying to change the political and economic institutions of our society so that they will provide equal justice for all of its citizens; protect other animals and the environment; and end poverty for those who have been shut out of the American Dream. On the other hand, there are those who primarily preach a social gospel but are wondering if they have neglected that more personal connection with God that is so much at the core of contemporary evangelicalism. In both mainline and evangelical churches, congregations are coming to realize that if the whole gospel is to be lived out, it cannot be a matter of either-or. Instead, it *must* be both-and. Unless those who are won to a personal relationship with Christ are incorporated into local congregations, churches will die; and unless these local congregations are also equipping their people to work for justice issues, especially on behalf of any who are poor and oppressed, they are failing to live out biblical mandates, and their religious lives could become narcissistic.

That much seems clear, but how can we establish an organic connection between these two essential parts of the mission of the church so that they are fully integrated? This book seeks to answer that question. We believe that the nexus between evangelism and justice is to be found in the kind of Christian mysticism we are advocating.

We contend that being "fully devoted followers of Christ," a phrase popular with many evangelical churches today, involves commitment to what Jesus was committed to: maintaining a deep, mystical connection to God that empowered him to be compassionately connected to others, particularly the outcasts of society. Jesus wanted all to know God personally and enjoy the benefits of the "full life" that God intends for all people.

Jesus' times alone with God and the Holy Spirit resulted in his being "moved with compassion" toward others. Compassion always led to action. While in the wilderness for forty days and nights Jesus resisted the devil by quoting scripture. This was not because he had just *studied* scripture; he had drawn strength and power by having those holy words absorbed into his spirit. Jesus then "returned in the power of the Spirit" (Luke 4:14); two of his initial acts involved preaching and advocating justice. In Matthew 4:17–19, we learn that Jesus began to preach and also called his disciples to follow him. In Luke 4:18–19, Jesus declared his commitment to justice by proclaiming the year of jubilee—freedom for all, whether poor, oppressed, or captive. This theme of economic justice permeates the Gospels, especially the Gospel of Luke. As modeled by Jesus, mystical intimacy with God truly empowers our ability to carry out his mission of evangelism and justice.

From the earliest days of Christianity, when a mystical relationship with Jesus Christ was nurtured in accord with biblical guidelines, the result was the church zealously at work winning persons to a transforming relationship with Jesus and, at the same time, passionately pursuing justice. In the New Testament church, there was no disconnect between the two. Each naturally flowed into the other. We are told in Acts that

> they devoted themselves to the apostles' teaching and fellowship, to the breaking of bread and the prayers. Awe came upon everyone, because many wonders and signs were being done by the apostles. All who believed were together and had all things in common; they would sell their possessions and goods and distribute the proceeds to all, as any had need. Day by day, as they spent much time together in the temple, they broke bread at home and ate their food with glad and generous hearts, praising God and having the goodwill of all the people. And day by day the Lord added to their number those who were being saved. (Acts 2:42–47)

But that is not the norm in Christendom today.

What happened?

As time went by, and the church became more institutionalized, an inevitable consequence was to tone down the radical justice imperatives prescribed hundreds of times throughout the Bible. Emperors, kings, and other rulers seldom want to hear about a God who came into the world to bring justice by taking down the mighty and lifting up those of low degree. Nor do rich rulers want Christians to endeavor to follow the teachings of a Savior who would see to it that the hungry would be fed while the rich would be sent away empty (Luke 1:51–53). The directives to live Jesus' radical gospel are diminished when Christianity becomes a cultural religion, as it did under the Emperor Constantine in the fourth century and at other times since then. Philosopher Søren Kierkegaard said that in a society where everyone is Christian, no one is Christian.[17] In such societies, biblical imperatives get watered down to the lowest common denominator. The radical nature of Jesus' life and message becomes something of a curiosity at best, or a threat at worst, to those who are seduced into believing that following Jesus is nothing more than being a nice, honest, and decent citizen. It is much more than that.

A Holistic Gospel

Donal Dorr, a Catholic missionary, theologian, and philosopher, in his book *Spirituality and Justice* talks about conversion as having three components: personal, interpersonal, and societal or political. He bases this idea on the verse that says, "And this is what God requires of you: to do justice, love tenderly, and walk humbly with your God." (Micah 6:8)

Dorr defines a personal conversion to Christ, whether sudden or gradual, as involving the awareness that one is loved by God, who shows this incredible love through the life, death, and resurrection of Jesus. I am required not only to understand this love intellectually but also to experience it in a subjective transformation of my inner self, which comes as a consequence of yielding to being possessed by God's Spirit. In other words, to be "personally" converted to Christ and thereby to "walk humbly with our God," I need to accept and then live intimately connected to this life-saving love.

In the interpersonal component of conversion, I become convinced that my relationship with Christ calls me to "love tenderly" in relationship to my friends, family, community, and even casual acquaintances. I become more other-centered, even to the point of experiencing Martin Buber's "I-thou" encounters. Both Mary and I have seen numerous examples of this kind of loving, interpersonal component in our own communities. Whenever someone expresses a need, the church and university communities in both Spring Arbor and Saint Davids come together in loving, practical ways to help one another. It might be anything from providing meals to someone who is sick to helping out a family with financial needs. And these are not atypical examples. Christians seem especially good at "loving tenderly" in their own communities.

In addition to the emphasis on caring for one another, we add to Dorr's second component a need to intentionally share the gospel story with those who have not heard, based on Jesus' mandate to go into the world and make disciples (Matthew 28:10). This interpersonal component would also then include helping those who commit to this gospel story connect to a faith community in which they can grow in Christ-likeness.

The third component, to "do justice," is societal and therefore also political. That means I not only realize I am to love others in my local or interpersonal sphere, but in my work in the broader world as well. This does not only entail trying to be honest and nice in business affairs; it is about something much bigger—being converted to Christ requires that my eyes be opened to how society is structured, particularly in ways that favor certain groups to the detriment of others. This conversion implies that I am to work at a systemic level to build societies that are intrinsically just, with just infrastructures. Dorr's third component is about "constructing a society in which minorities such as homeless people are not discriminated against either in laws or in practice; and a society in which women are not second-class citizens. It means struggling against the bias in our present society, a bias which enables the better-off people to widen the gap between themselves and the poor."[18] We also expand on this component to include being advocates for the world beyond humans. God created the sky, water, land, vegetation, and animals, and God called them good. If we love God, we are to value and restore whatever God created and called good.

When we read about these three components, we may be tempted to consciously or unconsciously rate them, depending on our own or our church's emphasis. The first (a personal connection to God), for example, we see as essential. The second (interpersonal relationships) probably is too, since even if it is not manifested in our attitudes or actions, we still most likely pay lip service to its importance. But the third (doing justice) is optional for far too many of us; and even those who see its value may still think it is a calling for others, not for them. Dorr, however, contends that none is optional, and Mary and I agree. These are not components from which we pick and choose. To do that is to distort the Christian faith. Being personally converted to Jesus Christ means having the interpersonal as well as the social and creation justice components, or there has been no conversion to the whole gospel of Jesus Christ. As our friend Jaime, who lives in Oakland, California, said in a letter sent to Mary, "Too often Christians are so busy trying to fight for people's salvation, they forget to fight for their lives. It is not just about people saying a magic phrase that invites Jesus into their hearts. . . . I want them to experience Jesus' love in a way that not only impacts their eternity, but in a way that impacts and changes their *now*."

Saint Francis is someone who not only understood this holistic gospel but lived it in an empowered simplicity. He was unencumbered with the kinds of philosophical and theological subtleties that enable so many of us to escape from its requirements. Can we, too, live in such a way that we do not escape its requirements? Can we live in harmony with all three parts of the gospel—spiritual intimacy, evangelism, and justice? Is everyone called to develop mystical intimacy with Jesus? Is everyone expected to share Christ through evangelism and justice? Although the answer to these questions is *yes,* that does not mean that we give equal weight to all elements in our lives. Each of us is called by Christ to manifest some ways of living for Jesus more than others, as Paul talks about in his discussion of spiritual gifts in I Corinthians 12–14. But living with our spiritual gifts does not mean we pay exclusive attention to only one part of the gospel. For example, we may be called to teach what it means to have intimacy with Christ; we may be called to share Jesus through evangelism; we may be called to work more intentionally for social or other earthly changes. But no matter our calling, each of us is to be involved in an ongoing intimate relationship with Jesus, each of us is to always be ready to give "an accounting for the hope that is in [us]" (I Peter 3:15), and each of us is to minister to the poor and to whoever or whatever in God's creation is oppressed. This means not only working to meet any short-term needs, but also being willing to work toward building a world that is more just. All three are part of Jesus' gospel, and each of us is called to express all three. The degrees to which these are conveyed in individuals' lives may differ, but none is optional, even if we are not attracted to one or more of them.

We must all be in the business of connecting how we live with how we are affecting others who may be lost in their souls or in the system but are no less loved by God—no matter why they are lost, since Jesus came to save and serve us all. We therefore connect by asking ourselves questions such as these:

Are we sharing the loving, redeeming message of Christ with others?

Are we caring for our own family, our friends, and others in our social sphere?

Are we championing the rights of those who cannot champion their own rights?

Are we using our resources, such as our time, money, and our right to vote, to help the oppressed—both human and nonhuman—have a more acceptable quality of life?

These are not just individual questions, since we cannot carry out Jesus' holistic gospel single-handedly. We and others, as the body of Christ, can only accomplish this mission by being incorporated into vital churches wherein people with differing gifts and callings can complement one another, encourage and build up one another, and support one another's respective ministries, all in the context of helping God's Kingdom to come, God's will to be done, *on earth* as it is in heaven. To do this, we believe these Christian communities need the kind of mystical spirituality that early Christians practiced and that gives impetus both to evangelism and to justice efforts. In this book we outline how that spirituality can be developed.

The Body of Christ

There is something crucial that we need to add when talking about this holistic worldview: the meaning of the biblical phrase "Christ in us" in relation to our being the body of Christ. There are no believers who will question that Christ is always *with* us. As a matter of fact, before Jesus was ever born, Christ was. Christ is the Alpha and Omega, the beginning and the end. Christ was before the creation of the world, and Christ is the one who created the universe, as we are told in the beginning of the first chapter of the Gospel of John. But two thousand years ago the Christ that always was took on human flesh. He was born in Bethlehem's manger. He lived among us as a human being and we called him Jesus. Jesus was the body of Christ; the body through which the eternal Christ brought personal and social transformation into human history. It was through that body—the body of Jesus—that Christ lived out love and rendered compassionate service to those who were in need.

> *Christian communities need the kind of mystical spirituality . . . that gives impetus both to evangelism and to justice efforts.*

In John 14:20, Jesus tells his disciples that he will be leaving them but that when he returns he will be *in* them. The same Christ who was in Jesus would be in those disciples and in anyone who would surrender to being invaded by his presence, all for the purpose of becoming "completely one" in God (John 17:23).

Being converted is allowing ourselves to become the body of Christ. Just as Jesus was the "then" body of Christ, so we are the "now" body. If you are thinking that it is one thing to say that Christ was alive in Jesus but quite another to say that Christ is alive in us, you are wrong! The Bible says that to be converted is to become the body of Christ (I Corinthians 12:27). The Apostle Paul in Romans 8:11 made it clear that the same Spirit that was in Jesus will be alive in our "mortal bodies." As shocking as this may appear, it is true. In light of this reality, we can begin to understand why Paul was so adamant when he said in Ephesians 4:1, "live a life worthy of the calling you have received" (NIV). All of us are called to be so mystically possessed by Christ that we become Christ's "now" body through which the gospel is preached to the lost and through which the poor and oppressed are blessed with hope and justice.

2

CHRISTIAN MYSTICISM
AND PERSONAL
EVANGELISM

Go therefore and make disciples of all nations,
baptizing them in the name of the Father
and of the Son and of the Holy Spirit,
and teaching them to obey everything
that I have commanded you.

—Matthew 28:19–20

ALTHOUGH I GREW UP in a Christian home and cannot remember a time when I did not believe in God, there was one decisive evening when I surrendered my life to Jesus. It was during a Bible study gathering of teenagers held at a friend's house in West Philadelphia. Scores of young people gathered weekly on Saturday evenings in private homes to listen to Tom Roop, an accountant by trade, whose avocation was to explain scripture to kids like me. Squeezed together with my friends on Burt Newman's living room floor, I listened with intense attention as Tom unpacked the meaning of Romans 12:1–2: "I appeal to you therefore, brothers and sisters, by the mercies of God, to present your bodies as a living sacrifice, holy and acceptable to God, which is your spiritual worship. Do not be conformed to this world, but be transformed by the renewing of your minds, so that you may discern what is the will of God—what is good and acceptable and perfect."

I can still hear Tom's words as he said, "It's not enough just to believe in Jesus, you must present yourself to Jesus and seriously give yourself over to his will for your life."

He then told us all to bow our heads in prayer and asked if any of us were ready to make the decision to offer ourselves to Jesus without reservations; if so, we should do so right then and there. So I did. I made a commitment to be what Jesus wanted me to be; to go where he wanted me to go; and to say whatever he wanted me to say.

What happened to me that night is the result of what is called "evangelism." Evangelism is, in the words of my own church denomination, "introducing people to Jesus to become His disciples."[1] Mary and I are not using the word evangelism in the sense that it is only for a segment of Christianity called "evangelicals." The kind of evangelistic fervor we are advocating is for anyone who enters into an intimate relationship with Christ.

Evangelism and First Love

That evening with Tom Roop, I was introduced to a Jesus I had never known. I experienced an ecstasy in the Spirit that is quite impossible to put into words. The rush of joy that I felt that evening was so intense that I thought that I would explode from the excitement.

I remember that my immediate response was to join up with a friend and go out that very night and tell everyone I could about who Jesus is and what he had done for me—and what he could do for them. Living at that time in West Philadelphia, the two of us went to Fifty-Second Street and walked along that busy shopping district, where there was a bar on almost every corner. We went into each one of them. At the time it did not seem surprising to me that so many of the men and women sitting on barstools would be fascinated by what we had to say. The two of us must have come across as vibrant and sincere, and those traits are apt to gain a hearing wherever they are evident. We expected people to be thrilled with what we had to tell them—and they were!

The Bible refers to the kind of exuberance that my friend and I possessed that Saturday evening as having a spiritual "first love" (Revelation 2:2–4). And it was that. Just as romantics cannot constrain themselves when they first fall in love and must tell everyone who might listen what has happened to them, so the excitement of having a mystical experience with Jesus generates a passionate desire to talk about what has happened. Indeed, for my friend and me, even our adolescent sex drive was not as strong as our desire to tell the world of Christ's love and salvation.

When trying to explain ecstatic spiritual experiences, the ancient Chinese would say, "Those who know do not say. And those who say do not know." I have heard others try to describe what it is like to feel invaded by God's Spirit. There are converts out of the drug subculture who have told me it is like a psychedelic high, but without the drugs. A fellow player on my college basketball team said it is more exciting than when he scored the winning field goal against our archrivals just as the time was running out. Blaise Pascal, who had such an experience, wrote in his diary:

> FIRE! God of Abraham, God of Isaac, God of Jacob,
> Not the god of the philosophers and scholars—
> Absolute certainty—beyond reason.
> JOY! PEACE! Forgetfulness of the world and everything, but God.
> The world has not known Thee, but I have known Thee,
> JOY! JOY! JOY! JOY!
> Tears of JOY![2]

The spiritual empowerment that is evident in the lives of those who experience an infilling of Christ explains the explosive growth of certain new mega-churches, at a time when most long-established mainline churches have a difficult time attracting new people. A church like the famous Willow Creek Community Church in Barrington, Illinois, is one of those thriving mega-churches, and its success is linked to the fact that so many of its members are new converts. With little or no previous affiliation with any church prior to joining the Willow Creek congregation, these new converts have that "first love" with Christ that always translates into a zealous commitment to share testimonies with other people. Sunday after Sunday, these spiritually excited Christians bring friends and relatives to become part of the church where they experienced the Christ who changed their lives.

It is a sad but true fact that many mainline denominational churches are not as Spirit-filled as churches like Willow Creek. Many of the members of these traditional congregations grew up religious but, for the most part, never went through the kinds of mystical transforming encounters that lead to evangelizing. I have talked to several leaders of mainline denominations who bemoan the fact that a lackadaisical disposition toward sharing their faith is common among their church members. Even when their churches are not growing, church members do not see the importance of evangelism. They see it as someone else's job—the clergy or missionaries. With this kind of attitude, there is little likelihood that they will be ignited by intense desire to bring their acquaintances and relatives into saving, transforming relationships with the resurrected and living Christ.

The good news is that if taken to heart, the spiritual practices Mary describes in Part Two of this book should help mainline denominational folks want to share their faith.

A Disclaimer

I am well aware that numerous Christians do not have the kind of sudden infillings of God's Spirit such as I had when Tom Roop asked those of us in his Bible study group to bow our heads and surrender our lives to Jesus. Perhaps for many of you, the kind of spiritual aliveness and transformation that is at the core of this book comes gradually. Most Christians who come into "aliveness in Christ" and sense a oneness with God do so over extended periods of time. For them it often comes through dedicated efforts to follow the spiritual practices that have been explored and explained by historic saints of the church. There is no doubt in my mind that those who develop intimacy with God in less dramatic ways are no less alive in Christ than those who have sudden born-again experiences. But for them, the same concern emerges: how to keep their enlivened soul ablaze with the zeal and enthusiasm of the "first love" for Christ.

Losing and Renewing Our First Love

That is the downside to all of this. Aliveness in Christ, and the sense of evangelistic drive that accompanies it, fade away for many of us. That is what happened to the church at Ephesus, described in Revelation 2:1–7. They were doing so many things that were technically "right," but they were doing these things without the love and power that comes from a first love relationship with Christ.

Without a revitalization of a spiritual first love, evangelism becomes nothing more than a legalistic lifestyle to uphold or a duty to be performed. All of us have known Christians who, in sharing the gospel, say all the right words and go through all the right motions, but are devoid of the love and intensity that effective evangelism requires. In the words of Saint Paul, they are "holding to the outward form of godliness but denying its power" (II Timothy 3:5). It should be noted that I do not want to be completely negative about evangelism done out of duty or misguided motives. After all, even the Apostle Paul said, "What does it matter? Just this, that Christ is proclaimed in every way, whether out of false motives or true; and in that I rejoice" (Philippians 1:18). But if we Christians believe that our fellow human beings' salvation and fate, as well as the fate of all of God's creation, is truly at stake, it should be hard for us not to tell the salvation story to those who are spiritually lost. Mary told me that years ago she had a dream about the end of the world that still haunts her to this day. In her dream there was a line of people walking toward whatever hell was. Mary remembers that in the dream she was standing outside the line, as people walked by. The former manager of the jewelry store she worked in was in that line, and as he approached where she was standing, he looked right into her eyes and said to her, "Why didn't you tell me?" Mary told me that she had not witnessed to him, out of fear of not being liked, even though she knew she should. She now wishes that at least her sense of duty would have motivated her to overcome that fear and to talk to him about Jesus.

I wish I could say that my own enthusiasm for witnessing has always run hot. Within a month following that special evening when I surrendered my life to Jesus and experienced the "fullness" of God's Spirit, the zeal for witnessing for Christ was gone. How much it was gone came home to me later, at a reunion of my high school class ten years after graduation. One of my closest friends from my teen years was there. Jerry had played sports with me and generally hung out with me in high school. When I met him at the reunion, he was more than overjoyed to see me again. Throwing his arms around me, he all but shouted my name. Then he said, "I've got to tell you what's happened to me! Six weeks ago I had this incredible spiritual experience, and you've got to let me tell you about it!"

> *Without a . . . spiritual first love, evangelism becomes nothing more than a legalistic lifestyle to uphold or a duty to be performed.*

Jerry went on to tell me about coming into a personal transforming relationship with Jesus. He told me about how everything had changed for him; how he now sensed the presence of God within; how a lot of bad feelings that had been burdening him were gone; and how he could not wait to see me to tell me about it all.

I said, "Slow down, Jerry! I know what you're talking about. I had the same thing happen to me a long while ago."

Then Jerry asked, "When?"

"Back before I even got to know you in history class," I answered.

Without accusation or condemnation, but with much puzzlement in his voice, he simply inquired, "How come you never told me, Tony? How come?"

Many Christians have told me similar stories of how the zeal they once had to spread the gospel story has died in them. Regret and sadness are often expressed when they talk about how they never had, or have lost, their evangelistic fervor. These stories make me only too aware of how some of us never experience a first love with Jesus that results in a desire to witness, or of how blasé we can become about witnessing. We may even talk about Jesus from time to time out of a sense of duty, but any sense of urgency we might have had is all but completely dissipated.

Jesus yearned to establish a spiritual connectedness with people that would relieve them of the burdens of their souls.

The good news is that there are spiritual practices that enable us to be renewed spiritually and have that "first love" with God again and again. That is what this book is about—how to regularly reexperience a joyful and fulfilling oneness with God through spiritual practices done in the context of a body of believers. But please note that I am not saying that a joyful and fulfilling oneness with God means that we will always have strong feelings toward God. There is a common misperception when talking about mystical intimacy with Christ that it is synonymous with positive emotional feelings. It is not; we talk more about this in later chapters.

We are advocating the kind of intimacy and friendship with Jesus that creates the same empathy with spiritually lost people that Jesus himself had some two thousand years ago when he walked the earth. Back then, he looked down on the city of Jerusalem and cried, "Jerusalem, Jerusalem, the city that kills the prophets and stones those who are sent to it! How often have I desired to gather your children together as a hen gathers her brood under her wings, and you were not willing!" (Matthew 23:37).

Jesus yearned to establish a spiritual connectedness with people that would relieve them of the burdens of their souls. He said that he came to seek and to save those who were lost (Luke 19:10). Those of us who surrender to Jesus' Holy Spirit and allow that Spirit into the depths of our souls in the here and now will experience freedom in Christ and will be possessed with that same Christlike drivenness to alleviate the soul sicknesses of all those we meet who need salvation.

In response to the masses of people weighed down by guilt and anxieties, Jesus sought to create an array of disciples who would carry on his ministry of deliverance after he ascended into heaven, and he promised to empower them with the Holy Spirit. Those of us who follow in Jesus' footsteps by yielding to a mystical infilling of Christ's presence know that Jesus kept his promise to his disciples: "But you will receive power when the Holy Spirit has come upon you; and you will be my witnesses in Jerusalem, in all Judea and Samaria, and to the ends of the earth" (Acts 1:8).

Those who are empowered by the Holy Spirit often report a drivenness and an irresistible urge to tell the salvation story so that people will commit to live it. In the Bible we read about how Peter and John tried to explain to Annas, the high priest, and Caiaphas, the captain of the Temple, how helpless they were in trying to assuage the inner compulsion to share the gospel. They told these Jewish leaders, "For we cannot keep from speaking about what we have seen and heard" (Acts 4:20).

Mystical spirituality brings Christians into such an intimate relationship with Christ that we empathize with Christ, and in that empathy we enter into what the Bible calls "the sharing of his sufferings" (Philippians 3:10). Christ agonizes when looking upon those who are lost and whose lives are destructive, not only to themselves, but to others around them. Mystical unity with Christ, we believe, will create some of that same Christlike agony within us. Our empathy for the lost that God's presence within us can create will drive us to reach out to those who do not know that there is hope and healing for them in an ongoing, personal relationship with Jesus.

Learning from Other Saints

Mary and I believe that it is possible to learn from saints, old and new, how to connect with God, or how to reconnect in such a way that the aliveness and vitality that has cooled in so many hearts can once again flame into a blazing fire. We know that such spiritual renewal can make us into driven evangelists who want to see people commit to becoming like Jesus.

For centuries, Christian saints and mystics such as Saint Ignatius of Loyola and Saint Teresa of Avila have sought and found ways to revitalize our souls. In more recent times, there have been prominent Christians such as Thomas Merton, a Trappist monk, and Richard Foster, an evangelical Quaker, who offer us a great deal of guidance about how to experience this kind of spiritual commitment and renewal. And, while that kind of aliveness and vitality of the Spirit is important to us personally, to our own faith lives, it is even more important to our sense of urgency in spreading the gospel message so that people can find abundant life in Christ.

What we are pressing for is that all Christians, whatever the process whereby they come to know Christ, take steps to generate or regenerate that first love fire in their souls. Mary and I hope you will commit yourself to those spiritual disciplines that will allow the Holy Spirit to explode within you and generate evangelistic zeal. What is more, we pray that readers who have not yet experienced Jesus Christ in their lives will not be deterred from practicing the spiritual disciplines that we describe. These disciplines hold great promise for those who hunger for intimacy with God. They can be a means for bringing you to where God can continue to be real in your life and you can repeatedly experience that "first love." In fact, Richard Foster, who writes and speaks extensively on spiritual disciplines, says that "in practicing the Spiritual Disciplines we are simply learning to fall in love with Jesus over and over and over again."[3]

The Mystical Basis for the "How-To's" of Evangelism

Not only does being spiritually connected to God generate a zeal for reaching others with the gospel, it also increases our sensitivity to just when and how to talk about Christ. Many of us have been in situations in which some fellow Christian chose to witness for Christ, and it was clear that it was bad timing and the results were negative. At one time or another, we have watched as a sincere fellow believer, while trying to be faithful to the Great Commission, was only turning people off and hardening them against the salvation story. We realized that the witnessing was not being carried out either at the right time or in the right place.

Once, a woman who lived next door to me decided to have a cocktail party with the express purpose of having an opportunity for neighbors to get to know one another. She wanted to generate congeniality and friendship with all of those who lived on our street. Unfortunately, an earnest Christian man who attended that party decided that this would be a great opportunity to do some preaching. One by one, he accosted everyone who was present and did a hard sell of the gospel on each of us. Some of those who were there that evening were so offended that they left early. Eventually, our hostess turned to me and said, "If he doesn't shut up, I'm going to go over there and punch him out!"

A couple of days later, another Christian couple who had attended the party and were sensitive to what had happened prayed long and hard about how to do some damage control. Eventually, the husband had a strong spiritual leading that he and his wife should take the upset hostess out to breakfast and try to make amends for what had ruined her party.

At breakfast, the hostess and her husband felt comfortable enough to ask what the preaching going on that night was all about. Halfway through an explanation, this sensitive Christian brother became sharply aware that this would be a good time to explain who Jesus was and what the Holy Spirit could do for all of those who trust in Jesus. Within the hour, the neighbor and her husband made decisions to surrender their lives to Christ. The timing was right, so it was no surprise to the man who was doing the witnessing that decisions for Christ quickly followed.

It is not enough to be driven to share the gospel with others. Sometimes we can do more harm than good if we lack sensitivity to the situation and the people. Being "in Christ" through disciplines such as prayer and fasting is essential to give us a sense of when the *kairos* moment has arrived (*kairos* is the Greek word indicating the optimal moment for something to happen). In witnessing for Christ, it is of utmost importance that we be led by the Holy Spirit (Romans 8:14) to speak at the right time and in the right place. Throughout the Bible we come across verses that emphasize the importance of timing, and Ecclesiastes 8:5 says that "the wise mind will know the time and way." This verse indicates that God acts with perfect timing; we can join that timing if we are in tune with God. An intentionally developing mystical intimacy with Christ makes us more sensitive to the timing for witnessing. That is why all those who are driven to witness need to be spiritually empowered—because it is the Spirit who prompts us when it is right to speak a word for Christ.

There is something else needed for effective evangelism, along with being at the right place at the right time. We need to use the right words. When we are mystically endowed with the Holy Spirit, the right words can more easily come to us when we need them.

Over the past several years, I have been recruiting college and university students to join a program called "Mission Year." On campuses across the country, I challenge young people to come and join with other students to form teams that will serve poor people who live in derelict neighborhoods in urban America. They are required to put in at least 20 hours a week in some form of community service, such as tutoring children, working in soup kitchens, building houses with Habitat for Humanity, and visiting shut-ins. They are also asked to get to know as many people in their neighborhoods as possible, and in addition to learning about them and their joys and struggles, they are to do their best to share the gospel with them.

When I ask these Mission Year volunteers to do the witnessing thing, I almost always notice some fear and trepidation on their faces. Eventually I am asked, "But what do we say? What if people ask us questions and we don't know the right answers? What if we don't know how to relate to people?"

I jokingly answer, "Do what I do as a university professor. If I don't know the answer, I just start talking. That's what you should do, just start talking. Something will come to you!"

In so many instances, I later have Mission Year volunteers say to me, "You know what you told us to do? Well, we did it, and it worked—we really did end up having something to say!"

If such a methodology seems a bit "off the wall," consider what Jesus said to his disciples when he sent them out to witness: "When they hand you over, do not worry about how you are to speak or what you are to say; for what you are to say will be given to you at that time; for it is not you who speak, but the Spirit of your Father speaking through you" (Matthew 10:19–20).

I really do believe that when we develop an intimate mystical relationship with Christ, the Holy Spirit can become a guiding presence in our lives, putting the words in our mouths that need to be spoken when the time for witnessing is at hand. Jesus told his disciples not to worry about what to say or how to say it, even when witnessing before governors and kings and risking the possibility of getting arrested! There is, no doubt, something wonderfully mysterious and mystical about witnessing.

Karl Barth, the famous Swiss-German theologian, aware of such Spirit-filled speaking, contended that there are times in preaching when words become sacramental. He believed that at such moments the Holy Spirit takes control of what is being said and gives the words special effectiveness and meaning for those who hear them.

I have known such times when what I was saying transcended anything that I could have planned to say. At those times I have been aware that my words are connecting with the audience in ways that are having a miraculous effect. I have a sense that at the end of my message, if I give an invitation for people to accept Christ into their lives, there will be many who will respond. During such sermons, there is a sense that the Holy Spirit is in charge. That is why, before I speak, I always spend time in silence so that the Spirit might flow into me and take possession of what will be said.

From time to time I am invited to speak at one or another of the many "Jesus Festivals" that are held across the country. These gatherings bring together tens of thousands of young people who have come to hear a variety of popular Christian rock bands. All of these festivals include speakers, but too often we are only "fillers" while the next band sets up their sound equipment.

I really do not mind being relegated to the secondary role of filler, as long as I get a good shot at preaching the salvation story to the many teenagers who are there. At one of these festivals, however, things got out of hand. The rock band that preceded my preaching had worked the crowd up into a frenzy, and the young people were not about to settle down to listen to a bald-headed university professor call them to repentance with a plea to surrender their lives to Christ.

When it was my turn to take the microphone, the vast audience hardly even noticed that I was there. Thousands of young people were yelling and screaming for the next band to do its set. To say they were ignoring me would be an understatement. A few who were quite honest in expressing their feelings yelled for me to "shut up and get off the stage."

I had a prepared message in hand, but I realized it would not work with that raucous crowd. I certainly had a sense that I should scrap what I had planned to say and spell out a simple message of salvation. I used the "Four Spiritual Laws."[4] These are simple, propositional truths developed by Bill Bright, the founder of the parachurch organization Campus Crusade for Christ. These simple statements had always seemed a bit trite and simplistic to me, but at that moment they were all that came to my mind. Looking back on that evening, I realize that the Spirit guided me in the decision.

Earlier in the day, through my time of stillness, I had experienced an unusually powerful encounter with God. It was one of those times when I felt my entire being saturated with the Holy Spirit. Later, when I was preaching, I found myself praying at the same time. I was less conscious of the words coming out of my mouth than I was of simultaneously praying, over and over again, "Dear Jesus, help me! Dear Jesus, help me!" That simple prayer was echoing in my mind the whole time I was delivering my message to the crowd.

After a few minutes, it became obvious that something mysterious was happening. The noise of the crowd gradually disappeared, and a deep stillness fell over those young people.

When, at the end of my message, I gave the invitation to surrender to Christ, the response was overwhelming. Hundreds of young people came forward and followed me to the prayer tent where counselors and I would talk and pray with them.

The next day, when I returned to the fairgrounds where the festival was being held, there was an extensive buzz about what had happened the night before. People were telling me how fantastically effective my sermon had been. But when I asked what they had heard me say, no one seemed to remember a thing. Members of the festival's leadership team told me that, because they were aware of how bad the situation was when I got up to speak, they prayed for me the whole time I was on the platform.

Later, when I had a chance to listen to the recording of my message, I cringed. What I had said that night was unimpressive. There was no eloquence to my words. My message was so boring and didactic that I found it tedious to listen to the entire thing.

Upon reflection, it became obvious that my own words were in no way decisive in generating the crowd's significant response. The Holy Spirit had taken control of that meeting and had been in control of me. It was the Spirit that had made thousands of rowdy teenagers open up to a simple declaration of the gospel. Since then, there has never been a question in my mind that mystical spirituality is at the base of effective evangelism and that intentional silence before God is the best preparation for a sermon.

Mystical spirituality is at the base of effective evangelism.

In addition to the right timing and the right words, we must also be attuned to the right actions, since we can turn people off to the message of Christ with our actions even more than our words. Communication scholars tell us that the greatest portion of our communication is nonverbal, even to the point that if our verbal and nonverbal messages conflict, people will believe the nonverbal.

The story is told that Charles Spurgeon, the famous British preacher, once visited a prominent scholar from Turkey who was on the faculty at Oxford University. He traveled there with two of his deacons.

The man ushered them into his drawing room, opened a box of his prized cigars, and offered them to each of his visitors. The two deacons refused the cigars with great indignation while Spurgeon took one of the cigars, lit it up, and comfortably sat down and enjoyed a pleasant conversation with his host.

On the way back to London, as they rode on the train, the deacons scolded Spurgeon, claiming that he had compromised his testimony as a man of God; to which Spurgeon answered, "Well, one of the three of us had to act like a Christian."

Actions really do speak—and witness—louder than words. Perhaps the most often paraphrased advice from Saint Francis is that we are to preach the gospel and, if necessary, use words. We need to allow the Holy Spirit to inspire our actions, as well as our words, for effective evangelism.

Some Help from Frank Laubach

Decades ago, I read a little book that radically altered the way I think about how the Holy Spirit controls what happens in effective evangelism. The book was written by Frank Laubach and is titled *Prayer: The Mightiest Force in the World.*[5]

In this book, Laubach validates the traditionally held belief that prayer involves making requests of God. He clearly affirms the scripture that tells us that "the prayer of the righteous is powerful and effective" (James 5:16). This, he claims, is especially true when it comes to praying for the salvation of persons who are of special concern to us.

All Christians would support that claim because both personal experiences and church history provide ample testimonies to the effectiveness of such petitions. For instance, in the fourth century a woman named Monica, living in the North African city of Hippo, had a reprobate son named Augustine. Monica never let a day pass without imploring God to rescue Augustine from his libertine lifestyle. She got all of her Christian friends to join her in praying for him. One day Monica begged her son to go with her to church, and while she was on her knees praying, Augustine sneaked away, boarded a ship, and headed for Rome. In those days, Rome was known for its debauched ways, and Monica was brokenhearted when she learned what her son had done. But she never gave up praying.

While Augustine was in Rome, Monica's prayers were answered. Augustine happened to meet up with Ambrose, a saintly leader of the church. Ambrose, in turn, was able to lead Augustine into a transforming relationship with Christ.

Years later, when the city of Hippo needed a new bishop, Augustine was chosen to fill that role. It is hard to imagine Monica's joy as the members of her church went to the dock to greet their new bishop, who turned out to be none other than her wayward son. The prayers of a faithful woman had availed much.

While pointing out how important it is for Christians to pray for others, Laubach makes a bold and intriguing proposal for another way of praying. He suggests that in addition to praying for someone in need of God, that we should consider praying to that person as well. He tells us that God may want to work through the praying Christian as a channel to reach into the heart and soul of the person who is in need of saving grace. Laubach proposes that a person who is resisting God might be open to the spiritual impact of a Christian concentrating God's power on him or her. It is as though, according to Laubach, a praying Christian might be a lens through whom God focuses saving power into another person's life.

Call it a kind of mental telepathy, but what Laubach is suggesting is that the Holy Spirit flowing into a Christian, as a result of prayer, can stir up spiritual energy in that Christian that can then be directed toward a person who needs Christ's salvation.

Imagine, if you can, being in a meeting where someone is preaching an evangelistic message. Sitting next to you is a deeply loved friend who has been resisting God for years. You are desperately yearning for that friend to be open to the gospel message and respond to the preacher's invitation to surrender to Christ. As your friend sits next to you, you concentrate God's saving love and grace on her. You focus all your psychic energies on her, nonverbally pleading with her to decide for Christ right there and then. Now consider what might happen if this psychic communication could be heightened because of steps you took to equip yourself for the task. Is it possible that the spiritual practices you have been carrying out in your devotional life could give you an unusual effectiveness in connecting with your friend? Might your mental pleas, energized by an indwelling presence of Christ, enable you to get through to her and make her ready to make a decision for Christ?

This kind of nonverbal connecting is what Laubach is promoting in his little book. I have come to believe in what he says and have made nurturing spiritual energy through this kind of praying an essential preparation for evangelism.

Without a doubt, when it comes to sharing the gospel, there is a realization that "it is God who is at work in you, enabling you to will and to work for his good pleasure" (Philippians 2:13). There is a special anointing that comes through times of mystical intimacy with Jesus Christ, generated through the spiritual practices we describe. When it comes to personal evangelism, this empowering anointing makes witnessing effective.

More Than Personal Evangelizing

Mystical spirituality provides an incredible impetus to evangelize. The Holy Spirit makes us sensitive to the right time and place to witness, as well as giving us the right words and actions. The Holy Spirit flowing through us enables us to connect with people, making them open to the gospel we try to communicate. But we must remember that this gospel is not about us personally evangelizing and then being done with our perceived duties. Evangelism is not meant to end with an initial commitment to live for Jesus. As crucial as that is, it is not any less crucial to help those who commit to live out that commitment. We must never forget that the purpose of evangelizing is for making disciples, which means being formed into Christ-likeness. Jesus' purpose in having us preach the good news is to get others to commit to living out Jesus' commands (Matthew 28:20). Those who respond and commit are, like the New Testament church, to get involved in a community of believers committed to a variety of ways to live out those commands. Those "ways" are spiritual disciplines or practices, as Mary later discusses in more detail. But what must be pointed out now is that these spiritual practices are to help us live out all of Jesus' commands—which include addressing the needs of the "the least of these," described by Jesus himself in Matthew 25 as the poor and oppressed, as well as caring for all of God's creation. These are the aspects of the cultivation of mystical Christianity that we turn to next.

CHRISTIAN MYSTICISM
AND WORKING
FOR JUSTICE

For I the Lord love justice.

—Isaiah 61:8

SAINT FRANCIS OF ASSISI took literally Jesus' words in Matthew 25:40 that whatever we do for "the least of these," we do for Christ. One way Francis lived out this conviction, born out of his intimacy with Jesus, was by reaching out to lepers. All of his life Francis had regarded lepers with disgust. But all of that changed one day when he encountered a leper who blocked his way while he was traveling to the city of Perugia. Francis stopped and gave the man, whose face and hands were already rotted by that dreaded disease, all the money he was carrying. The diseased man took the money, but did not move and continued to block the path.

Francis then decided to give the leper his cloak, thinking that the cloak would protect the suffering man from the chills of the Umbrian hills. Putting the cloak lovingly over the leper's shoulders, Francis thought that this gift would suffice. But the leper still stood motionless in front of Francis. Not knowing what else to do, Francis closed his eyes, braced himself, and then kissed the leper on his decayed lips.

When he opened his eyes, Francis was stunned to discover that the leper had vanished. It was then that he realized the miraculous nature of this encounter. He understood that the leper had been none other than Jesus in disguise. From that day forward, Francis resolved to treat every leper as though he were Christ—because for Francis that was who each leper really was. From henceforth, lepers would always be sacramental to him.

Consider what it would mean to live out the spirit of Francis today. I can, with some degree of certainty, imagine how Francis would react to gay people afflicted with AIDS because, in so many ways, these AIDS victims in our day can be compared to those lepers Francis met in Assisi.

Back then lepers were ostracized by those religionists who believed such persons were stricken by disease because of their sins. The plight of lepers was viewed as God's punishment for perversity, and all those who met lepers would deem them "unclean." I am convinced that far too many Christians among us today react to homosexuals with AIDS in much the same way. Francis, on the other hand, would embrace these modern-day lepers and treat them sacramentally.

You should ask yourself how your own commitments to AIDS victims, and to other ostracized and oppressed peoples, would change if every time you looked into their eyes you had a Francis-like sensation that Jesus was staring back at you. When this is the case, simple acts of charity are not enough. When the Spirit of God moves you to unfathomable depths of love and the suffering of others becomes yours in a mystical way, you will have an irresistibly urgent compulsion to speak on behalf of those who suffer and to fight for a world that is more just.

You will not ask yourself if you are noble enough to embrace these social "rejects." Instead, seeing Christ, the King of Heaven, waiting to be loved in them, you will ask yourself, "Am I worthy to be their servants?"

Another way Saint Francis lived out his commitment to "the least of these" was to care deeply for all of God's creation. It might be comfortable for us to talk about Francis as an advocate for lepers and other humans who were poor and oppressed, but we may get a little nervous when we learn about his pronounced spiritual affinity with animals and the Earth.

Francis has long been known as the patron saint of animals, and stories abound about his close relationships with many different nonhuman animals. One tale is told of a brother who brought Francis an unfortunate little rabbit who had gotten trapped in a snare. "Be more careful the next time," warned Francis to the rabbit, as he ushered him back to freedom in the woods. But, sensing the warmth and love radiating from the saint, the rabbit jumped onto Francis's lap, repeatedly! Francis had to ask another brother to carry the rabbit far into the woods.[1]

A similar story of Francis's kindness relates his encounter with two ill-fated doves who were being carried to market to be sold for someone's dinner. Francis purchased them with his own money and set them free, reminding all who heard him that these birds were created to praise God.

Birds were very special to Francis. He loved their singing and saw it as their own special way to praise God. One time, it is said, Francis spoke gently to a flock of birds whose song was so loud his human listeners could not hear Francis's sermon. He asked the birds to be silent while he preached, and promised that after he had finished it would be their turn to sing. And they *did* keep silent until it was their turn. On many occasions he preached to flocks of birds, who listened politely.[2]

One well-known anecdote chronicles the pact Francis arranged between the people of Gubbio and the wolf who had been terrorizing them. Francis, always a peacemaker, went out to the forest to meet with the wolf, who had been killing livestock and humans alike. After their conversation, the wolf and Francis returned to Gubbio. The townspeople promised not to harm or hunt the wolf, and the wolf lived in the city for the rest of his life, begging for his food and never killing humans or lambs again.[3] When he died—so the legend goes—the wolf was mourned by the townspeople and was given a Christian burial in the consecrated cemetery.[4]

Saint Francis's intimacy with God extended beyond love for animals to awe for all of God's creation. He taught that we are to live in harmony with nature and not to harm it in any way, as exemplified in this and other stanzas from his "Canticle of the Sun": "Praised be my Lord for our mother the earth, the which doth sustain us and keep us, and bringeth forth divers fruits and flowers of many colors, and grass."[5] Recognizing Francis as a genuine example of someone who valued the integrity of creation, Pope John Paul II in 1979 named him the patron saint for a host of twentieth- and twenty-first-century environmentalists.[6] And so today, when human pollution regularly assaults clean water and fresh air, it is beneficial for us to remember Saint Francis's reverence for the elements: "Praised be my Lord for our brother the wind, and for the air and cloud, calms and all weather by the which Thou upholdest life in all creatures. Praised be my Lord for our sister water, who is very serviceable unto us and humble and precious and clean."[7]

Working for God's Justice

As we see with these examples of Saint Francis, when we are mystically connected to Christ, the Holy Spirit urges us beyond our personal relationship with Christ and our love for one another to also care about, and work for, harmony and unity for all of God's creation. In the beginning God created the heavens and the earth, and called all of creation good. God calls us to be good stewards or caretakers of creation. That is why when we yield to Christ, Christ's Spirit presses us into efforts to bring this justice to all oppressed aspects of God's creation—people, animals, plants,

Christ's Spirit presses us into efforts to bring this justice to all oppressed aspects of God's creation.

and the entire Earth. Our job, in helping God's Kingdom to come on earth as it is in heaven, is to work to restore *all* that is no longer good, as well as preserve what is already good. As the Psalmist said, "The LORD is good to all, and his compassion is over *all* that he has made" (Psalm 145:9, emphasis mine). If we want to be committed to justice in its totality, then we need to become more aware of how to care not only for people but for the whole Earth.

It is the Holy Spirit who creates in us an awareness and a sensitivity to what victims of injustices—human and nonhuman alike—must endure, as well as a deep commitment to set things right for them. If we do not yield to that Spirit, we can succumb to the false notion that we are living for God when in reality we are not. As it is stated in Isaiah 58:2–9:

> Yet day after day they seek me and delight to know my ways, as if they were a nation that practiced righteousness and did not forsake the ordinance of their God; they ask of me righteous judgments, they delight to draw near to God. . . . "Why do we fast, but you do not see?". . . . Look, you serve your own interest on your fast day, and oppress all your workers. . . . Such fasting as you do today will not make your voice heard on high. . . . Is this not the fast that I choose: to loose the bonds of injustice, to undo the thongs of the yoke, to let the oppressed go free, and to break every yoke? Is it not to share your bread with the hungry, and bring the homeless poor into your house, when you see the naked, to cover them, and not to hide yourself from your own kin? Then your light shall break forth like the dawn, and your healing shall spring up quickly. . . . Then you shall call, and the Lord will answer; you shall cry for help, and he will say, Here I am.

Working for God's justice is a theme not only in Isaiah, but in numerous passages of scripture, including Amos 5:24, Micah 6:8, and Luke 4:18–19. Again and again Jesus confronts the ruling establishment of his day. In just one of many examples, he warned in Matthew 23:23, "'Woe to you, scribes and Pharisees, hypocrites! For you tithe mint, dill, and cumin, and have neglected the weightier matters of the law: justice and mercy and faith.'" God commands we work for justice, and it is our intimacy with Christ that ignites us to do what God commands.

I believe there are four basic consequences for a sense of justice that grows from mystical unity with Christ. Each of them is essential to actualize something of the justice and social well-being that are part of what the Bible calls the Kingdom of God. They are

1. An awareness that Christ is in the poor and oppressed, waiting to be loved and served
2. A call to challenge institutionalized religion
3. An understanding of the importance of entering into one another's sufferings
4. A plan for the world as it should be

Christ's Special Presence in the Poor and Oppressed

If you are empowered by the Holy Spirit, you will be sensitized to Christ, who is mystically present in the poor and oppressed, waiting to be loved and served. That sensitivity, I believe, inevitably creates a love for them and a conviction that in loving them you are loving Christ. As Jesus said in Matthew 25:35–40, whenever we feed the hungry, clothe the naked, attend to the needs of the sick, and visit prisoners, we are doing these things to him. This was no metaphoric language—Jesus said that he was the hungry one, the naked one, the sick one, and the prisoner that we served. Down through the ages there have been Christians who have understood this truth, but no one has exemplified this better—for all God created—than Francis of Assisi, as we saw in the stories earlier in the chapter.

Challenging Institutionalized Religion: A New Consciousness

Those who know anything about sociologists are aware that most of them are very down on religion—and for good reason. They have studied the indignities and injustices suffered by oppressed peoples and have recognized that religion was used again and again to keep people from throwing off their chains and enjoying the freedoms that were their just due as human beings. When slaves sought freedom, churches were often on the side of the slaveholders, quoting the scripture wherein God commanded slaves to be subject to their masters (Ephesians 6:5). Sociologists noted that when women sought social equality with men, the church often challenged female aspirations and told women to take subservient roles in their churches and homes. Even today when people bring up environmental concerns, often churches do not take these concerns seriously—as if caring for God's creation is outside the realm of a believer's responsibility.

The wrong use of religion must be challenged. True Christianity works to liberate oppressed people and heal oppressed creation, not to legitimate their oppression. The Holy Spirit, through the church, can help empower people to break the chains of oppression by enabling them to see through the ideological justifications that are used to keep them from recognizing how evil the oppressors really are. This is what Walter Bruggemann, the famous Old Testament scholar, calls "the prophetic imagination."[8] The Holy Spirit, he says, enables the oppressed to see through the justifications for the inequities within society and makes them aware of all that is wrong. This same Spirit, says Bruggemann, will drive the rest of us to weep over the injustices that they endure.

I know what Bruggemann is talking about. When I was in my late teens, my white Baptist church, with its comparatively affluent middle-class members, closed down, and I decided to join a neighboring African American Baptist church whose members were, for the most part, from poor backgrounds. When scripture was read in my new church, it took on a whole new meaning, because it sounded different from anything I had ever heard before. For instance, one Christmas the pastor read Mary's Magnificat from Luke 1:46–55. As he read, "He hath put down the mighty from their seats of power and exalted those of low degree" (KJV), an elderly man who had long been kept down by a racially discriminating society murmured, "Thank you, Jesus!" Old women, who had been denied the dignity that they deserved as they worked as maids and cooks, moaned, "Yes! Yes!"

> *True Christianity works to liberate oppressed people and heal oppressed creation, not to legitimate their oppression.*

When the pastor read, "He hath filled the hungry with good things; and the rich he hath sent empty away," I heard victims of undeserved poverty groaning, "Come quickly, Lord; come quickly." To this congregation, Mary's song sounded like the battle cry of an oppressed revolutionary rather than the sentimental utterance of a young woman about to give birth to her first child.

My pastor once preached about the Babylonian captivity of the Jews. He cried out, "They stole the children of Israel from their homeland and took them to a strange and distant land. They set the children of Israel down beside the rivers of Babylon and they said, 'Sing for us, children of Israel . . . 'cause you folks *sho'* can sing.'" I sensed the reactions of the people around me and realized that, as the sermon unfolded, they saw themselves in this story. I became painfully aware that these African American brothers and sisters were reflecting on the ways in which their own forbears had been ripped from their homeland, enslaved, and shipped to a land where, after three hundred years of suffering, they still were seldom appreciated for much beyond their ability to entertain.

The Holy Spirit created a new consciousness among the people of that African American church and enabled them to see through any attempt of the white establishment to justify itself. In the context of that worship service, my fellow church members recognized that they were God's people—a kind of new Israel—and that anything to "keep them in their place" was nothing more than the work of an evil system that could be likened to the empire of Babylon. This kind of consciousness raising is the first step toward freedom. It was the first step for me.

Then I went to seminary. I was told to study Hebrew and Greek. I was told that unless I could think in the verbal categories of those ancient Jews and Greeks to whom the Bible was originally written, I would not be able to fully understand what the Bible was all about. The problem was that they never told me *which* Jews and *which* Greeks. The way the rich people thought in the ancient world was very different from how the poor people thought, and what they found in scripture when they read it was different, too. So, when I was told that I had to get into the ancient languages to understand the Bible, my teachers didn't tell me the whole story. Each social class among the ancients spoke a somewhat different language.

When it came to the New Testament, this should have been obvious to me. I had been taught that the New Testament was not written in classical Greek—the language of the upper-class aristocrats. Instead, it was written in what is called "Koine Greek," which was the language of the lower classes. In a sense, it was what we might call "Rap Greek."

The Bible has to be read through the eyes of the poor and the oppressed, because it is primarily the story of a God who hears their cries and offers them deliverance. To limit the salvation story to spiritual deliverance alone, as more affluent folks are prone to do, is

To limit the salvation story to spiritual deliverance alone . . . is to fail to tell the whole salvation story.

to fail to tell the whole salvation story. Deliverance from social and economic oppression must also be part of the gospel story. The God of the Bible provides deliverance not only from sin and guilt, but also from the destructive effects of poverty and discrimination.

THE PROPHET'S ROLE IN CONSCIOUSNESS RAISING. Mystical Christianity has always challenged institutionalized religion. In many ways mystics have perspectives and make judgments on what is going on in society that circumvents the official ideology of religious leaders. It is easy to see that the prophets of the Bible were mystics. They proclaimed truths and pronounced judgments that came directly from God to them. Their thundering voices challenged those high priests in the king's court who too often served those who held political power rather than the God they claimed to represent.

Prophets do not preach a message that the religious establishment, which usually calls for passive submission to those in the ruling socio-economic order, would prefer. Instead, prophets pronounce alternatives to tyrannies of the status quo.

Consider the prophet Isaiah, who gave to the conquered and enslaved children of Israel an alternative vision for the future. The revelation he received in his mystical moments enabled him to challenge the way things were and to give hope to a people who had lost their hope. To an enslaved people he declared, "For I am about to create new heavens and a new earth; the former things shall not be remembered or come to mind. But be glad and rejoice forever in what I am creating; for I am about to create Jerusalem as a joy, and its people as a delight. I will rejoice in Jerusalem, and delight in my people; no more shall the sound of weeping be heard in it, or the cry of distress" (Isaiah 65:17–19).

Instead of legitimizing the social and political arrangements that leave so many people despairing and powerless to change things, a prophet like Isaiah gets these people to imagine another kind of world. Such prophets, through their mystical connectedness with God, communicate dreams and visions that enable those who are oppressed to imagine that they can rise above their downtrodden conditions. In fact, the prophets' spiritually inspired revelations of an alternative kind of society threatened the unjust kings in ancient Israel. Declaring God's judgment on oppression, they called people to commit themselves to the liberating God who offers a new and glorious future. That is why the spiritual mysticism of the prophets provided some of the most inspiring dynamic forces for justice that have ever been set in motion in human history. Certainly, leaders like Martin Luther King Jr. have taken courage from these prophetic visions as they seek to foster social transformations. Dr. King took his cue from the prophet Amos when he thundered, "Let justice roll down like waters, and righteousness like an ever-flowing stream!" (Amos 5:24).

Jesus proved to be the ultimate prophet. He came into the world declaring that a new kingdom was breaking loose in history, and that we should pray and work for its realization. Jesus' life, death, and resurrection were all designed to provide the means for creating God's Kingdom here on Earth.

THE RIGHT PERSON AT THE RIGHT TIME. We need to be working for that Kingdom *now,* and we need to recognize that God still sends prophets. They are raised up to challenge the political and economic injustices in dominant societal systems, as well as to cry out on behalf of all of creation. Mystically inspired prophets will not tolerate those who disengage from political efforts to end world poverty and the degradation of creation by saying that it is a positive sign that the world is coming to an end, or by quoting the verse, "You always have the poor with you" (Mark 14:7). True prophets know the whole verse Jesus was referring to: "Since there will never cease to be some in need on the earth, I therefore command you, 'Open your hand to the poor and needy neighbor in your land'" (Deuteronomy 15:11).

They will give no quarter to those who would disparage peacemaking efforts in the halls of Congress and in the assembly halls of the United Nations by declaring that there will always be "wars and rumors of wars." Prophets of God give birth to justice movements, and the gates of hell cannot prevail against them.

They will speak on behalf of any of the poor and oppressed who have no voice, including the poor and oppressed of nature, just as did the prophet Saint Francis who cared for all of God's creation.

Mystical prophets do not intend to struggle alone in their quest for justice. They call on others to join them in their efforts. But very few who are called to be prophets of God are, according to the scriptures, especially gifted for their calling, which may make them difficult to recognize. Saint Francis himself had Christians who disagreed with him and his methods. Even when prophets are gifted, we may not recognize them because of our conflicting societal or political values. Yet all of us who are followers of Jesus have a responsibility to discern who among us may have been given this mystical gift.

In our own time, many have believed that Martin Luther King Jr. was a prophet. There is little question, in retrospect, that God was at work through him, challenging racism. King was by no means a perfect man. We have a God who can draw straight lines with crooked sticks. God's choices of those who will be raised up to be prophetic voices, and through whom dramatic historical changes will be made, sometimes surprise us.

Often God chooses persons to be prophets who are not to our liking, whether because of personal lifestyle choices or political and ideological preferences. That is one of the reasons we need to be open to the kind of deeper sensitivities cultivated by the spiritual practices in this book. Challenging social injustice and violations of God's creation, and initiating changes that will actualize something of God's reign here on Earth can only occur when spiritually prepared people recognize and follow the ones whom God has anointed. A deeper connection to Christ and Christ's message and mission will spiritually prepare us to better recognize and receive a true prophet. But this preparation must be in the context of communities of faith. It is essential that we grow in intimacy with Christ as well as belong to communities of faith that can help us prayerfully "test the spirits" and discern true from false prophets of our time, so we know who to follow.

During the early days of the civil rights movement, in the 1950s, the African American community in Montgomery, Alabama, was confused and in disarray. Rosa Parks's refusal to give up her seat to a white man and move to the back of the bus, as required by Jim Crow laws, sparked a bus strike. African American people rallied to her support by refusing to continue using the public bus services of the city. The bus company was heading toward bankruptcy, but the strike began to lose momentum as the commitment of the strikers waned. Someone had to step forward to rally the flagging strikers, as well as draw national attention to the humiliation that black people in that city had to regularly endure.

The Black Ministerial Association of Montgomery met regularly to pray that God would raise up a prophetic voice among them. Little by little they agreed that a young, almost unknown minister should be their spokesperson. Martin Luther King Jr. was quite surprised when the group told him that they believed God had led them to choose him to be that person. Martin at first refused, but the group told him that they were all of the same mind on their choice. Eventually he said yes.

The rest of us know what happened after that. Martin Luther King Jr. not only gave voice to the humiliation suffered by his African American brothers and sisters because of segregation, but he pricked the consciences of people all across the nation and around the world. A praying community had discerned that he was God's man at the right time and in the right place, and they willingly followed him.

This kind of challenge to the world, born out of consciousness raising, is the first step toward freedom and wholeness in Christ.

The Importance of Entering into One Another's Sufferings

Through the prayerfulness that often marks those who suffer from oppression, the Holy Spirit can provide mystical revelations essential for liberation. When a group of people suffer together, they have a tendency to seek comfort and help from God and from each other. In the midst of their common agony, the Holy Spirit can create among them social solidarity and a shared vision of a future wherein present evils will be overcome and justice will abound.

In the scriptures we read how the Hebrew prophets gave voice to such dreams and visions, even as the people of Israel were tyrannized and enslaved by conquering enemies. Consider Isaiah's inspiring vision given to the suffering Jews during their captivity in Babylon:

> For I am about to create new heavens and a new earth; the former things shall not be remembered or come to mind. But be glad and rejoice forever in what I am creating; for I am about to create Jerusalem as a joy, and its people as a delight. I will rejoice in Jerusalem, and delight in my people; no more shall the sound of weeping be heard in it, or the cry of distress. . . . They shall build houses and inhabit them; they shall plant vineyards and eat their fruit. They shall not build and another inhabit; they shall not plant and another eat; for like the days of a tree shall the days of my people be, and my chosen shall long enjoy the work of their hands. They shall not labor in vain, or bear children for calamity; for they shall be offspring blessed by the Lord—and their descendants as well. Before they call I will answer, while they are yet speaking I will hear. (Isaiah 65:17–19, 21–24)

Such a vision of the future is what makes suffering people willing to take the risks required to create a more just world. They move from "false consciousness" that legitimates injustice and oppression toward a critical consciousness through which they see the world as it is, the world as it should be, and the difference between the two. Howard Thurman, a contemporary African American theologian and civil rights leader, as well as a classmate and friend of Martin Luther King Jr., brilliantly articulated this idea. In his book *Jesus and the Disinherited*,[9] Thurman described how critical consciousness and prophetic imagination emerge in the lives of people who suffer. He explained through his various writings how black people, because of their sufferings, often turned to God for the strength to endure their oppression. In yielding to God's Spirit they availed themselves of a power that enabled them to transcend the individualism that fosters a sense of helpless victimization. That same Holy Spirit, working in them in the midst of their sufferings, also created among them a collective empowerment that is essential for a people seeking liberation. The Holy Spirit transformed them from persons only interested in their own individual survival into a unified community ready to challenge the prevailing social order. The energy and power of such a unified people gives oppressed women and men the ability to sing, "We shall overcome."

Suffering, said Thurman, at first isolates the individual. Initially the sufferer is totally focused on the self and there is nothing else that gets his or her attention. Although many people are destroyed by the self-centeredness that suffering can generate, there are countless others who are able to rise above their suffering, and from them there is much to be learned.

Conquering suffering requires that sooner or later there must be an awakening to the reality that outside resources are needed, especially the fellowship of, and dependence on, intimate community. In a strange way, suffering can create spiritual community. Thurman wrote, "Despite the personal character of suffering, the sufferer can work his way through to community. . . . Sometimes he discovers through the ministry of his own burden a larger comprehension of his fellows, of whose presence he becomes aware in his darkness. They are companions along the way. . . . [This] is one of the consolations offered by the Christian religion in the centrality of the position given to the cross and to the suffering of Jesus Christ."[10]

Such fellowship among sufferers cannot be explained in psychological or sociological terms. I believe it is mystically inspired. The case can be made that when those who suffer enter into one another's burdens they transcend their own sufferings and even become heroic in their endeavors to alleviate the agonies that others endure.

Suffering does more than generate a sense of community, according to Thurman. It can also drive people to surrender and yield to God. When desperation results in someone falling into the arms of God, that person finds a means of triumph over the dreadful realities of life. Of the person who suffers, Thurman wrote, "If the answer to his suffering is to face it and challenge it to do its worst because he knows that when it has exhausted itself it has only touched the outer walls of his dwelling place, this can only come to pass because he has found something big enough to contain all violences and violations—he has found that his life is rooted in a God who cares for him and cultivates his spirit, whose purpose is to bring to heel all the untutored, recalcitrant expressions of life."[11]

In order to experience such spiritual fortitude, Thurman believed that sufferers must become saints, because only saints, he said, are people who are able to affirm life in the midst of a violent world. Thurman went on to say that this affirmation of life is the work of the Holy Spirit of God in the lives of those who suffer. In order to become saints, he claimed, those who suffer must surrender to a spirituality that comes from ecstatic experiences. Such a spirituality, said Thurman, transcends rational definitions or theological categories and "surpasses all understanding" (Philippians 4:7). Thurman went on to tell us that godly mystical spirituality, unlike that of New Age self-actualizing mysticism, brings the saints it creates into communion with the God who simultaneously connects them with all others in the world—especially with those who suffer. Given this conviction, it is easy to understand why Thurman believed that, inevitably, saints become people committed to love, mercy, and justice and dedicated to walking humbly with their God (Micah 6:8). Spirit-filled persons, Thurman said, will not be so focused on heaven that they are of no earthly good. On the contrary, the God that these saints feel in the depths of their being will be recognized as the God who shares in the agonies of those who are poor and who understands their pain when they are victimized by oppressive principalities and powers.

Though Thurman wrote primarily about human justice issues, he also taught compassion toward other living creatures. He recognized that non-human animals also suffer and, like humans who suffer, they hope to be released from their suffering. In his own childhood he playfully placed his bare foot on a small snake he saw in the woods. Feeling the snake writhe against the restraint of his foot, he realized that God instilled in all creatures—even snakes—the same impetus to seek liberation from suffering.[12]

A Plan for the World as It Should Be

The lifestyles of these saints, according to Thurman, are to be governed by Christ's radical teachings as set forth in the Sermon on the Mount (Matthew 5–7). These teachings are not unattainable goals to inspire us. Quite the contrary! Saints are expected to live out the values and principles set forth in that sermon. Thurman believed that with spiritual empowerment such things are possible. These saints are people who pray for, and work for, the Kingdom of God to come on earth as it is in heaven (Matthew 6:10), and they expect that Kingdom to become a historical reality.

The saints also know that the reign of God is not only about justice for humans. The Isaiah passage cited previously, prophesying "new heavens and a new earth," contains a promise for all of God's creatures: "The wolf and the lamb shall feed together, the lion shall eat straw like the ox; but the serpent—its food shall be dust! They shall not hurt or destroy on all my holy mountain, says the Lord" (Isaiah 65:25).

The radical lifestyle Jesus outlines in Matthew 5–7 starts with what are called the "Beatitudes" (Matthew 5:3–11). These Christlike attributes are not simply inspirational thoughts to be posted on the blackboards of Sunday school classrooms. They call all followers of Jesus—we ordinary saints—to do the following:

- Learn meekness in the midst of a power-hungry world
- Become poor by giving up wealth to respond to the needs of the hungry
- Develop mercy by affirming everyone's right to live
- Embrace what is required to be peacemakers
- Work for justice for all of God's creation
- Endure the persecution that results from speaking out for righteousness wherever injustice rules

The Beatitudes are the manifesto for a revolutionary lifestyle. If, as Christ's ambassadors, we follow them, they will turn society as we know it upside down:

- Those who cannot speak for themselves, born and unborn, will have saints advocating for their abundant life.
- Wherever the poor are malnourished and their children cry out because of aching stomachs, the saints will hear those cries and seek not only to feed them, but also to find ways to alleviate their poverty.
- When pestilence and war pervade the world, saints will work for health, well-being, and peace on behalf of all who suffer.
- Women and girls who are objectified and exploited in their homes, schools, jobs, or the sex trafficking industry, as well as any who are dehumanized through human trafficking, will have their cause championed, because the saints will feel Jesus' pain in their pain.
- When prejudices create racism, sectarian violence, and nationalistic prejudice, the saints can be counted on to stand up and shout, "No!"
- Gays and lesbians who are hated and persecuted for who they are will have saints respond by standing up for them and working to bring them justice.

- When God's nonhuman animals are treated in cruel ways, the saints will be advocates of lessening their sufferings.

- When pollution threatens and when land is selfishly used, saints will work to protect God's Earth.

The Holy Spirit enables saints to envision what could be, which creates a sanctified discontent with what is. Out of such, revolutions are generated. This Holy Discontent is the impetus for the kinds of revolutions that bring us closer to living out the reign of God on Earth.

JOHN WESLEY: A MODEL AND PLAN FOR RADICAL REVOLUTION. John Wesley, the founder of Methodism, serves as a model for the kinds of revolutions inspired by God. He serves as an example of how our spirituality creates zeal not only for evangelism, but for world reform.

Wesley was an Anglo-Catholic. While a member of the Church of England, he was part of that community that was more molded by Catholic theology than by Reformed theology. There was a specific time when Wesley experienced an overwhelming sense of being endowed with the Holy Spirit. This experience transformed him into a dynamic catalyst for a movement that changed Britain and eventually impacted the rest of the world. Historians say that the impact of the Wesleyan revivals alleviated various injustices and suffering, thereby saving Britain from violent revolution such as had taken place in France. The abolition of slavery, child labor laws, prison reform, a movement for universal education, and increased sensitivities toward nonhuman animals were just some of the direct results of the Wesleyan movement.

It is almost certain that Wesley had no carefully defined plan for changing Britain. All that Wesley really wanted to do was to bring people into personal transforming relationships with Christ. Primarily, he was committed to winning converts. However, the Holy Spirit had an even wider agenda, and it was only a matter of time before the spiritual liberation of souls was followed by social liberation for the poor and oppressed of the United Kingdom. The latter inevitably follows the former.

From his earliest days, Wesley was influenced by his family, and especially by his mother, Susanna, who was versed in the works of John of the Cross, Ignatius of Loyola, Blaise Pascal, and Teresa of Avila. She read, time and time again, *The Interior Castle*, which described Teresa's spiritual struggles and journey toward holiness and union with God. Through his mother, Wesley was drawn into a quest for mystical unity with God. He read the mystics she read and became convinced that the Catholic mystics were the only true Christians.

There were two spiritual benefits that Wesley sought in mysticism. One was the holiness that the mystics tried to achieve, and the other was assurance of his salvation. Although he would eventually abandon the mysticism of the Catholic saints, the holiness, or sanctification, that they held up as a realizable goal for the Christian would always be a part of his personal aspirations and hope, as well as an integral part of his movement. Just as important, Wesley sought assurance of his salvation and, initially, he thought that the Catholic mystics were the ones who could show him how to get it.

Wesley's intense efforts to achieve holiness and the assurance of salvation didn't work. Nevertheless, he pressed on in efforts to get close to God. He eventually would find help from Peter Bohler, a leader of the Moravian Church, a missionary-oriented denomination founded in Saxony in the eighteenth century. Bohler told Wesley not to get hung up on the intricacies of the mystical writers. His advice to Wesley was simply this: "Preach faith until you have it; and then, because you have it, you will preach it." It was in preaching, Bohler said, that assurance of salvation would become real to Wesley and the intimacy with God that he so desperately craved would come to him. So that's what Wesley did. Within months Wesley would be on board a ship headed for America, where he would preach the salvation story in a town just south of the city of Savannah, Georgia.

The trip across the Atlantic challenged Wesley in more ways than he could have imagined. While at sea a violent storm encompassed his ship, and Wesley was overcome with fear. As he trembled in the face of death, he heard singing coming from a section of the ship where a group of Moravian missionaries were quartered.

As he took note of the peace of mind and sense of security that they had about their salvation in these threatening conditions, he was driven into an even deeper awareness of his own spiritual insecurities and lack of assurance of a saving relationship with God. He wanted the confidence in salvation that the Moravians had.

Wesley's short time in Georgia did not go well. An ill-fated love affair, coupled with severe conflicts with the colony's governor, led to an early departure from America. But his time in Georgia was not a total loss. It was shortly after landing in America that Wesley met with August Spangenburg, who headed up Moravian ministries in Georgia. In Spangenburg, Wesley found a man with evangelistic fervor combined with an appreciation of the Catholic mystics. This was just the combination that Wesley needed as he was starting to rethink mysticism and to rework what he had learned. He began to separate what he referred to as the "dross" of mysticism from what he called the "gold." By then Wesley had become well aware that the mystics he had earlier revered were inadequate in explaining how to access the spiritual power to actualize God's presence in his life. The gold of the mystics, however, was their "practical and pietistic outworkings."

After his failed attempts at ministry in Georgia, Wesley returned to England feeling like a lost soul. Then, on the evening of May 24, 1738, he attended an Anglican "society" meeting being held on Aldersgate Street in London. The person leading the meeting that evening was reading from Martin Luther's *Commentary on Romans*.

To me that meeting seems like a setup for a boring couple of hours. I can imagine the man saying, "We haven't got a speaker tonight so I'm going to read some theology that Luther wrote a couple of hundred years ago." I wouldn't have been surprised if half of those gathered in that little meeting house dozed off. But there was one man present who was not sleeping, and what he heard, and how he reacted to it, would shake the British Isles. The next day John Wesley wrote in his journal, "About a quarter before nine, while he [Luther] was describing the change which God works in the heart through faith in Christ, I felt my heart strangely warmed. I felt I did trust in Christ, Christ alone, for salvation; and an assurance was given me that he had taken away my sins, even mine, and saved me from the law of sin and death."[13]

The man who had critiqued mysticism had, himself, had a mystical experience. Wesley would not have called it that, but William James would certainly characterize it as such. What happened at Aldersgate was the kind of spiritual experience Wesley had longed to have. The Holy Spirit seemed to explode within him, and convinced him from within that he *was* a child of God. Assurance of salvation *was* his, and he knew that he was on his way to the holiness that had hitherto evaded him. He and his brother Charles began to preach passionately and extensively. Their main themes were that a repentant sinner who trusted in Christ could have a conscious assurance that he or she was accepted by God, and that such a "new born" Christian could then take the steps to grow daily in holiness toward total sanctification.

The reason Wesley did not see Aldersgate as a mystical experience is that he felt the assurance of salvation, something he did not see mystics ever attaining. But this was not the only reason that Wesley said he broke with mysticism. He even went so far as to write, "I think the rock on which I had the nearest made shipwreck of the faith was the writings of the mystics."[14] Wesley had many serious theological concerns in his understanding of the mystics. These are the same concerns Mary and I address in this book. We warn of the dangers of viewing mysticism as just another form of "works salvation." We agree with Wesley that the good works that are the essence of justice are the result of what God is able to do through us because of the Spirit's transforming effects in our lives. They are not a means that guarantees becoming Spirit-filled. That is a grace from God. We also agree with Wesley that mystical experiences are not to lead to a life of quiet seclusion with God, but to action in the world. The saints and mystics we talk about were led by God to be very involved in helping to change the world. And we have already stated the difference between some mystics' views of union and ours of unity, as well as the importance of reading Christ-centered mystics. Wesley himself told people to read the mystics, but only his edited versions of them. In essence, that is what Mary and I are doing in this book. We want you to learn about intimacy with Christ from mystics who loved Christ and experienced the life-changing grace of God that empowered them to share Christ and work for justice—like Wesley.

Although Wesley said he broke with mysticism, he continued to be influenced by them throughout his life. Not only did his excursion in Catholic mysticism set him up for the overpowering encounter with Christ that made him into an unrelenting evangelist, but the drive for sinless perfection, so earnestly sought by the mystics, was a major factor in the development of the Methodist movement that led to great social reform.

While Wesley was still a student at Oxford, the group of young Christians who joined together with him to seek "holiness" promoted what they called a "mysticism of service." They visited those in prison, found ways to assist needy people, helped poor families to send their children to school, and even tutored some neighboring boys and girls. This group of friends, who called themselves "The Holy Club," showed many signs of the social activism that would come to full-blown expression in the Methodist denominations that emerged from that little club at Oxford. The Methodist churches of the next couple of centuries would be characterized by an activism that lived out a holistic gospel that advocated both evangelism and social reform.

Wesley wanted everyone to hear the gospel, and he was aware that there were social conditions that were keeping those who were socially and economically disinherited from hearing the salvation story. Furthermore, he recognized that if the poor were to get the good news of Christianity, the church had to change its attitudes and practices.

While he remained a priest in the Church of England until his death, he opposed his church's practice of selling pew seats to those who wished to worship. Wesley wanted to carry the salvation story to those whose poverty was keeping them from making such purchases, so he began preaching in the places where such socially disinherited people lived and worked, a common thread connecting him with Moses, Jesus, Saint Francis, and Martin Luther King Jr. This commitment led Wesley to the marketplaces and farm fields of Britain. Wesley was not above speaking on street corners and going into the coal mines. Any place he could get people to stop and listen to the gospel was a place where he would evangelize. His messages brought his hearers under the conviction of the Holy Spirit and led them into transforming relationships with Christ. In preaching Christ in accord with scripture, Wesley could not avoid the emphasis in Christ's teachings about helping the poor and standing against injustices.

Out of the small weekly prayer meetings that were mandatory for his followers came growing convictions that programs to help the poorest of the poor were necessary. Over the course of time these Wesleyans became aware that simply ministering to the victims of an oppressive socioeconomic system was not enough. The system itself must be changed so that it did not produce so many human tragedies. They realized that for every suffering needy person they rescued through their humanitarian efforts, the social system produced several more to take that person's place. It is no surprise, therefore, to discover that the Wesleyan movement eventually would become committed to changing the political and economic institutions of Britain. Commitment to social change would be the consequence of the mystical spirituality that characterized Wesley's followers.

But social change was not the only kind of commitment that came out of Wesley's ministry. Wesley believed followers of Christ should be committed to being good stewards of God's Earth, which included being humane to animals, a concept almost nonexistent at the time. He wrote, "I believe in my heart that faith in Jesus Christ can and will lead us beyond an exclusive concern for the well-being of other human beings to the broader concern for the well-being of the birds in our backyards, the fish in our rivers, and every living creature on the face of the earth."[15]

Wesley despised any cruelty to dogs, horses, and other creatures. As the Wesleyan revival unfolded, people in London even said, "We know who has been converted by the ways in which they treat dogs." In those days dogs roamed the streets of London and were not regarded as being worthy of concern. The Wesleyan converts, however, took compassion on the dogs and worked to have them treated in more humane ways. Wesley also cared for animals that were not domesticated. He believed that God "directs us to be tender of even the meaner creatures, to show mercy to these also."[16] It is no wonder that the Royal Society for the Prevention of

Cruelty to Animals (RSPCA), founded in 1824, is said to have been inspired by the teachings of Christians such as Wesley, abolitionist reformer William Wilberforce, and popular theologian C. S. Lewis, all of whom spoke out against cruelty to animals. C. S. Lewis even suggested that those animals will be with us in eternity. This may seem silly to some people, but not to an elderly woman I know, who in her aloneness, found her only loving companion to be her dog. She considered heaven to be undesirable if her animal friend was not there with her.

John Wesley did more than suggest that animals will be with us in "the new heaven and the new earth." Using Romans 8:19–22, where the Apostle Paul said that all of creation waits for redemption, as well as the creation accounts in Genesis, Wesley preached that animals *will* be with us in eternity. He believed that since God's creation was originally in harmony and unity, and since God will one day restore *all* of creation to that original state, then animals will be part of that new heaven and new earth promised in Revelation. But Wesley did not believe that we should just wait for that day to value all of God's creation. He believed that God is bringing all of creation "nearer and nearer" to the day it will be set free, so we too, in our lives *now,* should "imitate him whose mercy is over all his works."[17] We do this by treating all that God created in more compassionately just ways *because* they are valuable, in and of themselves, as God's creation.

When we Christians sing the doxology, we must remember that the second line calls "all creatures here below" to worship God. Saint Francis, Wesley, and C. S. Lewis would all say, "Amen" to that and, in agreement with Psalm 148, declare that all creatures, as well as all of nature, were created to glorify God, so that even if humans did not exist, God's creation would still have meaning in and of itself. If you read that Psalm, you find that the Psalmist certainly believed that this was true. Being sensitive to all aspects of God's created Earth is not simply a utilitarian necessity for the survival of the human race but is a way of preserving all of nature, whose ultimate significance is worship. To ruin parts of God's creation, or allow creatures to become extinct through our careless exploitation, not only has negative consequences for us, but because it interferes with worship it can be considered blasphemous. Is it any wonder, in light of all of this, that mystics such as Francis and Wesley had a deep sensitivity to the natural world?

As you seek to walk humbly with your God, we hope that these, as well as other models presented in this book, will help you not only to share the redeeming love of Christ more fully, but to be emboldened to do justice work on behalf of all of God's creation.

PART TWO

FUELING INTIMACY

THE MYSTICAL PATH

Mary Albert Darling

4

AWAKENING TO MYSTICISM AND A HOLISTIC GOSPEL (EVEN IF YOU'RE NOT A MONK)

Now the Lord is the Spirit,
and where the Spirit of the Lord is,
there is freedom.

—II Corinthians 3:17

ALTHOUGH I HAVE BEEN a Christian for a long time, I did not realize the importance of a serious commitment to evangelistic or justice work as early as Tony did. I was much more interested in cultivating my own personal relationship with Christ. I loved reading stories and writings of monks and nuns who had deep intimacy with Christ and through those readings felt inspired to deepen my own relationship with Christ. But as time went on, I realized I was reading selectively. I was focusing more on a particular saint's mystical intimacy with Jesus than on the service that inevitably arose in conjunction with that intimacy.

My readings did not lead me to the more formal life of a monk or a nun—although it was tempting when I realized that nuns like Teresa of Avila and monks like Francis of Assisi and Thomas Merton grasped something that for many years I caught only in glimpses. They seemed to have something deeply mysterious and freeing in their daily relationships with Christ, something that fueled them with relentless desires to share that relationship through their words and their work. Although their lives greatly inspired me to want that kind of relationship, with those kinds of outpourings, I had the mistaken notion that the realm of "mystical" in which they lived was reserved for others—those supersaints I loved to read about but who seemed so far beyond my own daily life.

I was wrong. I now realize that to be in an intimate relationship with Jesus means I *am* a mystic. It means that I can—and should—cultivate the kind of mystical intimacy with Jesus that empowers me to do Jesus' work: sharing my relationship with Jesus with others in ways that help God's Kingdom to come and God's will to be done on earth as it is in heaven. In fact, I now realize that I cannot really be a Christian without being a mystic. A person becomes a Christian by entering into a personal, intimate, transforming relationship with Jesus Christ who is ever-present, living *in* us—now that's mystical!

> *I now realize that I cannot really be a Christian without being a mystic.*

We Don't Know What We Don't Know

My students at Spring Arbor University sometimes tell me they want certain assignments to be optional so that they can decide what they need to read and learn. I usually respond to this request by telling them, "We don't know what we don't know." At first they stare at me, thinking that this is the stupidest thing they have ever heard. But then I add that if we don't know what we don't know, we have more to learn than we realize. Even so, as we mature, we tend to believe that we know the limits of what we need to learn. We might even think we have all the knowledge and resources we need for living. Except instead of really living, we stagnate and hit a false ceiling. In addition, we can get stuck thinking that life is about defending what we know, instead of being open to something more. A relationship with Jesus, however, should be anything but stagnant or stuck. It is not enough to live with what we think is sufficient in our walk with Christ if that means we have settled for less.

The summer after I graduated from high school I dated a really nice Christian guy. After a few dates we started to talk more about our faith. I told him that I did not want to "settle" in my Christian life—I wanted my whole life to be about following Jesus. I will never forget his response: "Why can't two people just be Christians, have a nice house, and live a normal life?" When he said that, my heart sank. That was not what I wanted. To me that was settling for something less than Jesus wants for me and for *all* of us. I wanted the abundant life that Jesus promised in John 10:10 and that Irenaeus, one of the early church bishops, expressed by claiming that "man fully alive is the glory of God." (And so is woman.) And although I did not know what that abundant life was, I

> *It is not enough to live with what we think is sufficient . . . if that means we have settled for less.*

wanted to find it. I knew in my heart that it is about more than personal happiness and self-gratification. I knew it is about loving God and loving others in radical, life-transforming ways. I sensed that spiritual vitality is meant to enliven and empower us to share the gospel of Jesus Christ and to work effectively for change and healing, so that we all can experience a full life in Christ. And although I was a Christian, I was sensing that I was not living that radically abundant life Jesus calls us to live. I didn't seem to know how to develop what I wanted—the kind of spirituality that led me away from my own disordered desires to the true desires of my heart—the ones that involve deep inward and outward transformation.

In the following chapters I tell you about my journey toward an awareness that I had to be in a mystically intimate, "Spirit-led" relationship with Jesus if I wanted to love and live for God more freely, boldly, and consistently. I tell you my story in the hope that no matter where you are on your journey, you too might recognize the wonder of the intimate love of Christ in deeply transforming ways that will not only mystically change you, but motivate you to help change the world.

My Journey as a Theological Mutt

My spiritual development has been anything but consistent. Instead, it has involved a mix of several theological influences. I had what I consider my first "evangelical" experience with Christianity when I was around age eleven. Our neighbor down the street, Mrs. Ulmer, asked if I would come to her backyard once a week in the afternoon for what was called the "Good News Club." Many of my friends in the neighborhood attended this club, where we played games and then talked about Jesus and the Bible. One day Mrs. Ulmer asked my friend Sue and me to stay after club so she could talk to us more about Jesus. I can still picture the two of us sitting on the bottom step of her stairs as she told us that Jesus came to save people from their sins so they could live for God and have eternal life. She then asked us if we wanted to pray to God for forgiveness of our sins and for Jesus to come into our hearts and be Lord of our lives. Even though at that point in my life I didn't think I had done anything so terrible as to send Jesus to the cross for my sins, still I prayed the prayer. Sue prayed it too. Mrs. Ulmer said we were now Christians. At the time, Sue and I hardly understood any of the implications involved in being Christian. And although from that moment on I identified myself as a Christian, we walked away from Mrs. Ulmer's house not quite sure what we were supposed to do now that we had prayed that prayer.

Right around this same time, my mom wanted our family to find a different church, because she felt that our minister was preaching too much "social gospel" and not enough "personal salvation." To her, preaching personal salvation—that is, giving a direct invitation to accept Jesus into our lives—was the crux of Christianity. But what my young heart and mind also heard, although I do not believe this was her intention, was that preaching about social and legal reforms was not a mandatory part of the gospel of Jesus. Because of these two early experiences, the stage was set for me to understand conversion to Jesus Christ very narrowly. My mom's theological opinion was truth for me, so I concluded that the personal side of my relationship with Christ and traditional evangelism—trying to get others to "pray the prayer"—were essential (even though the evangelism part didn't appeal much to me). And although my mom had a compassionate heart for the poor and oppressed, no matter who they were, as well as a gift for connecting with God's creation, especially animals, I viewed intentionally working for justice issues as at best second-rate to personal conversion.

This narrow view worked well for me because I was a very insecure, scared-of-almost-everything child. My sister remembers (all too often) not being able to get to her elementary class on time because I wouldn't let go of her hand to go into my kindergarten class. I wish I could say that was just first-day jitters, but some of those "jitters" stayed with me for too many years and in too many situations. So my personal relationship with Christ became personally focused on me more than on others. Christ became my friend over the next several years through prayer, Bible study, and the "Youth for Christ" organization. But my fears and insecurities caused the friendship to be fairly one-sided. Although I would venture out at times and nervously witness or do a one-hour service project, my relationship with Christ was still too much about me and my issues, preventing me from trusting Jesus enough to live more wholeheartedly for God's reign. I did not yet have enough resources at my disposal to understand that the holistic message of Jesus included sharing Jesus with the lost and needy as *the norm* of my daily life. Certain spiritual writings would draw me into times of intimacy with Jesus, and although these writings included talk about loving and serving others, much of the time my own relationship with Jesus involved just Jesus and me.

A devotional book that my mom gave me, *God Calling*,[1] helped me begin to experience Jesus in even more intimate ways—I felt so connected and close to Jesus when I read that book. The same thing happened when I read Hannah Hurnard's *Hinds' Feet on High Places*,[2] a powerful allegory about our intimate journey and surrender to God. The book featured a main character named "Much Afraid." I could definitely relate to that name, so her journey to a new name, "Grace and Glory," was very appealing. But the closeness I felt during those times of reading was not enough. When I stopped reading *Hinds' Feet,* I was still "Much Afraid." I hungered for a depth of relationship that made a difference in *all* of my life, one that would get me out of my own self-centered story and into God's other-centered story.

During my final semester in college, I was required to read a book that was unlike any other book I had ever read—Ron Sider's *Rich Christians in an Age of Hunger.*[3] Although I was sympathetic to the poor and oppressed, I had never taken Jesus' words about working for justice much beyond giving away some clothes, giving a little money, helping out in a homeless shelter for an hour, or volunteering an afternoon at a recycling center. As necessary as those things are, they are not enough. But I didn't know that at the time. I thought that working for the needs of the poor and oppressed was a more life-altering call that was only for some Christians. The message I thought I received earlier in life, that a social gospel was optional, had taken hold. But now Ron Sider was telling me something very different. He was telling me that if I truly loved Jesus, I must be committed to the poor and oppressed. More than that, Sider said those were not his own ideas and words, they were the words of Jesus. They were in the Bible.

So I looked up those words, and found out that he was right. My discovery was similar to that of Rick Warren, a leading evangelical pastor and author of *The Purpose-Driven Life,* who after being sensitized to the AIDS pandemic, reread scripture with different eyes. He said, "I found those 2,000 verses on the poor. How did I miss that? I went to Bible college, two seminaries, and I got a doctorate. How did I miss God's compassion for the poor? I was not seeing all the purposes of God."[4]

Neither was I. I was still lacking in the kind of daily, intentional mystical intimacy with Christ that could empower me to live a more holistic gospel. I was still too insecure and too self-focused to do much more than sponsor a Third World child. As important as that kind of sponsorship is, it eased my guilty conscience too much and too soon.

Looking back, I know that being sensitized to child sponsorship was one of the many ways the Holy Spirit was tugging at my heart, but I continued to be a very slow learner. I believe this was partly because I did not have many of the resources that I needed, and partly because I squandered the resources I did have. I read my Bible and prayed, but it was not enough. I often felt closest to God during praise and worship times or while reading certain spiritual books, but I did not seem to know how to live at this level of intimacy all the time. And that is what I hungered for—to know and love Jesus at much deeper levels. I wanted every day to live the Psalmist's words, "As the deer pants for streams of water, so my soul pants for you, O God" (Psalm 42:1 NIV). I also hungered to see others live more this way. I knew in my spirit that these depths of intimacy existed—I had read about them and had also experienced glimpses of them in my own life. Yet I knew there was a life God has for us all that encompasses something more than mere glimpses. I wish that much earlier in life I would have found those examples of many past saints who had the kind of committed, mystically intimate love that resulted in their being compelled to share the gospel and to initiate change in the way we treat all of God's creation. I wish I could say that the churches and youth groups I attended encouraged me to enter into that kind of relationship with Jesus. But I think those examples were lost somewhere along the way. We need to return to *intentionally* learning from and teaching about this rich treasure of ancient church testimonies and practices that can help us grow in intimate love with Jesus and others.

At this point you may be thinking that what I needed back then was one of the many discipleship programs designed to teach people how to live like Jesus. The truth is that I was involved in a few of them. But what I experienced in those discipleship programs was more about personal piety and rules for living a Christian life than about the kind of spiritual transformation that leads to seeing the needs of the whole world through different eyes. As Dallas Willard, who writes extensively on the spiritual life, says, "What sometimes goes on in all sorts of Christian institutions is not formation of people in the character of Christ; it's teaching of outward conformity. You don't get in trouble for not having the character of Christ, but you do if you don't obey the laws."[5] To me, the Romans 12:2 verse about being "transformed by the renewing of our minds" only meant in *my* mind that I was to be a better person; this included doing periodic service projects but did not include a depth of intimacy with Jesus that moves us away from more shallow, compartmentalized ways of living and toward more consistent involvement with those whom Jesus said he came to serve and save.

When I thought about what I needed for this depth of living, my brother Dave's boat came to mind. It has what is called a "depth finder" on it, which is a sensor that tells how deep the water is. Dave got it after he almost sent my sister-in-law, Jane, overboard when they hit shallow water offshore. Shortly after this incident, Dave had a depth finder installed so that he could more easily find the deeper water (and so that Jane would ride with him again).

What I needed in my walk with Jesus were spiritual depth finders—people and practices that would more intentionally help me move away from shallow, self-centered daily patterns and into depths of living that intimacy with Jesus offers. I needed opportunities that I did not know existed in the church: I needed to be consistently mentored in a variety of spiritual practices, especially planned times of silence for creating space to pray the kinds of prayers that would draw me deeper into Christ's radically transforming love. I needed friends and a church community who also were regularly involved in these opportunities, so we could share our journeys and encourage each other. I needed to experience Jesus in ways that would lead me away from pseudo-spiritual preoccupation with myself to the kind of Spirit-filled life of caring and compassion that results in more consistently sharing the holistic gospel of Jesus Christ.

The Awakening

Several years ago, when my two sons were in elementary school, a good friend, Bev, went through a powerful spiritual awakening. She told me she could not call it a spiritual *revival* because there was not anything left to revive—her relationship with God was pretty much dead. Then one day, at the invitation of a friend, Bev went to a local United Methodist church. The sermon that day was on trusting God. The minister, Pastor Barb, walked around the congregation with her roving microphone and asked people for their spontaneous responses to the question, "What do you think would happen if a person totally surrendered to the Holy Spirit and totally gave his or her life to God?" Bev said that what caught her attention and impressed her at the time was how unemotional the whole event was. The message was not a "You owe this to God and it will cost you everything" type of sermon. Instead, Pastor Barb told the congregation that whoever was at a place where they wanted to have this kind of total surrender to and trust in God could come to the front and she would lay hands on them and pray for them "to get that." Bev did not go forward.

Then the pastor said, "If there are people who did not come forward, but are feeling that they want to explore this surrender, then I am going to tell you to do what Jesus told the disciples to do before Pentecost: 'Pray and wait; pray and wait; pray and wait.'" Bev remembers leaving the church feeling sad because she did not go forward. However, she could not get "pray and wait," "pray and wait" out of her head. She said it was as if the Holy Spirit was "staying in me with these words." Even while making the bed or cooking dinner, Bev had a sense of waiting. There was no epiphany; it was just that joy, peace, and love started growing in her. She didn't think that anyone really noticed any changes except her husband, who thought she was just having a whole string of really good days.

As Bev and I regularly talked about what was happening to her, she shared personal reflections from books she was now drawn to, especially devotional writings of saints and mystics from a series called *Rekindling the Inner Fire* by David Hazard.[6] Through the words of saints like Teresa of Avila, John of the Cross, and Augustine, the Holy Spirit was speaking to her in profound ways about the love of God.

Although I had loved writings like these for a long time, as we talked something new started to happen to me. Each time Bev and I had a conversation about how a reading spoke to us, I was overcome with a calm feeling, as if I were getting a spiritual massage. Much later I would find out that these times of sensing a closeness with God are examples of what Saint Ignatius called "spiritual consolations."

As the Holy Spirit continued to massage my heart, I felt an increasing depth of joy that I had had inklings of in the past, but that had always eventually gone away. This time they did not. I am not saying that I was from that point on always *happy*—happiness is not the same as joy—but something took hold and began to change me inside, resulting in a more consistent kind of base-contentment, side by side with a strong desire to be and do more for Jesus.

Bev's mystical awakening had become my mystical awakening. We both began to experience a new freedom that was opening up in our lives because we were accepting what we had been told—that we were personally loved by God—in a way we had never known before. We began to experience freedom from the harmful things that were holding us back and the freedom to choose what drew us closer to God. Bev described it for herself as a deep desire "to move out of being the center of my own story." We both desperately wanted to be a part of God's story through learning to be more like Jesus.

As Bev put it, "We fell in love with God and our desire was to be with God and with others who were in love with God." Strangely enough, we found these others who were in love with God to be saints who had been dead for hundreds of year. Undoubtedly, we could have gone to some saints who were in our own everyday world; nevertheless, it was these saints to whom we were drawn. We wanted to read about them and experience all the fullness of an intimate relationship with God that they were expressing in their writings.

The Journey to Spiritual Direction

Over the next few years Bev and I kept meeting, and although we did not always *feel* the intensity we felt in those first several months of our awakening, we knew we were being transformed by the Holy Spirit through our prayer times, our reading, and our times of sharing. This included meeting and praying with a small group of women who also desired this inner transformation. We did not want this to end, but I was afraid that it would not last. Then one of my colleagues in the Communication Department at Spring Arbor University mentioned to me a program he was going through involving "spiritual direction." I had recently become aware of this term while reading a series of novels by Susan Howatch and was attracted to it, even though I didn't really understand much of what it was about. Bev also started talking to me about her own attraction to the program, and in the fall of 2000, we both joined the same spiritual direction program, titled "Internship in Ignatian Spirituality: Finding God in All Things," sponsored by Manresa Jesuit Retreat House in Bloomfield Hills, Michigan.

One of the requirements of this program was to commit to meeting regularly with a spiritual director. My journey with spiritual direction that would lead me into a deepening mystical intimacy with God had begun. For the next two years Bev and I met with our spiritual directors and traveled an hour and a half away for classes and retreats that focused primarily on applying the teachings of Saint Ignatius of Loyola to our everyday lives and world.

Who Is Saint Ignatius?

Before I entered the spiritual direction program, I had very little idea of who Ignatius of Loyola was. What I learned during the next two years about Ignatius and his spiritual practices changed my life. Ignatius, the youngest son of a noble family, was born in 1491 in the Basque area of Spain. In his younger years, like Saint Francis of Assisi, he partied and was a soldier. Then at age thirty, Ignatius was hit and badly wounded in one of his legs by a cannon ball. He faced several months of recuperation, especially because his leg did not heal properly and had to be rebroken and reset. During this time there was nothing much for him to do but read. He asked for books on romance and knightly adventures, but instead was given a book on the lives of the saints, and a special book called *Life of Christ,* written by a monk of the Carthusian order.

Ignatius began to notice that he felt peaceful and content after he read about and then reflected on Christ and the lives of saints. He was surprised by how wonderfully different those feelings were from the feelings of restlessness and dissatisfaction he had been having while daydreaming of a noble lady to whom he was attracted. Distinguishing these feelings was the beginning of what he called "the discernment of spirits," the hallmark of Ignatian spirituality. This discernment involved learning to recognize and respond to the Holy Spirit as a presence in his everyday life. More than anything, he wanted to follow the examples of Christ and the saints.

Ignatius eventually went on to spend a year in Manresa, a town about 40 miles from Barcelona, where his relationship with God was powerfully deepened. During that year, he made a decision to live in a large cave to escape the distractions of the world and develop an even closer relationship with God. While in the cave, Ignatius prayed, fasted, and studied *The Imitation of Christ* by Thomas à Kempis,[7] a book that urges Christians to take Christ as our daily example of how to live. As a result, Ignatius experienced God in mystically intimate ways that changed his life.

Ignatius came from the cave with a new and intense desire to share his Manresa experience, which he had started to put in a written form called the "Spiritual Exercises." These exercises consisted of a manual of prayers and meditations intended to draw people into experiencing Christ in personal and world-transforming ways. Although Ignatius passionately desired to share what he had learned and experienced, at that time unschooled laypeople did not usually speak about religious matters. So Ignatius went to various schools to get the credentials he needed to preach his message. He ended up at the University of Paris, where he found six spiritual companions, including Francis Xavier; this group went on to form a new type of religious order called the "Society of Jesus." An outsider would later call them the "Jesuits"—a nickname that stuck.

Based on Jesus' commissioning of his disciples to "go out into all the world," the members of this society could be sent, at a moment's notice, anywhere in the world where there was great need. These men, who became missionaries in all parts of the world, were known mainly for their contributions to service and to learning that came out of their experiences with the Ignatian Spiritual Exercises.

The Spiritual Exercises of Ignatius

If you want to gain a better understanding of the purpose of the exercises and what they have to do with a holistic Christianity, it is important to first know that Ignatius had a motto that was the focus of his spirituality, as well as the motto of the Society of Jesus: *Ad Majorem Dei Gloriam,* or "For the Greater Glory of God." This motto was Ignatius's mission statement in a nutshell. Everything he taught revolved around how to live out this statement every day. That is why the Spiritual Exercises were so important to him. Ignatius wanted his whole life to be taken over by God, as indicated in this prayer of his: "Take, O Lord, and receive all my liberty, my memory, my understanding and my will; all that I have and possess. You have given them to me; to you, O Lord, I restore them. All things are yours: Dispose of them according to your will. Give me your love and your grace; for this is enough for me."[8]

The purpose of Ignatius's Spiritual Exercises is to lead us into the kind of freedom in Christ in which we too can pray to God to take our whole lives and restore them to God's glory so that we can experience and follow God in all of life. The exercises involve being guided by a spiritual director through four "weeks" of prayer and meditation on specific themes. It is important to note that *weeks* does not necessarily refer to actual weeks, but to *themes,* which means that the exercises can be done over an intensive several days a month or longer extended periods of time depending on the structure of the particular program.

The exercises focus on these four themes or "weeks":

1. Experiencing the unconditional love of God along with the sin in the world, including our personal sin
2. Identifying with Jesus' life and putting on the mind of Christ
3. Sharing in the sufferings of Jesus' last week before his crucifixion
4. Sharing in Christ's resurrection and mission to the world

In my spiritual direction program, the exercises were presented over a two-year period using these versions of the traditional themes:

• The essential act of coming to accept that God loves us and shows us this love by creating us, by calling us into friendship and partnership, and by being actively present in all of our relationships, including all of God's creation, animate and inanimate

• The mystery of sin and evil drawing us into a self-centeredness that moves us away from God's loving presence, and then God's ever-greater love and mercy in giving us Jesus to draw us back to God's unconditional love

- The call of Christ for each of us to share in God's great mission and work to heal a broken, hurting world and help bring the reign of God

- God becoming human in Jesus to show us the way of this mission of healing the world by identifying, as Jesus did, with those who are broken and need healing, and by getting involved in their struggles and poverty

- The pull of two different ways to live: either for God or for the world; learning to tell the difference between "the movements of the Holy Spirit" and things not of God, so that we can recognize and choose Christ's call for our lives in ongoing, daily ways

During the two-year program, I learned about these themes through classes, workshops, readings, and written reflections. But I did not just learn *about* God, and this is crucial: I was beginning to *experience* the transforming love of God during these regular, intentional times of reflection, in-depth sharing, and guided silent retreats. We also were required to experience an immersion weekend, in which we had to choose among three options for ministry: a prison, a homeless shelter, or a hospital emergency room. The purpose was to help us in discerning how we are being purposely called beyond ourselves and into the world. Our charge during this immersion weekend was to go and simply be present with people by listening to them.

All these intentional combinations of learning and experience gave me a taste of what I had always been looking for: the means for developing a more holistic gospel of lifelong intimacy with Christ that would empower me to help bring Christ's Kingdom to Earth.

Does everyone have to go through a spiritual direction program like Bev and I did to live Jesus' holistic gospel? No. All who are willing to follow through with the directions modeled on the spiritual practices of great saints like Ignatius can find indescribable life transformation waiting to be experienced.

Being willing to explore these practices implies being open to new or different ways to know and experience Christ. But that kind of newness can be very scary for many of us. Yet intimacy with Christ *begins* with learning new ways to live, which means we need to unlearn some old ways of living, since the lessons of the past can block us in understanding the lessons of the future.

Remedial Christianity—
Relearning the Lessons from the Past

Toward the end of my spiritual direction program, my friend Roger, who was spending a year in Kenya with his family, wrote and asked me what I was learning in the program. I responded with a long e-mail about the recent experiences that were taking me out of my comfort zone and into a deeper intimacy with Jesus. These experiences, I wrote, were resulting in a new awareness of how I was to intentionally be a worker for Jesus' mission in the world.

As I proofread my e-mail, I realized that everything I had written could be summarized in one statement: I had gone through this intense program in Ignatian spirituality to learn what I had already learned years ago in church and Sunday school: that I need to read my Bible and pray. What was different was that I was being taught to read the Bible and pray in new ways. Actually, they were not new at all—they were just new to me. The spiritual practices I was learning were steeped in hundreds of years of church tradition. Some I had never heard of; others I had read about but had not practiced and experienced until then. Even though they all boiled down to reading the Bible and praying, I still needed to *relearn*. That's because I had become stuck in how I was praying and reading scripture, and through the program I learned ways to pray and read that drew me into a greater intimacy with Christ.

This was not the only time that old patterns had gotten me stuck. During a swim class I took in college, I learned that the Red Cross had changed the technique of the kick for the breast stroke. Since I already knew how to do the old stroke, it was very difficult for me to physically relearn how to time my arms and legs with a new way to kick. Not only was it physically difficult to change the stroke, it didn't *feel* right to be doing it differently, even though the experts agreed that it was better.

We can have misguided loyalties to comfortable patterns because what is new to us does not always feel right. But that does not mean it is wrong. We may even believe that our firm resolve not to change a certain attitude or action is due to a strong Christian conviction when what is really driving us is fear of leaving our comfort zone. During these times we can look to others who have come before us to help us discern what is of God and what is not. We do not have to look far in the Bible for a good example of someone who had trouble leaving his comfort zone to learn to live more fully for God and others. When Jesus first called Peter to be a disciple, he said, "Follow me" (Matthew 4:19). Then after Peter had been with

Jesus for three years, and even denied Jesus three times toward the end of those years, Jesus once again bid him, "Follow me" (John 21:19). As Jesuit James Serrick notes, "It's the very same invitation. But what a world of difference. By that time Peter was a changed man and he could follow Jesus in a totally different way."[9]

Even though Peter followed Jesus as he walked the earth, Peter still had a hard time understanding Jesus' messages and intentions. Peter was the one who told Jesus not to wash his feet because he did not understand the meaning of servanthood. He is also the one to whom Jesus said in Matthew 16:23, "Get behind me, Satan! You are a stumbling block to me; for you are setting your mind not on divine things but on human things," when Peter chastised Jesus for saying he was going to die. Yet Jesus did not give up on Peter. He knew Peter's heart and desire to follow him, even though it was misguided at times.

> We can have misguided loyalties to comfortable patterns because what is new to us does not always feel right.

Jesus continued to push Peter to learn new ways to love God and others, just as Jesus does with us. Because of his continuing relationship with Jesus even in the midst of misunderstanding and failure, Peter kept learning what it meant to grow in love and in desire to follow Jesus. Perhaps his biggest challenge came the day he had a vision of a large sheet coming down from heaven, holding all kinds of animals (see Acts 10 and 11). Imagine being Peter, a devout Jew who had always followed strict dietary laws being told during this vision to "get up, Peter. Kill and eat." After Peter replied, "Surely not, Lord!" the voice came back and said, "Do not call anything impure that God has made clean." Just after this vision, Peter was told by the Holy Spirit to go with three men to see Cornelius the centurion, who wanted to know more about God. But Cornelius was not a Jew, and it was against Jewish law for a Jew to associate with a Gentile. Still, Peter realized that God was telling him through the vision that he was now to open up the gospel not only to Jews, but to *Gentiles*!

Because I have heard this Bible story since I was a child, I can too easily forget what was really going on here. What Peter saw and discerned from the vision went against everything his religious beliefs had taught him. Yet his openness to listening to God's Spirit led him to live in new, radical ways for God's reign. It took him a long time to realize that his expectations for following Jesus were not the same as the reality of following Jesus.

Like Peter, we are called to follow Jesus in new and radically different ways throughout our lives, as we learn to love and grow in him. For me, the new way that has changed my life in the past several years is learning and experiencing three different prayers that are not new at all. They are the prayer of examen, *lectio divina,* and centering prayer. All three of these prayers, which I discuss in later chapters, have changed me, connecting me more intimately with Jesus and others than I ever knew was possible. I didn't realize any of these changes until my friend Bev started mentioning some of them to me. I say that in part because admitting that I am changing feels a little too close to what my husband calls "shameless self-promotion." But it is not my intention to imply that I am responsible for the changes. My intention is to show that it is the Holy Spirit who changes us when we yield to that Spirit. That is a crucial distinction. (And during those times when I start to take credit for positive changes, the Holy Spirit reminds me that I am flawed; my sons are good at that too.)

It is essential for us to remember that it is God's Spirit who changes and even rewards us when we enter into intentional times of intimacy with God. Jesus, in his Sermon on the Mount, said that when you pray you are to go into your room, close the door, and pray to God, who is unseen. Then God, who sees what is done in secret, will reward you (Matthew 6:6). I have found that when I meet with God in quiet through these prayers, God *is* rewarding me—and God will reward you too. These rewards, however, are not personal or material—they are something much more valuable. The God you meet in secret with these prayers will reward you by transforming you into someone whose heart is being broken more and more by the things that break the heart of God. You will better understand what happened to Jesus that resulted in his being "moved with compassion" (see Matthew 9:36 and 14:14; Mark 8:2). You will become increasingly concerned about the lost and about injustices done to God's people and to all of God's creation. And that is what mystical intimacy with Christ is all about.

In the next chapters I share how we can learn from supersaints, as well as from saints who are more like the rest of us, to enter into and continue this mystical intimacy with Christ. Ignatius of Loyola, Francis of Assisi, and Teresa of Avila, along with ordinary saints whom Tony and I know, can help us experience God if we do not just read about them but make their spiritual practices our own. The deep desire of our hearts can then be realized as we enter into a transforming intimacy with Christ and we allow that intimate friendship to change us into people committed to changing the world. This holistic gospel is where the Spirit of the Lord is. It is where there is freedom and the abundant life that Jesus promised. It is the "something more" I had been looking for all my life. I hope it is what you have been looking for too.

5

CULTIVATING
HOLY HABITS

*The Christian ideal has not been tried and found
wanting; it has been found difficult; and left untried.*

—G. K. Chesterton, *What's Wrong with the World* (1910)

IN THE MOVIE *The Lion King,* Simba, the young lion, runs away after his
father, the Lion King, dies. Simba runs both from his past, believing he
was responsible for his father's death, and also from his future inheritance
as the next Lion King. One dark evening, gazing into a pool of water, he
thinks he sees his own reflection. His friend Rafiki tells him to look again,
and when he does, Simba's reflection becomes the reflection of his father.
His father's image then appears to Simba in the sky, and the deep voice of
James Earl Jones booms out: *"Remember who you are!"*

We, too, need to remember who we are. We need to reclaim our her-
itage and once again live as we were made to live—as children of God,
made in God's image.

Why Holy Habits Are Important

The ultimate model for how to live as God's child is the ultimate Child of
God—Jesus Christ. We need to continually learn how to be like Jesus.
Jesus passionately loved God and compassionately loved and worked for
justice for others. But consistently living this way of Jesus *is* difficult—just

like Chesterton said. His quote has haunted me since the first time I read it because he puts it so bluntly. But so did Jesus. Jesus told us to count the costs—and that is precisely because Jesus' gospel is a holistic one, requiring us to change inwardly and outwardly. Yet too many of us try living a Christian life without making any radical change. The Trappist monk Thomas Keating wrote that our "false self"—the self outside of God—adjusts "to the circumstances of the spiritual journey as long as it does not have to change itself."[1] We need to be aware of this all-too-common danger so that we do not leave Christianity untried.

How do we go about this radical transformation? Regularly engaging in spiritual practices or "holy habits" is what enables us to consistently live and love like Jesus. Their purpose is to help us remember who we are by drawing us into, and helping us stay committed to, the kind of intimate "first love" with Jesus that makes it possible for us to do God's work in the world.

Some of you might be wishing for a different answer to the question of how we radically change because the idea of spiritual practices is not all that appealing. My friend Jacki used to feel that way. When she first committed to engaging in some of the spiritual practices we are advocating in this book, she decided on half an hour a day, which she said was a "chore" and God was often no more than a "concept." A few years have passed since then, and Jacki recently told me that she often *wants* to be alone with Jesus now—in fact, some days she can't wait for those times. She even said half an hour isn't nearly enough anymore. I asked when that changed. She said it was a gradual change, due to spending intentional time in various spiritual practices that she hoped would make a difference—and they did. God is no longer merely a concept to Jacki; Jesus is now an intimate presence in her life.

> *Too many of us try living a Christian life without making any radical change.*

Even though we all recognize the importance of concentrated discipline in many other areas of life—whether brushing our teeth, getting an education, training for a job, being involved in a sport, or developing a musical ability—still, we often do not understand how necessary training is to our spiritual lives. The Apostle Paul told Timothy to "train yourself in godliness" (I Timothy 4:7). Just as we need to be intentional in other areas of our lives for optimal health, so we need to be intentional in growing in love for God and others for optimal spiritual health and wholeness. This is the only *consistent* way to be formed to the likeness of Christ and to walk as Jesus did.

Defining Holy Habits

Traditionally, "spiritual disciplines" is the term used to refer to the holy habits I am talking about. But for some of us, even hearing the word *discipline* conjures up negative images. That is why I prefer the term "holy habits" or "spiritual practices." Looking at the spiritual disciplines as practices or holy habits can take away possible off-putting connotations and motivate us to do them. Another reason we might have a negative image of spiritual practices is that we define them too narrowly. We have a certain idea in mind of what they involve, and for whatever reason, that idea isn't very appealing.

Anything is a spiritual practice or holy habit if done

- Intentionally
- Over time with regularity
- With the goal of being formed into Christ-likeness
- With the result (fruit) of growing in love for God and others

Such practices include praying and reading the Bible in a variety of ways, worshiping alone or in a group through music and other forms of art, confessing our sins and shortcomings, living more simply, and giving of our time and money, to name only a few. Their purpose, in the words of the Dutch Catholic priest and writer Henri Nouwen, is to "create some inner and outer space in our lives" where we can practice the kind of obedience that Jesus had toward God when Jesus walked the earth.[2] As such, spiritual practices or holy habits are a means of receiving God's grace. They are the stimulus to create sacred space that can then be filled, through God's grace, with love for God and others. Love, grace, and holy habits always go together. As we will see later in this chapter, without love and an understanding of grace, engaging in spiritual practices can too easily lead to self- and works righteousness. But *with* God's love and grace, holy habits produce good works.

Intentionality

Over the years, I have noticed a questionable assumption in the area of discipline and planning versus spontaneity in our spiritual lives. Although spontaneity has its place, at times Christians can appear to value spontaneity over intentionality in some very curious ways. As just one example, take evangelicals and public prayer. It seems as if many of us who are evangelical put more value on spontaneous rather than planned, written-out prayer. I learned this through my personal experience with the fear of speaking, and therefore praying, in public. Whenever asked in advance to pray in public, I always used to be so nervous at the time I was to speak that I would draw a blank and have nothing to say. So I started writing out my prayers ahead of time and reading them when the time came. I remember feeling guilty for doing that, since others told me they often prayed on the spot "as the Spirit led." There seemed to be some underlying assumption of a lack of connection to or trust in the Spirit if I had to write out my prayer and read it.

What was really being said here? That if we are asked to pray ahead of time, is it better to assume that the Holy Spirit will work *best* in us spontaneously rather than leading us as we more intentionally ponder what we want to say? Although we know that the Spirit can move at any time, anywhere, we should never use that as an excuse not to discipline ourselves spiritually, for specific events as well as for lifelong discipleship to Christ. We do not want to become spiritually lazy. As the Apostle Peter taught, "Always be ready to make your defense to anyone who demands from you an accounting for the hope that is in you" (I Peter 3:15).

The philosopher Søren Kierkegaard illustrates how lack of intentionality leads to spiritual laziness in the following story.

> Every Sunday the ducks waddle out of their houses and waddle down Main Street to their church. They waddle into the sanctuary and squat in their proper pews. The duck choir waddles in and takes its place, then the duck minister comes forward and opens the duck Bible. He reads to them: "Ducks! God has given you wings! With wings you can fly! With wings you can mount up and soar like eagles. No walls can confine you! No fences can hold you! You have wings. God has given you wings and you can fly like birds!"
>
> All the ducks shouted, "Amen!" As the ducks left the service they commented on what a wonderful sermon it was. *And they all waddled home.*[3]

How many of us waddle through our weeks, after so many repeated proclamations to act on what we have heard, without forming the habits that will help us to do those actions? How many of us do not recognize the "wings" that free us to soar with God?

Dallas Willard, who writes extensively on this issue of spiritual practices, contends that we will not get far in our spiritual life if we do it haphazardly. We need to intentionally train, just like Jesus did. I love how

Richard Foster puts it: "Jesus did not all of a sudden one day start spouting nice sayings about God."[4] Instead, he came from a life of being intensely taught and trained. Jesus *is* our supreme example. We read in the Bible that from his early childhood Jesus "increased in wisdom and in years, and in divine and human favor" (Luke 2:52). He did this in great part by devoting himself to the reading of scripture and to prayer. Jesus absorbed the scriptures. For example, many times he quoted from the Hebrew Bible by starting with the phrase, "You have heard that it was said . . ." (see Matthew 5:21, 27, 33, 38, 43). Jesus also knew that to be intimately connected to God, he needed to go off alone to pray (see Matthew 26:36; Mark 1:35; Luke 5:16).

If we want to be like Jesus, we too must be intentional in our spiritual growth.

Over Time, with Regularity

I used to think that some followers of Christ had a special link to God because they appeared to be driven by a tremendous love for God that required no discipline. But as I studied some of those lives, including supersaints like Francis and Teresa of Avila, I discovered hours and hours of devotion directed toward opening up space in their lives to growing in that love. They were doing what the Apostle Peter told us to do when he wrote that we are to "*grow* in the grace and knowledge of our Lord and Savior Jesus Christ" (II Peter 3:18, emphasis mine).

All of us, no matter who we are, are continually formed through the daily, even hourly, choices we make that lead to habitual ways of living. As Richard Foster contends, just as we have made a thousand decisions to form certain habits in our lives, we can also make a thousand decisions to train to live a different way. Thomas à Kempis, in *Imitation of Christ*,[5] encouraged us to "fight bravely, for habit overcomes habit." We fight and overcome our harmful habits by regularly engaging in holy habits. Paul told the Colossians, "As you therefore have received Christ Jesus as Lord, continue to live your lives in him, rooted and built up in him and established in the faith, just as you were taught, abounding in thanksgiving" (Colossians 2:6–7). I don't think any of us would argue that Paul meant *daily* when he said to continue to live in Christ. This kind of daily living involves daily training.

We can be intentional in spiritual growth, but without daily training, our growth will be greatly inhibited. I remember talking to my friend Bev once about my frustration with engaging in certain spiritual practices only a few days a week or month, but not every day. Her response to me was, "Well, I guess it just depends on how long you want it to take." We both knew that growing in Christ-likeness is a lifelong process, but with those words she helped me more clearly see how I was stunting my own capacity to love God and others due to my lack of more consistent and regular spiritual practices.

So what do you do when you don't feel like engaging in any spiritual practices on a given day, or a given week, or even a given month? First recognize that everyone has dry periods that may not be caused by anything they are doing or not doing. Ignatius called these dry times "spiritual desolation without previous cause" and urged people to keep doing the practices during those times. He taught that those dry periods would ebb and flow into times of spiritual aliveness or "spiritual consolations." So trust that even though you do not *feel* anything, God is still at work deep in your spirit.

But if you know of something in your life or spirit that is, or could be, contributing to a dry time (or even if you aren't sure, but wonder), talk with a spiritual mentor or other spiritual companion. And don't forget the most important thing: to pray. When you are having an especially difficult time being disciplined in spiritual practices, don't forget that you can take that reality to Jesus. Pray, first by coming into Jesus' loving presence and telling Jesus that you do not feel like doing the disciplines. Then ask for the help of the Holy Spirit, remembering that Jesus said that if you ask, you will receive (Matthew 7:7). Then "just do it." Keep showing up. Keep doing the spiritual practices for spiritual health, just as you would keep doing physical exercises for bodily health.

> *Even though you do not feel anything, God is still at work deep in your spirit.*

Try this for starters: Follow the spiritual practices I discuss in the next three chapters for one day. Then do them one more day. And then another . . . Although you will sometimes feel you have stalled out, keep going. You won't be disappointed. You will find that these spiritual practices are helping you to discover how deep and wide is the liberating, good news of Jesus Christ in its power to transform you and the world.

Being Formed into Christ-Likeness

Whether or not we realize it, we are all influencers and role models. That is not necessarily a good thing, since we can influence others not only positively, but negatively too. There is no better way to prepare ourselves to be influencers for good than to get to know the greatest role model and person of influence who ever lived.

To get to know anyone, and become more like that person, we need to spend time with that individual. As Christians, we are called to be imitators of God, by living in love as Jesus did (Ephesians 5:1–2). Living this way requires us to know Jesus. That is why we regularly engage in spiritual practices—to spend intentional time with Jesus so that we can be "transformed into the same image from one degree of glory to another; for this comes from the Lord, the Spirit" (II Corinthians 3:18). We engage in spiritual practices to conform to the character of Christ. But we can too easily forget that calling, especially if we focus only on the first two parts of the definition of holy habits. We are then in very dangerous territory.

DANGER 1: LOPSIDED CHRISTIANITY. Although a variety of holy habits are needed to live a holistic gospel, it can become all too easy for us to focus on only a few. We need to encourage one another to develop a broad range of habits; otherwise our understanding of what it means to be like Christ can become lopsided. We may, for example, attend church whenever the doors are open; however, we may not see the relevance of working for justice in the neighborhoods beyond our church doors. This kind of limited focus can greatly hinder God's work in our hearts and in the world. The Holy Spirit is alive in us, helping us not only to love God, but also to love others, including those beyond our interpersonal sphere. Engaging in spiritual practices should always lead us to that realization.

It might seem ironic, then, that the next chapters focus on only three spiritual practices: the prayer of examen, *lectio divina* (holy reading), and centering (silent) prayer. Since there are so many necessary spiritual practices, such as intercessory prayer and fasting (to name only two), I could easily be accused of contributing to lopsided Christianity when I write about how to find intimacy with God through only three disciplines. But my intent is quite the opposite. I believe that these three, in particular, are lost practices to many of us, resulting in too many lopsided Christians and Christian communities. As Jeremiah 6:16 says, "Stand at the crossroads, and look, and ask for the ancient paths, where the good way lies, and walk in it, and find rest for your souls."

Rediscovering these ancient holy habits can help us connect intimately with Christ in ways that foster Christ-likeness and therefore help us to reach out in compassionate love and justice toward the lost and needy. We do need to be involved in a variety of what Richard Foster calls inward, outward, and corporate spiritual disciplines. We especially need to be open to fostering in our lives those ancient disciplines that have somehow gotten lost along the way for so many of us, causing us to lose sight of the radical nature of Jesus' gospel.

DANGER 2: WORKS RIGHTEOUSNESS. Another danger of an improper approach to the disciplines lies in using them as a way to be right with God in and of themselves, or what is called "works righteousness." Our motive should never be to do the disciplines only as a way to get to heaven, but instead to do them as a means for living out the two greatest commandments: loving God and loving others. If we use the disciplines as an insurance policy, they become an end in and of themselves, and our Christianity can become all form and no substance. Form can easily disguise itself as substance, and then we are not even aware of our wrong and harmful motives.

DANGER 3: PUTTING LEGALISM OVER LOVE. When spiritual disciplines become their own end, they can too easily turn into rules or legalisms, which then lead to a self-righteous, self-promoting pride—without our even realizing it. An older woman I knew grew up in a strict religious environment. One day when I was with her, she received a phone call from a local dance studio, asking her if she was interested in dance lessons. I heard her indignantly tell the caller, "*No, I do not dance. I am a Christian.*" One of her church's spiritual disciplines included abstaining from dancing, and she "witnessed" to the man on the other end of the line that dancing and Christianity did not belong together. This made me wonder: If the caller knew nothing of Jesus' gospel before the call, what did he know now? We can believe we are loving people, but when we put our spiritual rules above love, we become like the Pharisees who tried to accuse Jesus of breaking Mosaic law when Jesus was about to heal a man on the Sabbath (Matthew 12:10).

When legalism triumphs over love, we want others to see that we are living spiritually superior lives through our spiritual practices. But this stops us from living Jesus' radical message of love. Jesus warned the Pharisees, "Be careful not to do your 'acts of righteousness' before others in order to be seen by them; for then you have no reward from your Father in heaven" (Matthew 6:1).

What is worse is when we do not even live what we promote. Again, Jesus used the religious leaders of his day to warn us, "But do not do what they do, for they do not practice what they preach. They tie up heavy loads and put them on men's shoulders, but they themselves are not willing to lift a finger to move them. Everything they do is done for men to see" (Matthew 23:3–5 NIV).

When we engage in spiritual practices, we must continually be aware of the dangers involved in turning those practices into a set of rules in and of themselves. We must examine our motives, so that Jesus never says to us what he said to the Pharisees of his time: "You hypocrites! Isaiah prophesied rightly about you when he said: 'This people honors me with their lips, but their hearts are far from me; in vain do they worship me, teaching human precepts as doctrines'" (Matthew 15:7–9).

I do not think that any of us ever start out *intending* to worship God in vain or have our hearts far from God. I do not believe the religious leaders of Jesus' time intended that outcome either. But it can happen. If we allow our spiritual practices to become an end in themselves, instead of the means to the end, we will become hard-hearted and legalistic. We then forget that the disciplines are meant to help us develop the kind of deep love for God that compels us to reach out to others in selfless love instead of with self-righteous actions. We lose sight of the real goal of holy habits if we fail to recognize this crucial difference. As a matter of fact, if we start to believe we are doing pretty well spiritually by how spiritual we think we look to others, that may be a good indicator that we are not very spiritual at all. The point is not to do what we do for the sake of appearance. We do what we do for the love of God and others—all others.

Several years ago a student and I had a very disturbing talk. This young man was not a Christian, and he was confused and troubled by some comments he heard from Christian students about gay and lesbian people during a discussion in one of his classes. He told me he could not believe the hate in the room during that discussion. The rules these students had been taught about how we should live had triumphed over love. Sadly, that day several students identified themselves as Christians by their hate instead of by their love.

At this point you may be thinking of other examples of people you know who are too legalistic and self-righteous in their faith, with their lists of dos and don'ts. Although it is much easier for us to point the finger at someone else, we need to be open to the possibility of our own legalisms and lists. Here's how Stephen, one of my students, expressed this problem to me: "No wonder those whom God has called us to love and care for are forgotten when we're focusing all our attention on the things that we should not be doing. It would seem that if we instead focused on the things we should be doing, we would find ourselves so constantly being used by God that we wouldn't have any time to do the things that we shouldn't."

Developing holy habits helps us focus on the things of God if we remember that their purpose is to open up space in our lives to love God and others, not to give us a set of rules to make us feel virtuous. Making rules the end instead of the means stops us from having the power of God in our lives.

I believe this is what happened to the rich young man whom we read about in Matthew 19. One day this man came to Jesus and asked what he could do to inherit eternal life. Jesus responded by telling him to obey the Ten Commandments. "I have kept all these," the young man said. "What do I still lack?" "Boy," Jesus then said, "if you wish to be perfect, go, sell your possessions, and give the money to the poor, and you will have treasure in heaven; then come, follow me." The man walked away sad because "he had many possessions." Jesus then told his disciples that "it is easier for a camel to go through the eye of a needle than for someone who is rich to enter the Kingdom of God."

When I hear a sermon on this passage or read it myself, the stopping point of the story is often the metaphor about the camel and the needle. But one day, I kept on reading: "When the disciples heard this, they were greatly astounded and said, 'Then who can be saved?' But Jesus looked at them and said, 'For mortals it is impossible, but for God all things are possible'" (Matthew 19:25–26).

As I silently reflected on these words, the realization came to me: with the Holy Spirit it is possible! Then it hit me: *he walked away too soon.* The rich young man was trying to obey and follow God all on his own strength. He had disciplined himself to keep the Ten Commandments since he was a child (Mark 10:20), but he had lost sight of the real purpose and goal of that kind of discipline—as a means of selflessly conforming to Christ-likeness through the power of the Holy Spirit. So when it came to that last demand of Jesus, to sell all he had, that was his breaking point. It was just too hard. And he was right—it was too hard for him. But what he did not see was that it was not too hard *if* he allowed God's Spirit of love and grace to work in and through him. The ending of the story could have been very different if the man had realized that he could trust in the dynamism of the Spirit. But he walked away too soon.

This story makes me wonder how many times I walk away too soon. How many times am I guilty of, as Paul says in II Timothy 3:5, "holding to the outward form of Godliness but denying its power"? How many times do I try to live a spiritual life without the Spirit? When I do this, I settle for living by a set of rules, and transformation in Christ is not possible. But Christianity is not too difficult as long as we allow the Holy Spirit to transform us into the likeness of Christ. With God, *all* things are possible. If we open ourselves up to the power and love of the Holy Spirit, God will do "abundantly far more than all we can ask or imagine"

(Ephesians 3:20). We can continue this abundant life through intentional spiritual practices. That is what they are for—to create space for God to meet us and for us to meet God—all to the end that we might grow in love for God and become lovers of humanity.

John Wesley understood love's place over *everything* else—including truth. In his *Preface to the Sermons,* he wrote, "For, how far is love, even with many wrong opinions, to be preferred before truth itself without love! We may die without the knowledge of many truths, and yet be carried to Abraham's bosom. But, if we die without love, what will knowledge avail? Just as much as it avails the devil and his angels."[6]

Real Fruits and False Fruits

When we engage in spiritual practices intentionally, over time, with the goal of being formed into Christ-likeness, we *will* grow in love for God and others. The fruit of the Spirit will be produced in our lives as a by-product of this love. We must always remember this necessary progression; otherwise we could unintentionally short-cut transformation and produce false fruit.

In the summer of 2000 our family took a road trip out west. Because we were going to be traveling in a van together for three weeks, my husband Terry and I decided we should be more intentional with the spiritual growth of our two boys: David, then eight, and Michael, then seven. I came up with the idea of having them each pick a fruit of the Spirit and practice that particular fruit for a day; then the next day they were to pick another. I was pretty proud of this plan. I ran it by Terry, and he thought it was worth trying. The first day David picked joy, and that did not seem difficult for him, especially since he was excited about the trip. Michael picked peace, and that worked too. But it was only day one.

Day two went reasonably well, except at times they forgot the fruits they picked. On day three, things started going rotten. I think David picked patience and Michael picked kindness. At one point, not far into the drive, they started bickering about something. I turned to them and said, in a voice that ironically did not resemble any fruit of the Spirit, "What fruit did *you* pick, David? And what about *you,* Michael? *Patience? Kindness?* Well you both certainly aren't acting like it."

And that is how it went for yet another day, until we decided the fruit thing just wasn't working. We stopped making them pick a fruit. I was frustrated because I thought it was such a good idea.

But as I thought about it further, I realized that what we had them doing was *so* wrong! It hit me: those things are *fruits!* By-products! We had David and Michael practicing something that is a product of something else. Just like telling a plant in early spring to give me a flower *now,* we were trying to "make" them act fruitful.

It started to sink in that it is often the other things we do that plant the seeds that bear fruit in our lives. Humility is a good example. Humility is a quality of spirituality, but we do not try to *practice* humility to become humble. That would be dangerous. Can you imagine what would happen if you intentionally tried to be humble? The by-product would eventually be pride. That is why your choice of focus when training to be spiritually disciplined is so important. You engage in certain practices to live more as Jesus wants you to live. Giving away money *in secret* to someone needy (even if you cannot get a tax deduction), or swallowing your pride and confessing a failure with your small group are just two examples. A possible by-product of actions like these is that you may become more humble, but that is not your goal in and of itself—your goal is to become like Jesus. Dallas Willard and Richard Foster call this process "indirection." You indirectly have the fruits of the Spirit produced in your life by practicing a variety of spiritual disciplines.

All of this talk about the dangers of disciplines and false fruit might obscure the reality that as we grow into an increasingly closer relationship with Christ, we will become more like Christ. Changes in our character will emerge, often without our awareness or acknowledgment. Although bushels of fruit were produced from the lives of saints and mystics, many, if not most, supersaints and mystics still saw themselves as great sinners—and they meant it. Teresa of Avila prayed, "I see in myself so many imperfections—I am so remiss in serving you!"[7] Teresa had a continuing dependence on God's love and grace. Even the Apostle Paul called himself the "worst of sinners" (I Timothy 1:15–16). Paul knew he was dependent on God's grace, as is evident in his words to the church at Ephesis: "Of this gospel I have become a servant according to the gift of God's grace that was given me by the working of his power. Although I am the very least of all the saints, this grace was given to me to bring to the Gentiles the news of the boundless riches of Christ, and to make everyone see what is the plan of the mystery hidden for ages in God who created all things" (Ephesians 3:7–9). Saints like the Apostle Paul and Teresa of Avila were spiritually disciplined, not so that they could become more spiritual, but because they saw these practices as their lifeline to Jesus, their Savior, who out of grace and love revealed himself to them. In turn, these holy habits guided how they lived, and bore fruits in evangelistic zeal and a passion for justice.

The Examples of Two Supersaints

For years I have been inspired by the descriptions of intense love and devotion that have led supersaints to live such holistic lives in Christ. Something mystical happens to me again and again as I read accounts of their intimacy with Christ. Even when I can barely grasp or remember what I have read, these writings create in me a craving for greater intimacy with Christ.

I am not alone in this reaction. It is common for those who read the saints and mystics to have similar reactions. As Tony mentioned, John Wesley was attracted to certain mystics not only because they experienced deep love of God through spiritual devotion, but also because they gave Wesley inspiration for his ideas on what he saw as genuine holy living. These mystics experienced the love of Christ in such a way that it could not help but flow out to others.

As Francis Howe, author of *The Saint of Genoa: Lessons from the Life of St. Catherine,* wrote, "In order to reach a moderate degree of perfection, models of superlative perfection must be set before us to increase our ardor, and inflame our desire for virtue. If we regard as saints those who have only attained this moderate degree, we shall fall far short of what an ordinary Christian life should be."[8]

I want to highlight two mystics whose love for God turned them into evangelists and social activists. One, Monsieur de Renty, was a favorite of Wesley's. Wesley wrote a book about this mystic that is included in his Christian Library.[9] The other, Catherine of Genoa, is a favorite of mine.

MONSIEUR DE RENTY. At a young age, sixteenth-century French nobleman Monsieur de Renty's reading of Thomas à Kempis's *Imitation of Christ* led him to a spiritual awakening. In the words of John Wesley, de Renty "resolved seriously to pursue the one thing needful, the working out his salvation."[10] Wesley saw de Renty's life as a "living testimony of one who truly loved the Lord his God with all his being."[11]

De Renty's intense love of God led him to pray often, which included times of silent contemplation before God. De Renty often described his love of God with the powerful metaphor of fire, common to so many saints and mystics. He once said to a friend, "I cannot conceal from you that I have a fire in my heart which burns and consumes without ceasing."[12] De Renty's burning love for God drove him to intense involvement in both evangelism and service. In the words of Wesley, "Mr. de Renty, being continually inflamed with the love of God, incessantly sought all ways and used all means to make him more known and loved by all men, both here and eternally."[13] One day he came upon a poor young woman and asked her "what" she was. She said she was a servant. Then de Renty said, "But do you know you are a Christian and to what end you were created?"[14] In that simple statement he made her think about the high status she had with Christ, beyond her earthly social status. He then told her about Christ, and she promised to continue to seriously consider who she was in Christ Jesus.

Another story involves a young woman who had been abused by her uncle. Because she had been so badly treated by her uncle, the woman believed that Jesus had abandoned her. Her sense of abandonment made her feel not only unworthy of God, but also angry with God. She even took communion several times a day to spite God, in the hope that she would provoke God to kill her.[15] When de Renty was told about this woman, he rushed out to find her. Wesley records that when de Renty finally found the woman, eight days later, he "took so great care both of her soul and body that she returned to herself and gave ample testimonies of her repentance."[16]

De Renty also had a passion for the poor and oppressed. One day a week, de Renty visited the poor, sick people in the hospital; another day he visited the poor of his own parish; and yet another day he visited prisoners. Wesley said that de Renty looked past the outward appearance of those he visited and "beheld under these with the eye of faith Jesus Christ present and dwelling in them."[17] De Renty would then feed body and soul, assessing people's physical as well as spiritual needs. No duty for the sick or poor was beneath him. He would do anything to draw them closer to Jesus.

Along with having compassion for the poor that resulted in trying to meet their immediate needs, de Renty also worked for justice for them, doing what he could for their "general relief."[18] He helped them find jobs and the necessary materials or tools to do those jobs. Then he would buy whatever product or service they were selling, give it away, and encourage others also to buy from them. He continued to check on the people he helped to encourage them and see if their jobs were still going well.

CATHERINE OF GENOA. Caterina Fieschi Adorno (1447–1510), who was born to a noble family in Genoa, Italy, deeply loved God and wanted to enter the convent at a young age. Instead, when she was sixteen, Catherine's parents arranged for her to marry a young Genoese nobleman, Giuliano Adorno. Over time Catherine's love for God dissipated. Her marriage was bad, and she was miserable. Her husband was not only unfaithful, but he had a violent temper and was a spendthrift. Feeling she had nowhere else to turn, Catherine began to pray that the desire and love for God she once had would return.

At age twenty-six, ten years into her marriage, Catherine's prayers were answered one day when she went back to church after a long absence. As she knelt in the confessional, Catherine had an intense mystical encounter with Christ. In a moment she was overwhelmed with God's love as she saw her own sinfulness alongside Christ's redeeming love. The effects of this divine encounter never left her. Catherine stayed intimately close to God through regular times of prayerful contemplation for the rest of her life (another thirty-seven years). She would eventually say of God, "I have no longer either heart or soul, but the heart and soul within me are that of my dearly beloved."[19] Catherine of Genoa's love for God took her from times of intense contemplation into what God loves—the world. She, like Mother Teresa of Calcutta, ministered to the poorest of the poor, including lepers. She frequently visited a hospital for lepers where she washed and dressed their sores.

Along with ministering to lepers, Catherine went to the homes of the poor in Genoa, giving out clothing, food, and medicine. Eventually Catherine worked in a hospital, and it is said that nothing was too low or repulsive for her to do. She made beds, swept floors, and "performed all the countless disgusting services that sickness involves."[20] The founder of this hospital made it a permanent condition that laypeople would be in charge of its daily operations. It provided employment for the working class as well as a place for them to intentionally serve God. After working there for eleven years, Catherine was asked to be in charge of the women's section of this hospital. That is what she did for the rest of her life. In this role she took great care to make sure that those in her charge had all they needed for their well-being.

As Catherine continued to regularly spend intimate time alone with Christ, her intense and growing love for God led her to spend much of her time leading people to Jesus. In one instance, a young Jewish woman was sent to Catherine. It is said that Catherine "filled her heart with the fervent love which burned within her own soul."[21] The woman converted to a relationship with Christ. Perhaps the biggest evangelistic task Catherine and God took on was with her own husband, Giuliano. One description of him was that he was "full of evil and utterly void of good."[22] Catherine pleaded with God to save him. She also strove to love, and prayed for the souls of, all the women with whom her husband had had affairs. Giuliano eventually returned to Catherine, became a faithful husband, and joined his wife in her hospital work for the rest of his life.

These are just a few examples of the fruits of the lives of Monsieur de Renty and Catherine of Genoa. Their love for Christ, intensified through their commitment to spiritual practices, produced in both of them intense desires to share Christ and help the poor and oppressed.

The good news is that you, too, can live in this kind of love. You can experience the overpowering love and commitment to the lost and needy that characterized de Renty and Catherine. Holy habits can do that for you. In the sacred space created by spiritual practices, you again and again open yourself to receive the grace and strength to do the loving work God has called you to do for the Kingdom. Holy habits are not always easy, but if you stay committed, you can keep in shape spiritually. As is the case with any discipline we undertake for better health and wholeness, it is a serious mistake to abandon your spiritual practices because you perceive that not much, if anything, is happening or because you think they are boring. If you find yourself experiencing these reactions, remember the words of Saint John of the Cross: "In general the soul makes greater progress when it least thinks so, yea, most frequently when it imagines that it is losing."[23]

> It is a serious mistake to abandon your spiritual practices because you perceive that not much, if anything, is happening.

Someone once asked Mother Teresa what her secret was that enabled her to work day in and day out with the "poorest of the poor." Her simple answer was, "I pray." She used to teach people that to work for the poor, they must develop a consistent prayer life. She believed that people could work for justice possibly for a year or two, but to willingly sustain that kind of difficult work day after day, year after year, in a spirit of joy, was not possible without the help from God that came through a consistent prayer life.

In the next several chapters we look at how to have that kind of consistent prayer life. My hope is that you will discover how the ancient spiritual practices of the prayer of examen, lectio divina, and centering prayer can transform you, as the powerful love and grace of Jesus Christ manifests itself in your life. These three spiritual disciplines continue to have a dramatic impact on my life and on the lives of so many others in helping us discover the holistic gospel of Christ.

Although the three prayer practices we discuss overlap, as you will see when you practice them, they also build on each other. First, the prayer of examen will help you to discover how you can be purified from things that hinder or block you from having more freedom to love and serve, in addition to helping you realize and grow in areas where you are already living for Christ. The next practice, *lectio divina,* will help you discover how praying the scriptures opens you up to a deeper understanding of what it means for Jesus to call you "friend," and how the Holy Spirit desires to speak to you in and through that friendship. Finally, centering prayer will help you experience further intimacy with Christ through developing a kind of silence that leads to a more unified life with Christ and with others on a day-to-day basis. Each of these practices helps create space for you to experience a depth of mystical intimacy with God that empowers you to live out the full gospel of Jesus Christ as you become more like Jesus, equipped to do his work in the world.

MOVING FROM SELF-AWARENESS TO GOD-AWARENESS

THE PRAYER OF EXAMEN

Search me, O God, and know my heart;
test me and know my thoughts.
See if there is any wicked way in me,
and lead me in the way everlasting.

—Psalm 139:23–24

THE FIRST NIGHT of my spiritual direction program, we were all handed a brochure called "The Daily Faith Awareness Prayer." I was told to "do" this prayer every day as an important step in experiencing God in all things. It is a form of a prayer that has been historically referred to as the "prayer of examen," in which you intentionally reflect on your day, calling to memory what you did or thought about. You try to remember the blessings you gave and received, thanking God for each of them. You also consider all the good you *might* have done but did not, and repent of those sins of omission. Finally, you repent of each harsh word and unloving action and ask God to help you act in more loving ways. Taking stock of the day, with the goal of living more fully for Christ and others each day, is the purpose of the prayer of examen. Some of you may already be familiar with forms of this prayer, but to many Christians this is a new kind of praying.

It certainly was new to me. And honestly, the idea of examining my life in this way was not that appealing, so I did not do it at first. I later found out that the prayer of examen is such a vital way to daily grow in and for Christ that Ignatius taught his followers, the Jesuits, that if they had to abandon any prayer during the day, never to abandon this one—*not even for one day*. To this day, Jesuits are taught that this practice is essential. That caught my attention, so I started to practice the prayer of examen on a regular basis. It is not the most heartwarming kind of praying, since part of the prayer includes an examination of our weaknesses and failures. And since this is to be a *daily examination*, it can seem a little tedious at times. But it is worth it. Many other spiritual practices draw us into intimacy with Christ but do not help us as directly to deal with our weaknesses and build on our strengths.

> *Ignatius taught his followers . . . that if they had to abandon any prayer during the day, never to abandon this one.*

If practiced regularly, the prayer of examen will help you to be purified of those things that deter you from living more for Jesus. It is a daily gateway for the Holy Spirit to reveal areas of strengths and weaknesses to help free and empower you to live out a more holistic gospel.

What the Bible Says About the Prayer of Examen

When Ignatius told his followers never to forsake the prayer of examen, he was telling them to do what scripture already tells us. Here is a sampling of the many verses on examining our lives:

"When you are on your beds, search your hearts and be silent." (Psalm 4:4 NIV)

"Prove me, O Lord, and try me; test my heart and mind." (Psalm 26:2)

"Let us test and examine our ways, and return to the Lord." (Lamentations 3:40)

"I the Lord test the mind and search the heart, to give to all according to their ways, according to the fruit of their doings." (Jeremiah 17:10)

> "The Spirit searches everything, even the depths of God."
> (I Corinthians 2:10)

> "Search me, O God, and know my heart; test me and know my thoughts. See if there is any wicked way in me, and lead me in the way everlasting." (Psalm 139:23–24)

These scriptures make it clear that this prayer is not simply a process of self-examination. It is a prayer in which *God* examines our hearts, minds, and motives. As Paul told the church in Rome, "We do not know how to pray as we ought, but that very Spirit intercedes with sighs too deep for words. *And God, who searches the heart, knows what is the mind of the Spirit,* because the Spirit intercedes for the saints according to the will of God" (Romans 8:26–27, emphasis mine).

The Role of the Holy Spirit in Self-Awareness

Recently, when I was reflecting on the italicized part of the verse just quoted, the idea of the Holy Spirit searching our hearts reminded me of how good antivirus software regularly searches a computer for possible harmful programs. After our computer almost crashed twice in six months due to viruses, we realized that our antivirus software wasn't one of the good ones. By the time we could see what the viruses had done, it was too late—they had infected so many files that our computer was close to being inoperable. We needed a program that searched regularly and well.

Like a computer virus, a lack of self-awareness can block our sensitivities, and thus our love and service for God and others. We need to regularly ask the Holy Spirit to search our hearts and help us to become more aware of our attitudes, actions, and reactions, as well as the reasons and motives behind them. Then, with the Holy Spirit's guidance, we can change what needs to be changed so that we can live more fully in and for Christ.

There is a note of caution to be sounded in all of this. Self-awareness alone can too easily lead to self-centeredness. We need always to remember that our goal should be to move from self-awareness to awareness of who we are in God. Richard Foster points out, in his book *Prayer: Finding the Heart's True Home,* that the purpose of any intentional introspection is to journey "through ourselves so that we can emerge from the deepest level of the self into God."[1] This is where true freedom is found, and it is the kind of awareness Jesus possessed. My pastor, Mark Van-Valin, once said in a sermon that "Jesus had a self-awareness that set him free." The prayer of examen can help you have this kind of awareness.

Through this prayer God's Spirit can daily search you and make you more aware of your patterns of living. It will not always be pleasant to take more notice of certain things in your life, but if you do it anyway, the Holy Spirit will help guide you to discern when you are acting in love toward Christ and others and when you are not. It is learning to act in love that will set you free.

The Role of Feelings

As you get into this prayer you will notice that a crucial part of the exercise is to pay attention to feelings that surface from your reflection, and then weigh those feelings in your mind and heart. But for some of us, especially those of us who see ourselves as reasonable, rational thinkers, a red flag goes up with the word *feelings*. We may be doubtful that paying attention to feelings will help us become more aware of who we are in Christ. We know that countless people have been hurt, or have hurt others, by acting on their emotions. Perhaps we have learned the hard way that we cannot trust our own feelings, and we may even block them. But we cannot afford to discard our feelings if we want to live for God; Jesus was often "moved with compassion," and we should be too. If we block our own feelings, we can become hard-hearted, unable to feel the kind of compassion that leads to working for a more loving and just world.

On the other hand, some of us see *all* of our feelings as legitimate. This also can hinder us from living a holistic gospel, because focusing too much on feelings is emotionally exhausting, leaving us little time to focus on Christ and others. We need to learn to rein in and discern a variety of our feelings, including those that seem justified or even altruistic. Writer and speaker Joni Eareckson Tada, a paraplegic since age seventeen, told the story of several men who, after reading her story, each wrote to her saying that they felt the Lord told them to marry her. We can appreciate their hearts but still not believe those feelings came from the Lord. Even sincere hearts can be sincerely wrong.

> *Even sincere hearts can be sincerely wrong.*

The Bible tells us that we must "test the spirits to see whether they are from God" (I John 4:1). Our feelings must be tested, which means that we must carefully consider whether what we feel is in harmony with Jesus' holistic gospel, and whether our Christian friends and community agree. Even though the prayer of examen is something we pray in our alone times with Jesus, we need to be sharing what we are learning with a trusted friend or mentor so that we are not trying to discern without any accountability. In Chapter Nine we discuss further guidelines for discernment.

Preparing for the Prayer of Examen

The prayer of examen is meant to be done every day, so that you can become aware of daily patterns of living—and not living—more fully for God and others. Ignatius taught that the examen should be prayed twice a day, once after lunch and again after supper, but today it is often taught as a once-a-day prayer. If you choose to do it once daily, nighttime may be preferable because you can review the whole day while it is fresh in your mind. However, since this prayer takes only 10–15 minutes, you can pray it anywhere and at any time—during lunch, on a walk, while waiting in the car, at the park, or even at an airport—as long as you find a place where you can block out distractions. It is still a good idea, however, to have a regular daily time and place allocated for it, since that is the best way to develop this prayer into a holy habit. John Wesley wrote that a favorite mystic of his, Monsieur de Renty, "made an exact search into his smallest faults" each day before his noon meal and again in the evening.[2] My friend Dave does an examen of his day while he brushes his teeth—for most of us, this wouldn't be enough time, but Dave brushes his teeth for *at least 10 minutes* every night.

I have, however, met a few people who are exceptions to the specific time rule. One person I know often thinks about and analyzes what is happening to her as events occur throughout her day. She has found that it works to do a form of the examen as she goes about her day. When she notices and feels a certain reaction from an encounter or event, she tries to immediately take that reaction to God, asking God to help her discern whether or not what is going on leads to more or less love for Christ and others.

If you find that this more informal approach to the prayer of examen works for you, I still suggest you bring these events back to God in a brief 3- to 5-minute "summary examen" at the end of the day. The Holy Spirit may reveal to you events and patterns you missed as you prayed this prayer a little at a time.

Although there are several different ways to pray for God to examine us, over the years many people have found Ignatius's steps and directions to be particularly helpful in learning to listen to and obey God in their daily lives. His specific steps have often been paraphrased while still keeping the essence of the prayer. I have attempted to do this by combining and adapting Ignatius's guidelines for what has been called the "examen of consciousness" and the "examen of conscience" into three steps.

The Three Steps of the Prayer of Examen

If the following steps seem too structured or burdensome, just give them time. After following these guidelines for a week or so, you will feel more comfortable with them and may want to adapt them to your own wording; just be sure to hold on to their essence. Continue to practice all three of the steps, even if you do so in ways that fit your own personality, since the steps intentionally build on each other.

As you regularly engage in this prayer, you will become better able to recognize your inward and outward responses, even as they happen. Still, there will be many times when you may not understand *why* you are

THE PRAYER OF EXAMEN

STEP 1. Prepare yourself by quietly focusing your attention on God.

In him we live and move and have our being. (Acts 17:28)

STEP 2. Review your day with thankfulness and a spirit of reconciliation.

When the Spirit of truth comes he will guide you into all truth. (John 16:13)

- When did you live out of love and freedom in Christ?

Whatever is true, whatever is honorable, whatever is just, whatever is pure, whatever is pleasing, whatever is commendable, if there is any excellence or if there is anything worthy of praise, think about these things. (Philippians 4:8)

- When did you *not* live out of love and freedom in Christ?

Let us test and examine our ways, and return to the LORD. (Lamentations 3:40)

STEP 3. Thank God for what is happening through this exercise, and ask for guidance and grace for tomorrow.

Now to him who by the power at work within us is able to accomplish abundantly far more than all we can ask or imagine, to him be glory in the church and in Christ Jesus to all generations, forever and ever. Amen. (Ephesians 3:20) feeling or reacting to something in a particular way. The good news is that further insights come as you continue to do the prayer of examen. Remember to share those insights or questions with trusted Christian friends or a spiritual mentor to help you further discern what is from the Holy Spirit and what is not.

STEP 1. *Prepare yourself by quietly focusing your attention on God.*

Begin by sitting comfortably and breathing slowly and evenly so that you can focus on being in the presence of the One who loves you the most and wants to give you the true desires of your heart. After a few moments pray these words:

> Dear Jesus, help me to see myself and my life through your uncondi-
> tional love and acceptance of me so that your love and power can flow
> in and through me. Help me to remember that *nothing* can separate
> me from your amazing love.

Stay in silence for several seconds, repeating the prayer or reflecting on the verse shown with Step 1 in the box.

At this point, if you find you are at a place in life where it is especially hard to accept yourself and to accept God's unconditional love, you may want to consider putting the rest of this spiritual practice temporarily on hold. I have taught the prayer of examen to people who continue to live with guilt and shame over their pasts, and some who struggle with serious addictions. Many of these people find it hard to accept God's unconditional love and forgiveness. If you are one of them, it may be difficult for you to go to the next step, since guilt and shame can destroy the emotions of thankfulness and keep you from experiencing the wonder and joy that this prayer provides. It is therefore important to stay at this first step of the prayer of examen until acceptance of Jesus' love for you begins to take hold. Otherwise you may not be open to learning what the Holy Spirit wants to teach you through the rest of the prayer. You might ask a friend, spiritual mentor, or counselor to help you better discern whether or not you should continue this prayer at this time.

STEP 2. *Review your day with thankfulness and a spirit of reconciliation.*

Start by reading the first verse shown with Step 2 in the box and then praying:

> As I begin the review of my day, I ask for wisdom and courage to see
> what you want me to see. Help me first to recall and thank you for the

> gifts of the day. Then help me remember what you want me to remember, and notice what you want me to notice, including my motives—with thankfulness. I want to accept with gratitude what your Spirit reveals to me because I know you love me and want your best for me. When I see areas where I have failed to live in love and purity of heart, help me to be willing to ask for, and accept, your forgiveness. Help me to be open to anything you want me to see and change so that I can more fully love you and others.

I cannot stress enough how important it is that you try always to start with a spirit of thankfulness for what the Holy Spirit will reveal to you, continuing that thankfulness even when something you see as negative is revealed. My friend Paul, a pastor, is convinced that cultivating a spirit of gratitude will change us more than any other spiritual practice. Let God govern your reactions to whatever surfaces, remembering that the Holy Spirit is present and can help you to do *all* of what you prayed.

For the entire Step 2 of the prayer, you are to review the events of your day, as if watching a movie. Do not worry about recalling everything; besides taking too long, this is not the point of the prayer. Instead, be open and trust God to help you bring things to mind. Start on a positive note by recalling external gifts from God such as the birds that may have awakened you (even if they did so too early) or the smell of coffee brewing. As you move through the events of the day, ask God to continue to bring to mind specific pleasures such as a really good laugh or uplifting conversation, a special smile, or the feel of a warm rain. Pay special attention to whoever or whatever especially touched your life that day. Remembering these things as gifts will help you cultivate a spirit of thankfulness to God who gives "every good and perfect gift" (James 1:17). Nurturing this kind of thankfulness helps you to live less selfishly and more generously for God and others.

Next, look to the inner gifts and strengths that you brought to the events of the day, such as your ability to listen, your humor, compassion, patience, or certain skills. Thank God for each of them that may have given love, joy, and freedom to others.

You are now ready to enter the longest section of the prayer, which requires that you address two important questions. The first is this:

1. *When did I live out of love and freedom in Christ?* Start this part of the day's review with the verse from Philippians, shown in the box. Then ask the Holy Spirit to bring to mind when you acted out of love (or what some call our true self, self in God, or moments of consolation). Here are some examples:

- You began an unusually busy day in quiet time with Jesus.
- You gave money or time to a certain cause.
- You spent time with an individual or group who inspires you to want to be a better person.
- You shared what Jesus means to you with someone.
- You did something that scaled down your use of the world's resources.
- You were friendly to the slow cashier in the grocery store even though you were in a hurry.
- You didn't raise your voice when you were angry at a family member.

Be especially thankful to God if you did the right thing when you felt like doing otherwise.

As you reflect on what comes to mind, pay attention to your feelings—particularly those deeper gut-level feelings that are possible clues for discerning your thoughts, actions, and motives. Pay special attention to when you had feelings such as these:

- Joyfulness
- Happiness
- Peace
- Hopefulness
- Generosity
- Compassion
- Gratefulness
- Satisfaction
- Faithfulness
- Being a part of something bigger than yourself
- Being energized or "fully alive"
- Love and acceptance

The point here is to recognize when you were drawn to living with what comes when the Holy Spirit is guiding you. Paying attention to these feelings can help you discern "the desires of your heart"—these are the true God-given desires that empower you to live in Christ-likeness the rest of the day, tomorrow, and every day.

A CAUTION. It is important to note a potential danger while practicing this part of the prayer. What you see as a strength in your life, could, in reality, be something that hinders you from fully living in love and freedom in Christ. For instance, you may feel good about your heavy involvement in other people's issues, or even your ability to confront when others don't, but God may want you to be less involved or less confrontational. You would then be wise to heed the advice of Thomas à Kempis, author of *Imitation of Christ*, to not become busy with those things not committed to your care. Your overinvolvement can hinder how God wants to work in a situation. I have seen this happen in the lives of some people I know. Unfortunately, I am one of those people.

Before I began teaching, I did some counseling with students. But counseling wiped me out. I felt that I had to solve all of their problems by giving just the right advice. And though I would exhaust myself during counseling sessions, I would walk away thinking that this was how God wanted me to counsel. But it was not, and any good counselor knows that. Counseling is a process, and counselors are guides, not people who have all the answers. It took my training in spiritual direction and practicing the prayer of examen to start driving this point home for me.

Ironically, spiritual direction is often very nondirective. The goal is to help people find God in all things, mostly through listening intently to them, reflecting back certain things they have said, and giving suggestions for spiritual practices. Regarding advice on a particular situation, the spiritual director trusts the Holy Spirit to bring insights. When appropriate, I point out any relevant biblical or traditional church directives I am aware of; but beyond those directives, if no insights come, I try not to give advice. That's hard for me, since I am still tempted to tell a person what *I* think they should do before either of us have made it a matter of prayer and discernment. I now try to resist that temptation by remembering the best thing I learned about spiritual direction. It was during one of our training sessions when I was busily writing down all the things we were being taught to do when listening. I started to feel overwhelmed. Then Lucia, the teacher, said, *"And when you are in a spiritual direction session with another person, don't forget that God is in the room, too."* I had forgotten. I was caught up in how to make sure I was good at spiritual direction and forgot that, unlike Elvis, the Holy Spirit really *is* in the building. Lucia's reminder was so freeing. It was that reminder, along with insights from doing the prayer of examen, that helped me continue to see that something I thought was a good thing (taking people's problems into my own hands) was actually hindering me and others from living more freely in and for Christ. Exploring motives, with the guidance of the Holy Spirit, is an important part of this prayer.

2. *When did I not live out of love and freedom in Christ?* The next section of the prayer may be the hardest, since it is where you focus on your weaknesses and failures. This part of the examen is not meant to depress you. That is why it's a good idea to start by praying the Lamentations verse in the box. It will remind you that this second question is to help you become more aware of when you might be moving away from God so that you can take steps to "return to the Lord." Still, there could be a temptation during this part of the prayer to get into a "woe is me" rut, and then you can stop yourself, as well as those with whom you come in contact, from growing in freedom. It is especially important to have a teachable spirit when focusing on this part of the examen; otherwise, you can get down on yourself and become preoccupied with self-loathing, which keeps you from reaching out to others and the world.

Another temptation during this part of the prayer is to blame other people or life situations for times when you did not live out of love and freedom in Christ. It can be too easy to avoid working on our own weaknesses and failures when we convince ourselves that it really is not our fault that we acted or responded in certain ways. These blind spots are the most difficult things to change in our lives because they are just that. It can be easy to point a finger at others and not even realize our own faults. Jesus warned about this in Matthew 7:3 when he told us to make sure we take the plank out of our own eye before taking the speck out of someone else's eye. For instance, perhaps you tend to see yourself as innocent, simply reacting to negative situations, rather than seeing how you might negatively affect those situations yourself. Or maybe you put too much energy into blaming others for negative patterns in your life instead of putting that energy into freeing yourself from those patterns. It is crucial, as part of the prayer of examen, that you ask God to protect you from going down these counterproductive paths of blaming others and instead help you to see and reflect on where and how you need to grow in love and compassion.

It will greatly help you to remember that "it is God who is at work in you, enabling you both to will and to work for his good pleasure" (Philippians 2:13). God is present and can work even in your failures—there is no area of life where God is not. As Paul wrote, "For I am convinced that neither death, nor life, nor angels, nor rulers, nor things present, nor things to come, nor powers, nor height, nor depth, nor anything else in all creation, will be able to separate us from the love of God in Christ Jesus our Lord" (Romans 8:38–39).

With the awareness that self-loathing or blaming others can get in the way, you now ask God to reveal to you the events and possible patterns in your day that do not lead to love and freedom in Christ (or what some call false self, self outside of God, or moments of desolation). Be open to those times when you might need to be purified or healed from the effects of dark deeds or thoughts, or from hurts experienced or caused.

Here are possible examples:

- You complained to others about a task you were doing.

- You cleaned your house more than your heart.

- You focused too much on looking good, rather than being good.

- You spent too much time with someone who dragged you down (or perhaps *you* are the one who, knowingly or unknowingly, dragged someone else down).

- You were wasteful.

- You said or did too much or too little.

- You didn't share Jesus with someone when the opportunity seemed right.

- You used money on new clothes you did not need instead of meeting someone else's need.

Again take note of the feelings your attitudes and actions produced in you, such as these:

- Anger or frustration
- Hate
- Pride
- Sadness
- Jealousy
- Confusion
- Fear or captivity
- Anxiety or turmoil
- Exhaustion
- Abandonment
- Embarrassment, shame, or guilt

Paying attention to what you did or did not do, and how you felt, will help you to become more and more aware of what hinders you, as well as how you might hinder others, from fully living a holistic gospel.

It is important to realize that this new awareness can lead to guilt and shame. Then, instead of focusing on living Christ's holistic gospel, your energies may become too focused on your sins. The good news is that Jesus, through his death and resurrection, delivers you from sin. With this truth in mind, ask God to forgive you and give you the strength to live more fully tomorrow as Christ would have you live out your day. You might want to picture yourself talking to Jesus, telling Jesus you are sorry, asking for, and then accepting, the freeing forgiveness of God. Carrying out this exercise could also lead you to ask forgiveness of someone you feel you wronged, and to seek further ways to restore any strained or broken relationships.

If this part of the prayer proves especially difficult, again ask God to help you see any new awareness as a gift and an opportunity for growth. If you stick with this more difficult step of the examen, you will feel increased freedom from the heaviness of heart and mind that often weighs you down and therefore increased freedom to find God in all things—including your failures and weaknesses. Although it is not easy to confront these things, it *is* liberating, as long as we recognize God's tremendous gifts of love, mercy, and grace in the midst of our sinfulness. "While we still were sinners Christ died for us" (Romans 5:8). Acceptance of this truth creates a desire for unity with Christ, which, in the words of the Jesuit priest and writer Joseph A. Tetlow, "is intensely personal and draws us to friendship with Jesus." He goes on to state that this desire for unity is also "widely social and draws us to love one another" because the Second Commandment "does not state a moral imperative but describes the way God lives in us."[3]

When you accept God's love, forgiveness, and grace, you are drawn in by Jesus' love and compassion to have love and compassion toward others. This is where the prayer of examen should always lead you—to a greater awareness of how you can serve God and others in the world. That is why it is a good idea to take a few minutes during this part of the prayer to focus more specifically on those who live beyond your world of experience, asking God to expand your heart and vision.

At times there will be an area or issue within Step 2 of the examen where God's Spirit will call you to a more focused self-examination. An example of this in my life is directly related to God expanding my heart and vision. Through the prayer of examen, the Holy Spirit continues to reveal something that in the past was not on my radar—that my fear of confronting and not being liked was stopping me from fully stepping out and speaking more boldly for Christ and for justice issues about which I felt strongly. I dealt with these fears by tuning into my own sphere of family, friends, and coworkers and tuning out many other needs in the world. Even when I watched the news or heard about horrible disasters and hurts, I quickly shut down emotionally so that I did not have to face uncomfortable feelings about those events. I felt better about this tendency after I was reassured by someone that we should, in fact, disengage when we hear or read about all the bad things going on in the world because it is "just too much." But then I heard someone else say that we must do the opposite if we want to enlarge our hearts to be more like the heart of Jesus. To develop the compassion and sense of justice for the world that Jesus modeled, this person believed that we need to engage emotionally and empathetically with what we hear is going on in the world. One way to do this is to pick at least one news story a day, pray specifically throughout the day for whoever or whatever is involved, and take action if possible—such as calling a political representative, sending money, or even volunteering yourself, depending on the situation.

Further reflection through the prayer of examen helped me realize that the latter advice is the more loving and just approach. I was reminded of what Karl Barth, the great German Reformed preacher and theologian, said about sermons: that they should be written with the Bible in one hand and the newspaper in the other. I realized that the same should be true for all of life—we should live as if the needs of the world are in one of our hands and the Bible is in the other.

As I continue to examine my fears and motives, the Holy Spirit gives me increased vision for helping those beyond my own personal and social spheres and increased strength to accept others' responses to me so that I have the courage to act and to speak out more than I used to. It is still not easy for me, but I am learning what it means to "speak the truth in love" (Ephesians 4:15).

I encourage you to take note of any special focus the Holy Spirit may be inviting you to notice through the prayer of examen. I also encourage you to ask the Holy Spirit to help you honestly confront any ongoing patterns that are hindering you from sharing Christ through your words and actions.

STEP 3. *Thank God for what is happening through this exercise, and ask for guidance and grace for tomorrow.*

Start by reflecting on the verse shown with Step 3 in "The Prayer of Examen" box. Then end your time in prayer, making sure you first thank God for what has been revealed to you before you ask for guidance and grace for tomorrow. Here is a possible prayer:

> Thank you, Jesus, for what you have shown to me today. Help me to accept with gratitude all you have revealed. Please give me the grace to be open to what you revealed to me now and to see what you will reveal to me tomorrow. Thank you for all the ways your love is already revealed in and through me. Help me to know what about me must change and give me strength and courage to change those things. Thank you that you have my true heart's desire in mind and work in me so that I can truly love and serve you and others. In Jesus' name, Amen.

You may also want to end this time by reciting the Lord's Prayer. Then, to help you remember, you could write down what you are discovering about what helps and what hinders your relationship with God and others. Again, I strongly recommended that you regularly share what you are learning with a trusted friend or mentor.

Patience Is a Virtue

Remember that you need to be patient and trust the Holy Spirit in this process of examination. This *is* a process, and you cannot know the vast benefits and mercies of God through this spiritual practice if you read about the prayer of examen and try it only once or twice. Commit to praying it daily, and if you miss a day, come back to it the next day, because you will learn through this prayer to develop habits of lifelong discernment of the Holy Spirit at work in the patterns of your life.

In addition, it is important to be aware that the connectedness with God that you seek through the prayer of examen will probably not happen right away. You may have to be into it for several days, and even weeks or months, before you sense the Holy Spirit bringing you into new awareness of how to live more wholly for Christ. But if you are patient and "wait upon the Lord," new awareness will come and, if you allow it, it will change the way you live.

The Prayer of Examen as a Gateway to Purification

When you engage regularly in the kind of holy habits we are proposing in this book, you will eventually notice that some things you used to spend your thoughts and energies on just don't matter anymore. As the hymn suggests, when you "turn your eyes upon Jesus," some things of the world do "grow strangely dim," without you even trying to rid yourself of them. They simply disappear as you focus more on loving Jesus, and that unexpected gift is incredibly freeing. But other things do not disappear without a battle. We still struggle with "things of the world" that distract us from living a more holistic gospel, even though Jesus told us to seek *first* God's Kingdom and righteousness, and all that we need will be given to us—Jesus said we don't even need to worry about anything else (Matthew 6:31–34).

To seek God's reign first and foremost, we need purer hearts. Søren Kierkegaard once preached a sermon titled "Purity of Heart" based on Matthew 5:8. To have purity of heart, he said, was "to will one thing." That one thing is what Saint Paul calls the "most excellent way," which is love—the kind of love that we live out toward God and all others with our words and our actions, like Jesus did.

Past saints and mystics knew this. They also knew that a process of intentionally deep purification is necessary on this path of love that results in unity with Christ and others. That is why they wrote not only about their intense love for Jesus manifested in their prayer practices and service to others, but also about additional external ways to give up or not seek after whatever distracted them from being more fully devoted to Christ. We can learn much from past and present saints and mystics about how to rid ourselves of what hinders us from the purity of heart that drives us to seek first God's Kingdom. They can teach us the importance of becoming more aware of how things can distract us and crowd Jesus out of the center of our lives; and they also teach us the need to simplify our lives by either removing those things or putting them in their proper place.

Becoming Aware of What Distracts Us

Through the years saints have taught that the "things" that distract us from living a holistic gospel are anything we value or desire that takes us away from more fully loving and serving Jesus, from possessions to pleasure to prestige to power.[4] We become preoccupied with, worried about, and possibly even addicted to some of these values and desires, which take our focus off of Jesus. That's what happened to Mary's sister Martha when Jesus was visiting their home. Although Mary had found that "one thing," Jesus told Martha that she had become "worried and distracted by many things" (Luke 10:41).

When my son David was old enough to hold something with his two little hands he started holding any sports ball he could find. It was a rare sight to see him without at least one or two in his hands. One day David and I went with a group of his friends to a kid-friendly place that had cages of colorful plastic balls. David was overwhelmed with how many plastic balls he saw and ran into one of the cages. At one point when I looked over at him, he had so many of those balls in his arms that several were dropping to the floor. He anxiously looked at me and in a very serious voice said, "Too many things." Even though David was visibly upset and even admitted that he had "too many things," he was still so focused on holding on to as many of those "things" as he could that he didn't even want to come out of the cage for pizza.

Trying to hold too many things in our lives keeps us from holding on to things much more important than pizza. These things distract and prevent us from holding on to God and can even create a false sense of security so that we no longer depend on God. When friends of mine were in Kenya, they met a Kenyan pastor named John. When this pastor visited the United States, his first stop was their home. While standing in the kitchen, Pastor John asked what several things were and what they did. My friend Deb pointed out the uses for the microwave, oven, and dishwasher. As Pastor John stood looking at all of these appliances, he said to her, "You have no need for God."

But we do need God—more than anything the world has to offer—and deep in our hearts we know that. Why then do so many of us, including myself, often live as if we believed that we really can love Jesus right along with loving all of the things we think we need? Contrary to popular opinion, we know we cannot have it all. More important, we don't need it all. Yet, as we try to live our lives for Christ, many of us back off of the radical nature of the gospel and embrace other perceived needs, values, and desires. We say Christ is number one in our lives, when in reality many of our choices are guided by selfish and social desires, such as making more money so we can buy more things.

Often we do not even see this happening. But Thomas Merton did. He wrote about the dangers of self-deception regarding false needs and desires. He contended that our deepest desires—for joy, harmony, peace, order, and meaning—have been co-opted by our culture's lie that we can

search for and find meaning in tempo-
ral things. We have been strongly conditioned our whole lives to believe that
pleasure, possessions, prestige, and
power will lead to true happiness and
give life meaning. Consequently, we
have settled for too little.

Several years ago a former student
stood in my living room and announced
to me that his life had been transformed. Through Jesus? No. It was
through a vacuum cleaner. He was trying to sell me a vacuum cleaner that he

> *We say Christ is*
> *number one in our*
> *lives, when in reality*
> *many of our choices*
> *are guided by selfish*
> *and social desires.*

claimed had changed his life. I do not doubt that a really good vacuum
cleaner can change my carpet, but if something like that changes my *life*,
I am in trouble.

Like the song that laments "looking for love in all the wrong places,"
we look for fulfillment in all the wrong places. We become blinded by the
illusion that we can be satisfied with things that are not of God. Yet when
Jesus was tempted in the wilderness with those things that only create an
illusion of a fulfilled life—power, prestige, and possessions—he denied all
of them. He was then able, "filled with the power of the Spirit" (Luke
4:14), to proclaim his true mission: "to bring good news to the poor . . .
release to the captives and recovery of sight to the blind, to let the
oppressed go free, to proclaim the year of the Lord's favor" (Luke
4:18–19), which was the year of jubilee or freedom. Jesus' message was
one of freedom from things that bind us all.

Can we have this same "power of the Spirit" that results in living with
the same focus Jesus did? Yes. When we become more aware of how our
disordered desires and needs distract us from the "one thing," we are then
able to look at ways to disengage from them to make room for that kind
of transforming power.

Simplifying Our Lives Through Asceticism

Asceticism is a word that has a bad name in many circles. But understanding the intent of the word can greatly aid us in simplifying our lives.
In the religious life, an ascetic is one who leads a contemplative life
full of rigorous self-denial for God, based on Jesus' words to deny ourselves, take up our cross daily, and follow him (Luke 9:23). But over the

centuries, some followers of Jesus have taken this much too far and have focused more on the rigorous self-denial part of the definition rather than the religious purposes part. Although we are called to deny ourselves and follow the way of Jesus, this particular kind of denial often leads to a suffering that really does not have much to do with Jesus.

We are not to take asceticism to an extreme as the Syrian monk Barsauma did by standing on a pillar high up in the air for days or sometimes wearing an iron tunic "for maximum discomfort in all seasons"[5] (he also refused to sit or lie down). Although the intention of these seemingly eccentric behaviors was for mortification (deliberately choosing a form of suffering to reverse disordered desires so as to live more for Christ), they often became much too extreme and lost their original purpose. As Paul said to the Colossians concerning regulations, "These have indeed an appearance of wisdom in promoting self-imposed piety, humility and severe treatment of the body, but they are of no value in checking self-indulgence. So if you have been raised with Christ, seek the things that are above, where Christ is, seated at the right hand of God. Set your minds on things that are above, not on things that are on earth, for you have died, and your life is hidden with Christ in God" (Colossians 2:23–3:3).

Living "one thing" by imitating Christ does not mean denying for denial's sake or suffering for suffering's sake—it means sharing in the sufferings of Christ (Philippians 2:10). This kind of sharing is for the sake of others. There is enough suffering in this world without inflicting irrational or extreme suffering on ourselves. Suffering is not to be an end in itself. We enter into the sufferings and injustices of others not so much to give up something, but to "set our hearts" on the things of Christ. The true purpose of ascetic practice, according to the Cistercian monk M. Basil Pennington, is "to free ourselves from the imperious domination of our own thoughts, passions, and desires, to free the spirit for the things of the Spirit. It is paradoxical, isn't it, that what seem to be life-denying practices actually open the space for new life?"[6]

We give up so that we can gain new life in Christ. As Jesus said in Mark 8:36, "For what will it profit them to gain the whole world and forfeit their life?" John of the Cross called this kind of giving up or asceticism "the active night of the sense." By "active night" he meant an intentional process, because he knew that after some time our affections and intentions toward Jesus could lessen, while our previous attachments to various things could again come to the forefront and keep us from Jesus. This active night, however, was not intended to be a giving up of everything. Saint John's way to exemplify this "active night of the sense" involved "being in the world but not of it." As Saint Paul said in I Corinthians,

"'All things are lawful,' but not all things are beneficial. . . . So whatever you do, do everything for the glory of God" (I Corinthians 10:23, 31).

But there is still another kind of asceticism that is of the highest order. It is the result of the kind of self-denial that is directly related to lovingly sacrificing ourselves and all that we have as we try to meet the physical and spiritual needs of others. We find this kind of asceticism in the life of Saint Francis, who often went without the basic necessities of life as he gave all that he had in ministry to the poor. Dietrich Bonhoeffer embraced an ascetic lifestyle as he endured hunger himself in order to give food to others who were confined with him in a Nazi prison.

Saint Ignatius called this kind of giving up or asceticism "detachment." He believed that we can hold on so tightly to possessions, prestige, power, pleasure—and even people—that all of our time is consumed with unhealthy, even addictive attachments. Ignatius believed that it is only through a proper spirit of detachment that we can be freed to truly love God and others.

Louis Dupré, in *The Deeper Life: An Introduction to Christian Mysticism,* described this same spirit of detachment when it comes to *people* in the following way: "No mysticism can claim to be Christian that does not include a spiritual love for the creature. . . . To love creatures requires no effort, particularly if they are lovable—we all do that as a matter of course. . . . But to love creation, to be deeply involved with it, and yet to remain detached from it, demands more than common virtue."[7]

There is a note of caution that should be sounded here. This use of the word *detachment* should not be confused with *uncaring.* Ignatius saw detachment as a way to love more selflessly. He talked about disengaging from unhealthy obsessions or codependencies so that we can freely love others without having selfish desires dictate how we treat them.

The most powerful example of detachment from possessions I have heard came from Gordon College art professor Bruce Herman. He and his wife, Meg, often had students live with them, especially when the students had limited funds for their education. Eventually, Bruce began to grumble a little about these extended stays. One night, Meg informed Bruce that she had invited yet another student to stay, even after Bruce had expressed the need for a break. She reminded him that before they built the house, they had prayed over the land and dedicated it to the Lord. Bruce said he came to his senses, "acknowledged this was right," and realized that he shouldn't complain.

The very next day their house caught on fire and burned; Bruce said he felt convicted for the bad attitude he had been harboring. As he and Meg watched the firemen try to put out the fire, which was taking most of their possessions, including many of his original paintings, Meg whispered to Bruce, "All this hangs lightly on us, doesn't it?" Bruce nodded. Meg already knew the real meaning of having a proper spirit of detachment that frees us to live that one thing—the most excellent way of love (I Corinthians 12:31b).

How do we allow the things in our lives to "hang lightly"? This is where the prayer of examen can help. It will help you give up your disordered desires to make room for the true desires of your heart.

Using the Prayer of Examen to Simplify and Purify

Allowing the Holy Spirit to examine your disordered desires through a slightly modified version of this prayer will help you to, in the words of Saint Benedict, "prefer nothing to Christ." Start by adding on a few minutes, or an even more extended time each day, during your regular prayer of examen. Better yet, if you commit to two examens a day, one of them could be for this more focused purification. Then follow these adapted steps of the prayer of examen:

1. Come into Jesus' loving presence and tell him you want to live a more purified, simplified life for him.

2. Thank Jesus for what will be revealed to you as you seek purification and simplification.

3. Ask the Holy Spirit to show you a specific disordered desire or perceived necessity in your life that needs purifying.

4. Reflect on how living with this desire or perceived need hinders you from living in more love and freedom.

5. Reflect on how giving this up would help you to live in more love and freedom.

6. Ask Jesus to forgive you for making whatever it is too important and to give you the willingness, courage, and determination, through the power of the Holy Spirit, to give it up. At this point you may need to pray, "Make me willing to be willing."

7. Thank God for what was revealed to you and ask for grace and guidance for tomorrow.

Continuing the Prayer of Examen

As you continue to pray the prayer of examen, you will find something wonderful happening. More and more, the things that once had such a hold on you will no longer have the same effect, and you will experience an expanding love for God and others. You will desire more time to seek to live like Jesus and less time with the things that used to be important to you. You will not be totally freed from all "things of the world," but you will be increasingly open to getting rid of whatever holds you back from fulfillment in Christ.

Purifying our lives is never a completed process this side of heaven—it is a lifelong journey into Christ-likeness. An image that has been useful for me in understanding this process is a spiral. As we grow in Christ, we may find that old issues and concerns that we thought we dealt with surprise us by coming around and resurfacing again. But when they do, because we have been spiraling upward into greater intimacy with Christ, those same issues and concerns are treated in a different manner. At times we may not even be consciously aware of these new ways we are handling certain circumstances.

The prayer of examen, if practiced regularly, will give you increased freedom from the things that hinder you from "making the most of every opportunity" (Colossians 4:5 NIV) and increased freedom to be more like Christ, every day, in your words and in your actions.

Even though this daily faith-awareness prayer plays a crucial role in empowering us to live in greater love and freedom for Christ, it is not enough. There are things in our lives that we will still not notice, or that will be difficult to change, hindering us from fully living a holistic gospel. That is why the focus of the next two chapters is on two more prayers that draw us deeper into Christ's transforming love and amazing grace. Through these prayers we will continue to spiral, in the words of C. S. Lewis, "further up and further in," as we help God's Kingdom to come on earth as it is in heaven.

BECOMING GOD'S FRIEND

LECTIO DIVINA

I do not call you servants any longer,
because the servant does not know
what the master is doing;
but I have called you friends,
because I have made known to you everything
that I have heard from my Father.

—Jesus (John 15:15)

I have hidden your word in my heart
that I might not sin against you.

—Psalm 119:11 (NIV)

THE FIRST TIME I flew on an airplane alone, I was petrified. I remember sitting in my window seat, frozen in place, anticipating all kinds of disasters even though my husband had reminded me that I was much safer in an airplane than a car (as if rational thinking would be helpful at a time like this). As I sat there anticipating my short future, a Bible verse I had not thought of for years came to mind: "Thou wilt keep him in perfect peace whose mind is stayed on Thee." The reason I knew I hadn't thought of it for a very long time was because this verse from Isaiah 26:3 came to me in the King James Version, a translation of the Bible I had not read since I was a child. I had long ago hidden these words from God in my heart. When they came back to me, I immediately felt an incredible calm wash over me, a calm that stayed throughout the flight.

I wish I could say that the right Bible verse always comes to mind just when I need it, but it doesn't. That is partly because I do not think God always works that way, but mostly because I have not always made it a habit to hide God's word in my heart. Yet if I want to live in further intimacy with Christ and if I want that intimacy to fuel my work in the world, then it is essential that I regularly hide God's word in my *heart* and not just in my mind.

The Holy Spirit invites all of us to develop an intimate friendship with Jesus Christ, the Word became flesh (John 1:14). Jesus wants to be our Savior *and* our friend. That's quite incredible. The God of the Universe not only invites us to follow Jesus but also to be *Jesus' friend*. We can dwell with God—our Friend—who has *always* loved us and who is *always* accessible and present, in ways no earthly friend could ever be. No matter where we are in life and no matter what our struggles are, God invites us, through Jesus, into a redeeming, life-transforming friendship.

The sixteenth-century mystic Saint Teresa of Avila understood this invitation. She saw prayer as friendship with Jesus. For Teresa, knowing Jesus in a deep friendship meant moving from superficialities to more intimate ways of knowing each other. For Teresa the purpose of this intimate friendship was to "produce good works," which were the only way to know whether or not our prayers were authentic.[1] Teresa, heavily grounded in the Bible, nourished her intimacy with God by regularly hiding God's word in her heart.

One of the best ways for us to do the same thing is through a special kind of Bible reading called *lectio divina*, which is Latin for "holy or divine reading." This kind of reading fosters a conversation with Jesus that can deepen our friendship and intimacy and empower us to have transforming relationships with others.

Before getting into the specifics of *lectio divina*, it is important to understand its connection to one of the most essential characteristics of true friendship—that of listening. As we know, real friends listen to each other—*really* listen. Just as two-way communication is crucial in any friendship, so it is in friendship with Jesus. As Jesus says, the sheep know the shepherd's voice (John 10:4). The only way to know a voice is to really listen to it.

Our task as friends of Jesus is to train ourselves to listen deeply to Jesus' words. By listening to Jesus' voice I do not mean trying to hear audible words from God; instead I mean listening to how Jesus might be prompting us to live and love through our holy reading of the scriptures. As we listen, we learn to recognize Jesus' voice, instead of false voices, and thereby discern what is and is not of God (see John 10:5). We then respond to Jesus, since the Hebrew word for *listen* comes from the word *obey*. In John 15:14, Jesus says, "You are my friends if you do what I command you." What does Jesus command? That we love God and others—these are the two greatest commandments. To learn to obey these commandments we need to listen to Jesus through deepening our interaction with scripture.

Lectio divina, or simply *lectio*, as a spiritual practice is one of the best ways we can learn to listen and thereby develop a deep and dynamically intimate friendship with Jesus and with those whom Jesus loves. Through lectio our eyes are opened to seeing the sacredness of others. We see Jesus in "the least of these," as he says in Matthew 25—the hungry, the thirsty, and those sick and in prison. Then we respond by sharing God's love through evangelizing and by working for justice for everyone, for that is what friendship with Jesus is about.

Listening to God Through *Lectio Divina*

Although many of us have grown up hearing how important it is to read the Bible, fewer of us know of the type of meditative and reflective reading called *lectio divina*. We know that we are to "get into the scriptures," but it is even more important that we allow the scriptures to get into us, and that is *lectio divina*. The difference is in *how* we read the Bible.

Lectio divina is much more than reading—it is the act of "praying the scriptures." In *lectio divina*, you combine reading with meditation for a deeper understanding of how to imitate Jesus in word and action through your deepening friendship with him. In just one time of lectio you can experience the friendship and love of Jesus in ways you never knew possible.

Lectio in its truest, broadest sense has three parts (with accompanying Latin names): hearing *(lectio)*, reflecting *(meditatio)*, and responding *(oratio)*. It implies a dynamic interplay among God, the reader, and the text. And since the Bible is the living word of God, this holy, meditative reading of scripture is all about relationships.

Before we go any further, it is important to define what we mean by "meditative" reading. The word *meditation* has different connotations, which often lead to confusion. With some New Agers, meditation is a form of silence with the purpose of emptying the mind. But the word also is commonly used as a generic term for methods of deep breathing and relaxation for, among other things, stress reduction. Describing meditation is like trying to explain postmodernism or evangelicalism—you could ask several different people their definitions and hear just as many different answers.

Biblically, the word *meditate* or *meditation* refers to reflecting on the scriptures and commands of God. It is not a state of inactivity or emptiness; instead it is a mindful, "heartful" reflecting on and pondering of a biblical text. It is the kind of reflecting that Psalm 1 refers to when it says blessed is the one whose "delight is in the law of the Lord, and on his law he meditates day and night." Here is a sampling of the many verses in scripture that illustrate how meditation refers to this kind of active reflecting for "getting the scriptures into us."

> *You know that you are to "get into the scriptures," but it is even more important that you allow the scriptures to get into you.*

"I treasure your word in my heart, so that I may not sin against you." (Psalm 119:11)

"I will meditate on your precepts, and fix my eyes on your ways." (Psalm 119:15)

"I revere your commandments, which I love, and I will meditate on your statutes." (Psalm 119:48)

"Your word is a lamp to my feet and a light to my path." (Psalm 119:105)

"Let the word of Christ dwell in you richly; teach and admonish one another in all wisdom; and with gratitude in your hearts sing psalms, hymns and spiritual songs to God." (Colossians 3:16)

The Biggest Lie in Christianity?

When we meditate on scripture, we do more than informational and instructional reflection, because although that kind of Bible study is necessary, it is not sufficient. As Jesus said in John 5:39–40, "You search the scriptures because you think that in them you have eternal life; and it is they that testify on my behalf. Yet you refuse to come to me to have life."

With any type of relationship, there is a world of difference between studying about what makes for a good relationship and actually experiencing one. For instance, we can talk about falling in love, but if it happens to us, our words do not begin to describe the experience. Meditating on scripture creates opportunities for us to come to Jesus in more intimate, mystical ways than ordinary study ever could. Perhaps the biggest lie in Christianity is that we can in fact be Christian without developing that kind of intimacy with Christ. *But we cannot.* As Thomas Merton wrote:

> The Christian is then not simply a man of goodwill, who commits himself to a certain set of beliefs, who has a definite dogmatic conception of the universe, of man, and of man's reason for existing. He is not simply one who follows a moral code of brotherhood and benevolence with strong emphasis on certain rewards and punishments dealt out to the individual. Underlying Christianity is not simply a set of doctrines about God. . . . On the contrary Christians themselves too often fail to realize that the infinite God is dwelling within them, so that He is in them and they are in Him. They remain unaware of the presence of the Infinite Source of Being right in the midst of the world and of men.[2]

For Merton, the kind of wisdom that comes from *lectio divina* is a "living contact with the Infinite Source of all being, a contact not only of minds and hearts . . . but a transcendent union of consciousness in which man and God become, according to the expression of St. Paul, 'one spirit.'"[3]

In lectio we are invited again and again into a kind of aliveness and empowerment in the Spirit that study alone cannot produce. Since reading scriptures *only* in analytical ways quenches the Holy Spirit's flame, in the Middle Ages lectio became an antidote to the preoccupation with study, analysis, and rational theological thought. Without disparaging scholarship, *lectio divina* adds something crucial to our relationship with God. For instance, when reading a passage of scripture on humility, such as Philippians 2:1–11, during lectio we are not so much concerned with analyzing what Paul meant as we are with what God can say to us

Perhaps the biggest lie in Christianity is that we can in fact be Christian without developing . . . intimacy with Christ.

as we silently meditate and let the Holy Spirit control our reflection. John 15:26 tells us, "When the Advocate comes, whom I will send to you from the Father, the Spirit of truth who comes from the Father, he will testify on my behalf." This is what happens in *lectio divina.*

When we read the Bible for study only, as Merton said, our Christianity can become too much about a set of beliefs and not enough about the kind of intimacy that leads to real transformation in our lives and in the world. If we know that Christianity is a relationship much more than a religion, why do we often live as if the opposite were true? Many of us continue to live with our system of beliefs *about* Jesus instead of living *with* Jesus. The terrible truth is that we may be blind to the difference. Yet as Jesus said in John 5:39–40, even though we may adhere to a system of beliefs from the scriptures, if we do not *come to* him, we do not have eternal life. Coming to Jesus means having a relationship with Jesus, surrendering to an intimate connection with him, so that Jesus can do his work in the world through us. *Lectio divina* helps us avoid treating the Bible as a rule book that replaces the Holy Spirit who speaks to us in the here and now as we meditate on scripture.

When we surrender to the Spirit during *lectio divina*, we get meanings specifically personal and relevant that build our friendship with God. That is why the same passage of scripture can speak to us in different ways when we read it at different times. As Basil Pennington wrote in his book *Lectio Divina,* "We come to lectio not so much seeking ideas, concepts, insights, or even motivating graces; we come to lectio seeking God himself and nothing less than God."[4]

Preparing for *Lectio Divina*

It is important to plan an intentional amount of time per day for lectio. It can be done in as little as a few minutes, although I recommend a minimum of 10 to 15 minutes a day. Since the purpose is to get the word of God into us, the more time we can spend doing it, the better. It is also best to find a quiet space so as to concentrate more fully on what the Holy Spirit wants to say to and through us.

It is a good idea to choose and read a passage the day or night before you plan to have a lectio session so that you can begin to have it in your mind and heart. Another reason to choose the exact text ahead of time is to resist the temptation to use time and energy reserved for Jesus to pick "just the right passage." The first time I did an extended form of lectio was during a five-day retreat. Father Bernie, my retreat director, gave me three passages from which to choose. He then gave me what I found to be very solid advice—don't spend a lot of time choosing one, but select the one that seemed to come to mind the most.

To choose a passage, you could get ideas from verses we have talked about in earlier chapters. You can pray for guidance from the Holy Spirit, or ask a spiritual director, trusted friends, or your small group for suggestions. Your church community may be studying certain verses in the Bible, or you might use a passage that stood out to you from a recent sermon. You could also start with a favorite chapter or verse or some other passage of scripture that has recently come to mind.

But I want to caution you about picking verses for your times of *lectio divinis*. Many people have a tendency to use passages geared mostly toward ourselves in relationship with Jesus, instead of also reading portions of scripture that focus on our responsibility toward loving and serving others. We might, for example, select verses like Matthew 11:28–30 on resting in Jesus, which can greatly comfort us; but if we never choose passages such as Matthew 5:43–45 on loving our neighbor, our holy reading and reflection will become too much about us and not enough about those others that Jesus also loves and has called us to love.

When doing lectio for 15 minutes or less, shorter passages of one to three verses are best, since it is difficult to read and absorb longer portions of scripture in that amount of time. Almost any section of the Bible can be used for meditation, but I recommend starting with Jesus' Sermon on the Mount, found in Matthew 5–7. You could do lectio on two or three verses a day until you have gone through the entire sermon in about 40 days. This sermon, which is to be taken as a sequential whole, is designed to help people understand what Dallas Willard calls the "present availability of the kingdom through personal relationship to Jesus"[5] and thereby live in God's reign *now*.

Here are some additional passages for lectio that have been helpful in my own life in drawing closer to Jesus and his mission. These verses are partially written out here for the sake of space and also because it is best to read the verses from a Bible, since the more familiar we become with using the Bible, the better.

> "The Spirit of the Lord is on me, because he has anointed me to preach good news to the poor. . . ." (Luke 4:18–19)

> "For I have learned to be content with whatever I have. . . ." (Philippians 4:11–13)

> "This is how we know what love is: Jesus Christ laid down his life for us. . . ." (I John 3:16–18)

> "Do not fear, for I am with you, do not be afraid, for I am your God. . . ." (Isaiah 41:10)

"The Lord is my shepherd, I shall not want. . . ." (Psalm 23:1–3)
"Create in me a clean heart, O God, and put a new and right spirit within me. . . ." (Psalm 51:10–12)

If you use up all of these verses and do not know where to go next, I suggest a Bible word search on some of the following words: *love, righteousness, one another, poor, oppressed,* and *justice.* Enough verses will pop up for each of these words to last you a lifetime.

I also recommend committing to lectio for a longer period of time, perhaps an hour during the weekend, and even periodically setting aside a half-day or a few days for a retreat. As with any friendship, the more quality time devoted to it, the deeper it will grow. Although you can choose shorter Bible passages, the following longer passages are possible suggestions for such intentional times with Jesus:

Matthew 25:31–46

John 15

John 20:19–29

Isaiah 43:1–7

Isaiah 58

Romans 8:31–39

Philippians 2:1–11

Philippians 3:7–14

LECTIO DIVINA

STEP 1. Lectio: Holy reading.

I treasure your word in my heart, so that I may not sin against you. (Psalm 119:11)

STEP 2. Meditatio: Reflecting on the reading.

Reflect on what I am saying, for the Lord will give you insight into all this. (II Timothy 2:7 NIV)

STEP 3. Oratio: Responding by taking a "word" with you.

Your word is a lamp to my feet and a light for my path. (Psalm 119:105)

The Steps of *Lectio Divina*

Now that your preparation is done, you are ready for the three simple steps of *lectio divina*.

STEP 1.   *Lectio: Holy reading.*

Always begin your session of lectio by focusing on being in God's loving presence, and then asking the Holy Spirit to meet you in and through God's Holy Word. A good way to start is with this prayer:

> Holy Spirit, please keep me open and humble as I seek to know you more through your word. Help me to be willing to see what you want to show me about myself and my place in the world as Jesus' friend. I don't want to be afraid of your intimacy and thereby limit what you want me to know and how you want me to love. In Jesus' powerful and precious name I pray, Amen.

Next, with the Bible passage you've selected in hand, begin by slowly reading it, or reread it if you read it the day or night before. Then slowly read it again, focusing more intently on the passage so that the words can flow into your heart and mind. I have been told by a spiritual teacher that it is a good idea to read out loud, even when alone, since the scriptures are meant to be heard. God spoke all of creation into being, and the Holy Spirit can mystically speak newness into us as we surround ourselves with the spoken word of God.

STEP 2.   *Meditatio: Reflection on the reading.*

After you've read the passage the second time, reflect on it and let the Holy Spirit speak to you as you "sit with" what you have read. In this sense, meditation is a more receptive than active process. You are simply creating reflective, sacred space for the Spirit to speak to you. Sacred space is an inner state of heart and mind in which all is driven out save a sense of God's presence. As you quietly reflect, open yourself up for the Spirit to speak through a certain word, phrase, image, or event that comes from the reading.

I have a note of caution at this point: It is during Step 2 that I sometimes catch myself analyzing the Bible passage instead of reflecting on it. I start thinking about what the passage might mean, which is understandable because I like to study scripture, but as we have seen, lectio is not the time for that kind of Bible reading. If you have this tendency too, be sure to stay aware of it so that you can catch yourself when you are turning reflection and meditation into biblical analysis. Then just stop and go back to quietly reflecting.

When the words or phrases from the passage sink into your consciousness, meditation then becomes more active as you yield to the Holy Spirit's opening of your mind and heart to expand on what has been given to you in the reading. Allow your thoughts and imagination to "go with" any insights from your reflections. In this sense, lectio is not a spectator sport. You are a participant, using your God-given imagination to enter into the scripture and to come to Jesus as the Spirit speaks into your heart and mind.

A few years ago I reflected on Matthew 11:28, where Jesus said, "Come to me, all you that are weary and are carrying heavy burdens, and I will give you rest. Take my yoke upon you, and learn from me; for I am gentle and humble in heart, and you will find rest for your souls. For my yoke is easy, and my burden is light." When this passage was first suggested to me for lectio, I remember getting ahead of myself and thinking that what I would probably focus on the word *yoke*, since I had heard interesting sermons on that term in the past. But when I did the process of lectio and reflection, the word that lifted off the page was *come*. So I sat with that word and the image that came to me was one of Jesus holding out his arms, palms wide open, simply saying, "Come." It was and continues to be a powerfully comforting and soothing image for me.

You can also become actively involved in a biblical scene that the passage brings to mind. Pay attention to what you hear, see, feel, think, and even touch or taste. Ignatius called this practice the "application of the senses." We apply our senses and visualize in detail what is happening in the passage. Ignatius advised people to try to feel as if they were witnessing the event or were even a principal character in the event, and then to use the experience as a motivation for loving God and others in more concrete, active ways.

Before I ever heard the term *lectio divina*, I was sporadically doing a form of this type of reflecting by entering into a biblical scene. Years ago, I was reading the resurrection story in John 20, where Mary encounters the risen Jesus, but thinks he is the gardener. Without really planning on doing what I now know is lectio, I "entered into" the story and pictured myself as the woman who saw Jesus. As I slowly read the story, I imagined myself "early on the first day of the week, while it was still dark" coming to the tomb, beside myself with grief because my friend Jesus had just died three days ago. When I came to the tomb, I "saw that the stone had been removed" and that Jesus' body was gone.

It was not hard to then picture myself weeping, as the other Mary did, because I realized I had really entered into the scene and had become very

emotional. So as I continued, I imagined myself bending over and looking into the tomb. I was surprised to see two angels and was even more
taken aback when they asked me why I was crying. I told them that they
had "taken away my Lord" and I did not know where they had put
him. I was so focused on finding Jesus' body that I am not sure I realized
that I was talking to angels. So instead of staying with them to see if I
could get any more information, I turned around to leave. And there
stood a man who I assumed was the gardener. I said through tears (I was
crying at this point), "Sir, if you have carried him away, tell me where you
have laid him, and I will take him away." The man said, "Mary." He
called me by my name, but how could he know? And in that same instant
I knew who it was. Through my excitement and tears I said, "Teacher!"
I could hardly contain myself; I was so overwhelmed with a joy I had
never known until that moment. Jesus was alive! I turned to hug him, but
he wouldn't let me, saying that he had not yet ascended to the Father. I
didn't know what that meant, and I really didn't care. Jesus was alive and
that was all that mattered.

I now engage in lectio on these same verses every Easter. But this past
year for the first time, I continued the story of Jesus' resurrection just
beyond those verses and found that they took me beyond my own personal encounter with Jesus. I found in passages such as Matthew
28:16–20 and John 21:15–17 that Jesus was not only presenting himself
to me, he was also urging me to go and spread his message to others.

We can have these times of reflection every day, even if only for a few
minutes, but if we want to go deeper into the amazing, life-altering love
of Christ, extended times of lectio are a must. I first did an extended time
of lectio and meditation during a silent retreat. One of the passages that
I stayed with and repeated for several sessions was from Matthew 14, the
story of Jesus walking on the water. I read the passage slowly, and then
pictured myself in the boat, with Jesus telling me to come to him. As I
allowed my imagination to go with the scenario, I visualized myself slowly
and reluctantly getting out of the boat, but then hanging onto the side,
refusing to let go, even though most of my body was in the water. As I
looked over at Jesus standing on the water, a little distance away,
he looked back at me and asked, "What are you afraid of?" I told him
that I was not sure. I love the water, so it certainly wasn't that. I then realized I did not believe I would actually be able to *walk* on the water; I was
afraid I'd fall in front of Jesus, a dead giveaway of my lack of faith. He
stood there, hand on hip, tapping his foot on the water, and said, "For
goodness sake, I'm the Son of God—if you can't trust me, who can you
trust?" What he said and the way he said it disarmed me and made me

smile. So I let go. We met halfway, and Jesus took my hand and hugged me. It was such a great hug. I treasure that image and carry it with me often. Again and again it has helped me move out of my comfort zone so I can do Jesus' work.

At this point, you may be having trouble with this idea of imagining as part of meditating on scripture. I was somewhat leery of this concept at first, in part because it was foreign to me and I had not taken the time to explore its possible value. One of the most insightful lines I have heard came from two very different movies—*Brother Sun, Sister Moon,* the story of Saint Francis of Assisi, and the popular 1980s film *The Breakfast Club.* In each of these movies, one of the characters admits, in so many words, "I always make fun of what I don't understand." Not taking the time to understand an idea or action has stopped too many of us from a fuller life with God and others.

But the foreignness of lectio was not the only reason I was hesitant. I also feared that imagining might take me into dangerous territory outside of what the text was "supposed to mean." I knew the verses in Deuteronomy that said we are not to add to or take away from God's commands in scripture (4:2 and 12:32), so I did not want to be a part of anything that might do that. But as I learned more about imagining, I realized that we often see these kinds of images used as book and sermon illustrations. Some of us have heard a sermon that challenges us to ask ourselves what is in our boat that is so important that we are reluctant to leave it to go *to* Jesus and to go to the world *for* Jesus. John Ortberg wrote a book titled *If You Want to Walk on Water, You Have to Get Out of the Boat*[6] that involves the type of imagining I did with this Matthew 14 story. If it is acceptable to use our imaginations in this way while preaching a sermon or writing a book, then it should be acceptable to use them in the context of holy reading and reflecting. This kind of meditation is steeped in hundreds of years of church tradition and has born much fruit in people's lives by drawing them into greater friendship and intimacy with God.

When we do lectio and meditation on events in Jesus' life and the life of the church, we are allowing the Holy Spirit to take us to an awareness that we either would not or could not go to on our own. Some people are afraid of letting go or losing control, forgetting that the "leap of faith" Søren Kierkegaard told us we need is not only a onetime leap. Teresa of Avila articulated this fear of letting go through her metaphor of our relationship with God as a journey into an interior castle. "The truth is," she said, that "some are afraid to learn what lies deeper within that splendid castle—for they know He is a Sovereign power and, if once they catch sight of Him, He will command their full allegiance. And then their own will—their very self—must be changed to become one with His."[7] Lectio takes us beyond our comprehension as we allow the Spirit to work in us, deepening our friendship with Jesus so that we can do everything Jesus commands—including giving him our full allegiance.

If you are experiencing *any* of the concerns or fears we have mentioned, hold on to the promise from Isaiah that God will be with you, strengthening, helping, and upholding you (Isaiah 41:10). Then be patient with lectio. Trust God's living word and trust that God wants to meet you and love you through scripture. Keep showing up, doing it, and asking the Holy Spirit to show you what you need in order to more fully know, experience, and love Christ and others through holy reading and reflection.

Saint Ignatius was well aware of how the use of the imagination in praying the scriptures created intimate connections not only between Jesus and us, but also between us and others. For example, in his Spiritual Exercises, he takes participants from imagining and accepting God's love for them to seeing their own sin in the world and how it has hindered others from fully sharing in all of God's resources. Ignatius asks us to imagine in prayer the role we play in buying into what the world says we need and deserve at the expense of those who do not have even basic resources. Therefore, authentic realization of God's love for us and our acceptance of that love gives us new ways of seeing how the manner in which we live needs to be transformed for the furtherance of God's Kingdom.

Recently when I was doing lectio based on the Ignatian Spiritual Exercises, the assignment was to pray on John 21:17, in which Jesus asks, "Simon, Son of John, do you love me?" I pictured Jesus saying to me, "Mary, do you love me?" And when I said, "Yes, I love you," Jesus looked into my eyes and said, "Then feed my sheep." The next line that came immediately to my mind and went straight to my heart was, "Do something!" The clear message was that if I truly love Jesus, I must act by helping others who are lost and oppressed.

The best test for knowing if what happens during lectio is from God is to discern the fruits, not the experiences, of lectio. If praying the scriptures does not lead to greater friendship and intimacy with Jesus, with the result of sharing Jesus through evangelism or justice, it is not true lectio and meditation. If we do not open ourselves up to the Holy Spirit in lectio, it can become a narcissistic way to get a spiritual high, a selfish means of feeding our spiritual pride by trying to show how spiritual we are, or another method by which we study Jesus but do not fully come to him. One way to avoid these serious dangers is by honestly praying the prayer suggested at the beginning of the first step of lectio.

STEP 3. *Oratio: Responding by taking a "word" with you.*

After reading and reflecting, the next step in lectio is to respond by taking what is called "a word" with you throughout your day. This gift from God refers to a word, phrase, or image that may have come to you during your reflection.

You might want to write down your word, as well as any other thoughts, feelings, or reactions you may have had during lectio, to help you keep a record of ways the Holy Spirit may be speaking to you. If not much comes to mind, you could make a note of that. Sometimes things come to us, and sometimes they don't. At times you may feel God at work in very loving ways; at other times the entire experience may be flat and God may seem absent. That's OK. Spiritually dry times are common, even when there are no particular sins causing them. Such times were even common with super-saints. The Spirit of God uses dry times to draw you into a kind of deeper, more trusting relationship with Jesus. Don't

If praying the scriptures does not lead to . . . sharing Jesus through evangelism or justice, it is not true lectio.

let those times stop you from doing lectio simply because you don't feel anything. Remember, engaging in spiritual practices is based not on how we feel but on our commitment to a decision. So keep showing up, asking the Holy Spirit to help you accept *any* way Christ chooses to be with you during times of lectio.

If, however, you do experience more than a week or so of dryness, talk to a friend, mentor, or spiritual director to see if there might be something in your life contributing to that dryness. Anything, from a sin to a lack of sleep, can have an effect on your spiritual practices.

After you have received a "word," you may need help in remembering to ponder that word during the day. For example, you might set your watch alarm on the hour or put a sticky note on your computer to help you periodically and intentionally focus on the word or image. I have a picture of an outstretched hand in my office, and when I look at it, I am taken back to my meditation on and image of Jesus saying to me, "Come."

I do have one caution about expectations for receiving insights and a word. You may be tempted to try to ensure that some profound thought emerges. I have struggled with this temptation to the point of stopping myself in the middle of my reflecting time to record an insight that just came to me. I have even thought, "Good. I have my insight, and I've written it down. My goal is accomplished. Now I can relax. Maybe I can be done for today." But the purpose of holy reading and reflection is not to acquire a meaningful insight; the purpose is to grow into deeper intimacy with Jesus. So at the beginning of lectio, I now try to remember to ask the Spirit to help me release any desire to come up with insights and focus instead on being with Jesus. If insights come, I see them for what they are—pure gifts of grace.

As part of an ongoing response to times of lectio, review every few weeks what you have learned, and look for possible patterns. Ask two important questions, remembering that the Apostle Paul advised that you "work out your salvation with fear and trembling; for it is God who is at work in you, enabling you both to will and to work for his good pleasure" (Philippians 2:12–13):

1. How am I growing in love for God and others?
2. What fruits are being produced in my life?

This kind of intentional recalling helps you remember how *lectio divina* is changing you, and remembering is crucial to your friendship with Jesus.

As a final part of the responding step, I recommend meeting at times with a friend or a small group who is also committed to doing this kind of holy reading and reflection. The accountability of regularly sharing struggles and insights together greatly helps you to know the deep friendship and love of Christ that reaches out to others. With growing awareness of what the Holy Spirit is saying to you, you can learn to respond to Jesus as friend during your work, your service, your play, and your other prayers.

The Rest of the Story: *Contemplatio, Compassio, Operatio*

If we intentionally commit to engaging daily in the three steps we have discussed—*lectio, meditatio,* and *oratio*—they will naturally lead into the three we focus on for the remainder of this book: *contemplatio* (silence), *compassio* (compassion and care), and *operatio* (action). We will see that the fruit of these holy habits we are discussing is a compassionate, active caring for others. As a matter of fact, if these spiritual practices do not take us to the kind of compassion that Jesus had for every person, then we must go back and discern, with the help of others, what is hindering us from this necessary outcome. I believe that Jesus' times alone with God and the Holy Spirit fueled his compassion toward others. Compassion always led to action. When he was in the wilderness for forty days and nights, Jesus resisted the devil by quoting scripture. This was not because he had only studied scripture; he had drawn strength and power by having it absorbed into his spirit. Then, as Tony mentioned in Chapter One, Jesus "returned in the power of the Spirit" (Luke 4:14), and two of his initial acts involved evangelism and social action.

So, too, our times of allowing scripture to get into us will result in action for God's Kingdom. As Tony has testified, his own evangelistic fervor flows in part from lectio, as this kind of holy reading helps energize him to preach the salvation message.

My own times of lectio have resulted in caring more for certain justice issues, such as those involving God's created Earth. Reflecting on creation passages leads me to use fewer of the Earth's resources so I can help preserve God's world.

An exciting context in which *lectio divina* has made a revolutionary difference over the past forty or more years is the Christian base communities of Latin America. Groups of Christians come together and, rather than being preached to by a priest or minister, practice lectio by exploring the meaning of biblical passages for their own lives. Many of these groups are composed of poor farmers and fisherfolk who immediately sense a connection between their setting and that of Jesus' original followers. Father Ernesto Cardenal, a priest in Nicaragua who collected and published many of the reflections of the Solentiname base community, observed that "the commentaries of the campesinos are usually of a greater profundity than that of many theologians, but of a simplicity like that of the Gospel itself. This is not surprising: The Gospel, or 'Good News' (to the poor), was written for them, and by people like them."[8]

As these communities read the Gospels and other scriptures aloud and reflect together, they have discovered their own power to work for justice in their villages, their churches, and their countries. Lectio has thus played a major role in producing positive social change in Latin America over the past several decades by giving farmers and laborers the vision and energy for democratic reforms.

As we see with just these few examples, *lectio divina*, if practiced regularly, changes people. It will change you, too. It will draw you into a deeper friendship with Jesus that creates in you a further desire to be like Jesus in your words and in your actions.

DEEPENING OUR
INTIMACY WITH GOD

CENTERING PRAYER

If you love truth, be a lover of silence.

—Isaac of Nineveh, seventh-century bishop

*But without the deep root of wisdom
and contemplation,
Christian action would have no meaning
and no purpose.*

—Thomas Merton, *Faith and Violence* (1968)

I ONCE BOUGHT a birthday card for a friend that said, "In honor of your birthday I spent a moment in silence." On the inside it read, "It was the hardest thing I've ever done." Although I was drawn to that card because of the humorous truth in it for me, it was a bit exaggerated. I could definitely spend a moment in silence—it was anything beyond a moment that was a problem. I always used to fill silence with *something* because too much of it seemed either uncomfortable or unproductive. If I was alone in the house or car for any length of time, I would always try to have music playing. I wondered how people endured driving alone if they didn't have a radio or CD player in their car. I would marvel at my husband, a counselor, who could spend several minutes in silence with someone.

I, on the other hand, was capable of telling people my entire life history to fill up even a brief silence. That all began to change just months after my spiritual reawakening, when I was introduced to *centering prayer* through my friend Bev. I noticed not only how she was drawn to this form of silent praying but also how she changed as a result of regularly engaging in it. I find that college students are also drawn to it. I recently asked a group of students who had just taken a class on spiritual disciplines to tell me about the course, specifically something memorable. Several singled out this kind of silent praying as something they had never done before but found so helpful to them spiritually.

Centering prayer involves sitting with God in intentional inward and outward silence, with the goal of yielding to the Holy Spirit's work in us. I found it curious that I was so attracted to this prayer, given my adverse reactions to silence. But I decided to try it anyway, and after practicing this prayer for a period of time, I began to realize how something so seemingly passive or empty as silence before God could be so powerful—powerful enough to change me in ways I had not been able to change through other means, even other types of prayer. I began to see that the Holy Spirit's transforming power works deep in our spirits through silence. One area where I started to notice change was with patience. A few years after I had been practicing centering, I remember sitting in the car, waiting for someone, and I realized that I was enjoying the time alone in the car, sitting in silence. That was not the norm for me because, as a general rule, I was not a very patient person. I hated to wait—for anything. I used to even want to make decisions quickly so I could get rid of the anxiety I had when they were hanging over my head. After doing centering for a few years, I realized that I was becoming much more comfortable with waiting, which included letting unmade decisions incubate within me, giving me more time to allow insights to come that could help me make wiser choices.

Centering Prayer and Contemplation

To understand centering prayer and its connection to living a more holistic gospel, it is important to first be aware of its connection to a deeper form of silent prayer called "contemplation." Contemplation involves entering into a deep and profound time of stillness with God that allows God's love and grace to mystically come into us and wash over us so that we are filled with the love and compassion of Jesus Christ. Sixth-century church father Gregory the Great referred to contemplation as "resting in

God." As was common in ancient church practice, it was for him the fruit of holy reading (*lectio divina*) and reflection, as well as a gift of grace from God. It is interesting to note that Saint Gregory the Great and Saint Augustine, as well as Saint Bernard, used the word *contemplation* to designate what we now more often refer to in the Christian tradition as "mysticism."

Trappist monk Thomas Merton taught, as did so many contemplatives and mystics before him, that to live for Christ, this contemplation must go hand in hand with action. Deep resting in God is supposed to energize and motivate us to do God's work in the world. Tragically, many Protestants and others have lost sight of the connection between contemplation and action. Our way of life is no longer geared toward cultivating the extended times of holy reading, reflection, and silence that were practiced in early church history. Most of us today cannot even begin to understand, much less know how to engage in, the kind of quiet to which this traditional form of contemplation refers—when we leave behind our multitude of thoughts and enter into a deep intimacy *with* Christ that then empowers us to go out into the world *for* Christ. Thomas Merton, in his book *Faith and Violence,* contended that contemplation "is so contrary to the modern way of life, so apparently alien, so seemingly impossible, that the modern man who even considers it finds, at first, that his whole being rebels against it. If the ideal of inner peace remains attractive the demands of the way to peace seem to be so exacting and so extreme that they can no longer be met. We would like to be quiet, but our restlessness will not allow it."[1]

Merton was right. Even though we pay lip service to the importance of the fourth commandment to have Sabbath rest in God, we seldom quiet ourselves for even 5 minutes of silence, much less take the time to enter into more profound stillness. Yet these times of silence can result in us living a more holistic gospel by helping us find the inner peace in Christ that equips us to bring peace to others. That is why we need to reclaim the intimacy with Christ, born out of silence, that results in greater compassion and service toward others.

This is where centering prayer can help us. It is a form of silent praying that can stand alone as a way for us to enter into greater intimacy with Christ, or it can set the stage for even greater depths of silence found in contemplative prayer. As one person put it in Thomas Keating's book *Open Mind, Open Heart,* centering prayer "sort of compensates for the lack of people's ability in our time to go from lectio into contemplation."[2] In this sense it could be called a precursor and a path to the deeper experience of silent contemplation.

It is possible that all of this talk about silence and centering sounds too monkish, like something reserved for the cloistered or the supersaints—not a practice for us "normal" Christians. But it is a mistake to think this way. Even Thomas Keating, who is a monk, agreed. Referring to this kind of silent praying, he writes, "The persons I know who are most advanced in prayer are married or engaged in active ministries, running around all day to fulfill their duties."[3]

The Basics of Centering Prayer

Although I often refer to centering as "silent" prayer, in reality the word *stillness* is what it is about, specifically the stillness that happens when we are emptied of everything but Jesus. This waiting on God in stillness helps us experience a deep, abiding awareness of God's love, through an intimate knowing of Jesus that goes beyond words, thoughts, and feelings. When we cultivate this kind of silence, we gradually focus less on ourselves. The love of Christ grows more deeply within us in ways that we are not even consciously aware of, ways that mystically free us to be more other-focused in word and action.

In centering prayer, we respond to Christ by sitting in silence and yielding to the presence and actions of God within ourselves. We defer to God, getting ourselves out of the way, to receive all that God has for us. It is a time to wait patiently for the Holy Spirit and surrender to what the Spirit wants to do in us, so that we can do for others in the name of Jesus. This kind of waiting involves learning to listen to what the Bible refers to as that "still small voice" that calls out to us in the depths of our being. In this form of silent prayer, we commit to quieting our hearts *and* minds to silently be in God's presence.

In Philippians 2 we read that we are to have the same mind that was also in Christ Jesus. Centering prayer is surrendering to the mind of Christ so that we think the way Christ thinks. The Apostle Paul makes it clear that if we do this, we will become a servant to others because Jesus thought of himself always in terms of service to others. And if we take on that same mind, we will be oriented to the same way. We will reach out to meet the needs of others, embracing both their spiritual needs *and* their many other needs.

This description of centering prayer may seem daunting—it was to me at first. But I came to realize that this kind of praying was essential for me if I wanted a deeper intimacy with Christ that could change me into a person better equipped to help change the world. I also realized that even though I was not a "natural" at silence, I could still learn to dwell in this holy stillness with God.

The Scriptural Basis for Centering Prayer

There are several verses in scripture that point to the importance of being still and finding God in silence. For example, this passage from I Kings 19: "Now there was a great wind, so strong that it was splitting mountains and breaking rock in pieces before the LORD, but the LORD was not in the wind; and after the wind an earthquake, but the LORD was not in the earthquake; and after the earthquake a fire, but the LORD was not in the fire; and after the fire a sound of sheer silence. When Elijah heard it, he wrapped his face in his mantle and went out and stood at the entrance of the cave" (I Kings 19:11–13). As we see in this story, God was to be found in silence.

Jesus often went off by himself to pray. Since the Bible Jesus read included verses that said we are to be still before God, I believe we can safely assume that Jesus' praying included silent yielding to God. Here are some of those verses Jesus would have read:

> "The LORD will fight for you; and you have only to keep still." (Exodus 14:14)

> "Be still before the LORD and wait patiently for him; do not fret over those who prosper in their way, over those who carry out evil devices." (Psalm 37:7)

> "Be still, and know that I am God! I am exalted among the nations, I am exalted in the earth." (Psalm 46:10)

> "For God alone my soul waits in silence, for my hope is from him." (Psalm 62:5)

> "But the LORD is in his holy temple; let all the earth keep silence before him!" (Habakkuk 2:20)

A Method for Practicing Centering Prayer

The specific method for centering prayer that I use was developed in the 1970s by three Trappist monks—Father William Meninger, Father Basil Pennington, and Abbot Thomas Keating. It was drawn from ancient prayer practices, especially from the desert fathers and mothers of the early church, as well as saints such as John of the Cross and Teresa of Avila. These saints knew what it was like to experience the kind of silent intimacy with Christ that led to profound changes not only in them but also in the world.

Before describing the method, there are three practical matters that need to be mentioned: a word, a place, and a timer.

CHOOSING A WORD. Those who teach centering prayer tell us to pick a sacred, Christ-centered word to help ward off distractions so that we can be drawn into the love of God through the silence. When my son Michael was four years old, he had a high fever for a few days that kept him wiped out, so he would lie on the couch for hours. At one point when I was sitting next to him, he said a single word: *Mommy*. When I asked him what he wanted, Michael replied, "I didn't say 'Mommy' because I need something. I said 'Mommy' because it makes me feel better."

We can also feel better and be drawn into the silent love of God just by saying a word like *abba* (meaning "father") as our sacred word. Other words that work well for centering include strong biblical words such as *love* or *peace*, or a word from *lectio divina* that has been personally comforting to us, like *remain*.

The Christ-centered word we pick best helps us to stay quietly in the silence if it is only one or two syllables, so that we can slowly and effortlessly repeat the word to ourselves. We may need to do this repetition often during the prayer period, since a sacred word helps us to stay with God or to come back to God in the silence when we find our minds wandering—and they *will* wander. It's hard to be internally still. Henri Nouwen likened the inner life during times of intentional silence to the image of monkeys jumping up and down in a banana tree.[4] I am so thankful for that image, since I thought I was the only one whose thoughts were all over the map during centering prayer. Often I will be saying my word, and before I know it, I am thinking about what sounds good for supper or I'm wondering how much time has gone by. One time I composed my entire Christmas list in my head. I have learned that when I realize I am off center, I begin saying my word and can come back in silence to Christ.

Some people get nervous at the suggestion to pick and repeat a sacred word, since they see this as "vain repetition"—something Jesus chastised the Pharisees for and warned us not to do when praying. This kind of repetition happens when we simply utter a word or words over and over without paying attention to what we are saying. To avoid this in centering prayer, we need to remember that we repeat our sacred word to keep us from being distracted by other thoughts, thereby helping us to stay with God in the stillness. There is nothing vain about that kind of repetition.

To further avoid distractions, it is a good idea to always use the same word, unless the Holy Spirit impresses a different word upon you, since even changing words can be distracting. When I first started centering, I became a little obsessed with choosing just the right word. I wanted the perfect word that would draw me into the silence and keep me there. But I was missing the point. The word is only the means to help us stay focused. It is a symbol of our willingness to yield to God in silence. Beyond choosing a sacred word, the exact word is not that important. I confess that I did change my word one more time after my friend told me that her word was *Jesus*. I decided that choosing *Jesus* was just what I needed to stop obsessing over different words.

There are, however, some people who get distracted by a sacred word. For them, thinking in terms of what is referred to as "a gaze upon Christ" might be more helpful. In this practice, instead of saying a word, we turn inward toward God, picturing a scriptural image of Christ, such as Light or Shepherd, and then we gaze on that loving image. After we choose how we gaze upon Christ, we then follow the same guidelines as we do for the sacred word.

CHOOSING A PLACE. Although you may not be able to create an ideal place for silence, it does need to be as quiet as possible, where you won't be disturbed. If possible, continue to use that same place, since continuity is helpful for staying committed to centering. Although a quiet space is important, many who do centering have wordless music playing softly in the background so they are not distracted by other sounds. In addition, you'll probably want the place to have a comfortable chair or cushion so you can sit in a relaxed, undistracted manner—but not *too* comfortable if you are prone to fall asleep when that relaxed!

USING A TIMER. Unlike the word and place, choosing a specific kind of timer is not that important, as long as it is not too loud, since going from silence to a loud ringing bell might startle you. The reason you time yourself is so that you are not distracted by looking at the clock to see how long you have been praying in silence.

A minimum of 20 minutes once a day for this prayer is recommended, but most who teach this method recommend two 20-minute periods a day: one in the morning, and the other in the afternoon or evening. This amount of time draws us more deeply into God's presence and action, and thereby allows us to maintain interior silence throughout our day better than shorter periods do. Even so, I encourage you to regularly "show up" for this spiritual practice even when you have not allotted yourself enough time and have only 5 or 10 minutes.

The Steps of Centering Prayer

Now that we have our word, our place, and our timer, we are ready to enter into centering prayer.

CENTERING PRAYER

STEP 1. Pray for protection.

For God alone my soul waits in silence, for my hope is from him. (Psalm 62:5)

STEP 2. Come into God's loving presence.

Be still, and know that I am God! I am exalted among the nations, I am exalted in the earth. (Psalm 46:10)

STEP 3. Become quiet; say your word when you need help in being still.

In quietness and in trust shall be your strength. (Isaiah 30:15)

STEP 4. End with the Lord's Prayer.

STEP 1. *Pray for protection.*

We first start with a prayer of protection, because as we open up space in our spirits for "God alone" (Psalm 62:5) to meet us in silence, we do want to be shielded from any other influences. The good news is that at the name of Jesus, all evil spirits flee, and that is why a prayer of protection is the first step. I suggest one of the following two. The first comes from Richard Foster's book *Prayers from the Heart.*

> Loving Lord, as I begin this journey into a prayer-filled life, please be with me—guarding and guiding. Protect me, O God, from all evil. Surround me with the light of Christ; Cover me with the blood of Christ; Seal me with the cross of Christ. This I ask in the name of Christ. Amen.[5]

The second is adapted from the way my friend Michaella often prayed at a centering prayer group I attended:

> I cover myself with the precious blood of the Lord Jesus Christ and I direct myself to the True and Living God in the Name of the Father, Son, and Holy Spirit.

STEP 2.   *Come into God's loving presence.*

As with any type of prayer, we must first remember that God is love and therefore God meets with us in love. So as you sit comfortably, and as you breathe slowly and evenly with your eyes closed, picture yourself in God's loving presence, surrounded by the light and love of Christ. I often have to consciously remind myself to breathe in a more relaxed manner. One way I do this is by slowly repeating "Be still" a few times. It continues to amaze me how quickly this simple act can slow down my heart rate and calm me, helping me to enter into silence with God. Then, as I slowly breathe, I focus on the Holy Spirit surrounding me with God's love. Sometimes that is all I need to do to enter into the next step of becoming quiet. Sometimes I need more. When I feel I am having a hard time acknowledging and accepting God's unconditional loving presence, I then picture myself in "the palm of God's hand" or in "the shelter of God's wing." I actually see myself resting in a big hand or surrounded by a gigantic wing, and these images help take me into the next step.

STEP 3.   *Become quiet; say your word when you need help in being still.*

While picturing yourself in God's loving presence, continue to breathe slowly and evenly and begin to say your word silently from time to time. When your mind wanders, don't get down on yourself, since that is just another distraction. Instead release all thoughts and feelings. A suggestion that has been helpful to me is to picture myself putting distracting thoughts in an imaginary balloon and releasing that balloon into the air. Then go back to your word. There may even be times during the prayer when you do not need your word to stay in God's presence. Don't force the word if you do not need it; you can always go back to it if distractions come.

STEP 4.   *End with the Lord's Prayer.*

When the timer goes off, stay in silence for another minute or so, with eyes still closed. End this time of centering by slowing saying the Lord's Prayer. There is something mystical about praying the very words that Jesus taught his disciples to pray.

Fears About Centering Prayer

I hope that you won't be dissuaded from this powerful form of praying because of some well-meaning but misguided warnings you may hear. Some Christians fear centering prayer because it seems too close to "New Age" or to some other religion's spiritual practices. Although it might seem similar, it is not the same. Even though other religions find value in times of deep silence and have claimed similar practices (with much different outcomes), that does not mean times of silence are not for us. In fact, the real danger and temptation to our spiritual lives is refusing to engage in certain spiritual practices because we are suspicious of anything that appears to be anti-Christian. We then live in a fearful cocoon, unable to experience the depth of God's love and mission for us that become known in silent intimacy with Christ. We are also unable to recognize many of the fruits of the Spirit that are manifested in so many lives as a result of these silent, wordless prayers.

It is essential . . . that we not succumb to the dangerous fallacy of avoiding something that is of God because others have laid claim to parts of its truth.

Francis of Assisi, Teresa of Avila, Catherine of Genoa, Thomas Merton, Howard Thurman, and countless others were led to evangelize and serve the poor and oppressed as a result of their times of deep silence with God. It is essential to our relationship with Christ that we not succumb to the dangerous fallacy of avoiding something that is of God because others have laid claim to parts of its truth. We also do not want to be responsible for advising others against this prayer and thereby preventing them from experiencing all that Jesus has for his followers. Jesus himself cautioned us against attributing to evil what comes from the Holy Spirit.

Centering prayer is, first and foremost, Christ-centered. That makes it distinctly different from New Age and other forms of silent meditation. *It is not New Age.* And we are not emptying ourselves in silence so as to achieve emptiness and thus to experience Nirvana. Jesus himself talked about the dangers of this kind of emptying in Matthew 12:44–45. He warned that if we create a vacuum in our soul, things that are not of God can quickly enter in. In centering prayer we are yielding to Christ by trying to rid ourselves of any distractions, so that our spirits can be still and become focused on Christ and more in tune with God's Holy Spirit. This yielding begins with a prayer of protection, as we saw in Step 1, and with an understanding that God, through Jesus Christ, is in the beginning, middle, and end of centering prayer. My spiritual director, Tom Ball, explained it to me this way:

> Centering prayer starts and ends with prayer to Jesus, asking for his presence, his angels to fill the room, his protection. It is surrender to

Jesus, being filled with Jesus, that we seek. There is a big difference between seeking emptiness and nothingness, and seeking to be with Jesus.

We are told in Psalms 46:10 to "be still, and know." Centering *does* bring us closer to God. It works because God made it work.

That others may also use silence for additional purposes to further their own theological worldview is up to them. Christian centering prayer practitioners need not subscribe to their thinking.

Other Struggles with Centering Prayer

Fear is not the only thing that can stop us from engaging in centering prayer. Our preconceived notions of what prayer is can keep us from silence with God even more than our fears do. I grew up thinking that prayer was only about my saying things to God with words, either out loud or in my head. Even though I had read about other people's experiences with God in silence, I did not understand how they were praying and what it meant to be in the kind of wordless silence that is at the core of centering prayer.

A few years ago a friend of mine wanted me to do an afternoon mini-retreat with her and a few of her friends that included a time of centering prayer. I gave them some explanations about it and then we entered into 20 minutes of silence. After we were finished, my friend opened her eyes, looked at me, and said, "OK, so what were we supposed to be *doing*?" I laughed, mostly because I understood the question too well, since my friend, like me, strives to be an A student. We want to make sure we do the assignment right. But during this time of centering, my friend was not sure if she *was* doing it right, especially since she was not clear about what was supposed to be happening—or not happening. This kind of prayer was not like what either of us had been taught growing up.

The good news is that there is very little to "get right" for this prayer, since what we are doing is learning to quietly sit in God's loving presence. That's all. When I was first doing centering prayer, I, like my friend, was trying too hard to be in silence "just right." Sometimes I would even focus so much on not focusing on anything that I would exhaust myself. Then I talked to my friend Michaella, who had been doing centering prayer a long time. She helped me see what was happening and told me that all I had to do was sit and do nothing but be with God by yielding to the presence of the Holy Spirit.

Forgive me for a canine analogy here, but this process reminds me of how our dog trainer, Terri, told us to quiet Amelie, our yellow Labrador retriever, when she is out of control and using her energy in counterproductive ways (such as chewing on us). Terri showed us how to carefully position Amelie on the floor and firmly but gently hold her down until she "settled." After just a few seconds Amelie always goes limp, in total submission to us. That is what we need to do in our prayer life with God— yield to the Holy Spirit and go limp. We can hope that God will not need to wrestle too much with us to get us there.

When I settle and submit to Christ, centering prayer is not so hard. Letting go and yielding to Jesus' loving presence by simply sitting, without expectations, without trying so hard to not do anything, is incredibly freeing. Like a trust fall, in which we allow ourselves to fall backward, trusting there is someone behind us to catch us, centering is a trust prayer. We silently fall into God, trusting that in the stillness the Holy Spirit quietly catches us deep within our spirits. The fruit of allowing the Holy Spirit to catch us then becomes evident in how we live our lives more holistically for Christ.

Just Show Up

Although I do have several friends who love this type of silent praying, and cannot wait until their prayer time, that has not typically been my experience. Since getting things done has always given me a great feeling of satisfaction, every day I have to fight the temptation to stay busy instead of entering into times of silence with God. And when I do sit down, I have trouble sitting still.

The best piece of advice I have ever received about doing centering prayer was when my spiritual director told me to "just keep showing up, no matter how it goes." So I show up. And though I continue to struggle, every time I do centering, I am so glad I did. The more I regularly engage in this practice, the more I sense the peace of Christ in my life—the peace that gets the focus off of me and on to working for peace in the world. I also find that I can access a sense of calm, even in the midst of a busy and frustrating day, by remembering to quietly yield my spirit to God.

If you find you have trouble committing to this prayer, you may want to talk to a spiritual director or friend. It is a good idea to join a centering prayer group if one is available. After I started doing centering, I joined a group that met weekly to engage in centering prayer. This may sound silly. Why would someone need a group to meet just to sit together in silence? But there was something about those times that drew me into centering in a way I was not able to do on my own. Those group times mystically connected to my own times alone with God in a way that encouraged me to center more on my own. Remembering my times of silence in that group setting helps me to enter into and stay in centering prayer.

Fruits of Centering

Centering prayer can create an intimacy with Christ that many who practice it say they rarely find elsewhere. This intimacy often results in a more eternal perspective that gets us beyond ourselves and into God's story by helping us more clearly see our place in the grand scheme of God's reign; gives us a sense of unity with God and others so that we are able "to do justice, love tenderly, and walk humbly with God" (Micah 6:8); and helps us resist burning out because of the type of peace that this intimacy creates.

> *Centering prayer can create an intimacy with Christ that many who practice it say they rarely find elsewhere.*

When I initially began to do centering, I usually felt a sense of calm for at least a few minutes afterward. Beyond that I could see no other fruits. I was hoping for warm and fuzzy feelings of peace to permanently invade me, and it was not until much later that I realized that the peace that comes from yielding to the Holy Spirit is not that kind of peace. In the words of Norman Shanks, an ordained minister in the Church of Scotland, it is not "a frothy, feel good, be-nice-to-everybody" kind of peace.[6] To pursue the peace of Christ means to be in the business of fighting whatever blocks God's reign of love and justice. It is the peace of Christ that gets the focus off of me and onto working for love and justice. But I didn't know that at the beginning. I was too busy focusing on getting my own peace.

It has taken me a long time to see how the Holy Spirit works deeply in my spirit to bring more of a desire for Christ's peace in my life. The change has been gradual. I liken it to daily living with my sons, who have grown so many inches over the years, yet I have never once *seen* them grow. The process of centering prayer is much the same. We change through times of stillness with God, but we do not necessarily see those changes right away.

One of the areas where I desperately needed change was with worry. As far back as I can remember, I struggled with worries that blocked the peace of Christ in my life. My mom used to say that if I did not have something to worry about, I would worry about that. I desperately wanted to feel calm and content, but I rarely did. My worries left me with little time for anything else, including Jesus and his mission. Even when worry got me on my knees to pray, my prayers were mostly focused on me rather than on others. I couldn't even think of going out of my comfort zone and living more holistically for Jesus, since my comfort zone didn't exist much beyond my house and immediate family. No matter how I tried to deal with all my worries, they would not be tamed. That's why years ago a daily devotional really struck me. It was about a man who said he worried every day of his life; then one day he read the verse that tells us, "Do not worry about your life" (Matthew 6:25). From that day on he said he stopped worrying. I was so inspired by that devotional reading that I decided to stop worrying too. It didn't work.

> *The peace that comes from yielding to the Holy Spirit . . . is the peace of Christ that gets the focus off of me and onto working for love and justice.*

My worries seemed to only get worse. When my dad died suddenly several years ago, I hit a level of anxiety I did not know existed. My focus on worry and lack of trust in God could no longer be hidden. I felt nervous much of the time and turned inward. Living for others was no longer on my radar. I developed abdominal pains that I was convinced indicated a serious illness, even though two doctors told me otherwise. One doctor temporarily put me on a mild form of an antidepressant. Concerned about me, my husband, a psychologist, recommended I see a psychiatrist. The psychiatrist said I was showing symptoms of panic disorder, and I needed to be careful or the symptoms could get worse. But they did not. I attribute that to the subsequent spiritual awakening that got me into centering prayer. After several months I realized that my reactions to things had started to change. I was experiencing increased freedom from worry and anxiety.

The most telling example of change came less than two years after I had been doing centering prayer. I got a call from my sister telling me that the horrible headache my mom had been having for two days was due to a brain aneurysm, and she was being airlifted to Chicago for a special procedure that the doctors hoped would save her life. I was scared, not only for her, but for myself. I could not forget how I had fallen apart after my dad's death four years earlier, and since I had always been much closer to my mom, I was worried about how I might react after the initial shock of what was happening wore off. I called my friend Bev to tell her what was going on, and this is what she said to me: "This is the time to see if what has been happening to you spiritually the last few years, and the advice you have been giving others, really means anything. I am going to be praying for you, picturing you in the palm of God's hand."

For the next two weeks my sister and I lived in a hotel in Chicago, near the hospital. Although my mom survived, there were several times when even the medical staff did not know if she would make it. Still, in the midst of all the uncertainty, I did not react in the ways I did after my dad died. Even as my mom was being wheeled into the room for a procedure they said she might not survive, I had a calmness that I knew had to be from God. It certainly couldn't be from me. I believe it was the fruit of my spiritual reawakening, specifically the result of my times in stillness with God.

When I was praying in stillness, the Holy Spirit was changing me from the inside out, calming my spirit in such a way as to help me not be so focused on myself. Every time I sat in silence before God, I was creating mystical space in my life for God to meet and to enter into me, and that was what was making a difference. I was slowly realizing that I needed to see that space as fertile soil in which the Holy Spirit works to free me from things that hinder me from living more wholeheartedly for Jesus and his kind of peace that can change the world.

This kind of praying, if done regularly, will change us—as long as we keep showing up. When we don't show up, that shows too. A friend of mine recently told me that she saw a direct correlation between doing centering on a regular basis and her awareness of the importance of working for justice. She was reading her journal from a few years ago and realized that she had gotten away from her commitment to certain social justice issues. Those journal entries, from a time when she was consistently engaging in centering prayer, showed much more care for the poor and oppressed than she currently was demonstrating. She decided to get back into regular centering, believing that it would once again fuel her to work for justice. It has done that for many other people, including Tony's friend Jonathan Wilson-Hartgrove. Jonathan, who lives in intentional community in Durham, North Carolina, says his daily practice of contemplation "provides the spiritual strength to do ministry work."[7]

"They who *wait* upon the Lord shall renew their strength," states Isaiah; "they shall mount up with wings as eagles, they shall run and not be weary, they shall walk and not faint" (Isaiah 40:31). When we wait for God by yielding in silence to God's Spirit within us, we not only become more sensitive to those things that Jesus was sensitive to when he walked the earth, but we will have the strength we need to do Jesus' work. That's a good reason to keep showing up.

9

COMMITTING TO
A HOLISTIC GOSPEL

Henceforth, Lord, I want to forget myself
and think only of how I can serve you,
and have no will other than your own.
But my will is weak: you alone, my God,
are powerful.
All I can do is to make a firm resolve
to serve you as I have said
and do it from this very moment.

—Teresa of Avila

For everyone must keep in mind
that in all that concerns the spiritual life
his progress will be in proportion
to his surrender of self-love
and of his own will and interests.

—Ignatius of Loyola

And this is my prayer:
that your love may abound more and more
in knowledge and depth of insight
so that you can discern what is best.

—Saint Paul (Philippians 1:9–10 NIV)

I LOVE TO READ about the spiritual lives of those who are committed to the kind of intimacy and unity with Christ that empowers them to do God's work in the world. They inspire me to want that intimacy too. But inspiration doesn't necessarily lead to action. It took me a long time to realize that I preferred reading about others' encounters with God to creating space in my own life to encounter God. It wasn't until my first silent retreat that I saw the seriousness of this difference. Because I was uncomfortable being in extended silence with God, I was instead reading a book about the prayer life of Teresa of Avila. As I was reading, these words came to me: *"Put the book down."* But I didn't want to do that. In that moment I realized that I preferred living vicariously through the saints' experiences of deep intimacy with Christ rather than engaging in that intimacy myself. Putting the book down was very hard for me.

You may not be able to relate to my experience. But if you are convinced, like I am—and was, even at that time—that living a holistic gospel is what Jesus wants for us, that does not mean you will actually live that way. We all need help in discovering, and committing to, the radical life Jesus wants us to live.

Discovering New Ways to Live

When we are developing intimacy with Christ through centering prayer, as well as through the prayer of examen and *lectio divina,* our ideas about ourselves, others, and the world change. We find we are no longer satisfied with the way things are in the world. Promptings from the Holy Spirit begin to lead us to new, more loving, compassionate, and just ways to do what we are already doing, or even lead us to life-changing directions and decisions involving more intentional personal, interpersonal, and world change.

What might these new ways of believing, thinking, feeling, and acting look like? Since Jesus calls us to deny ourselves, and tells us in Luke 16:13 that "'you cannot serve both God and Money,'" one main area of change for many people involves their view of money, since money is often such a stronghold—whether we think we have a lot, a little, or just enough. So many verses in the Bible talk about money in terms of economic justice, which involves not only corporate but also private use of earnings. If you find that you need to change the way you make, spend, save, and give away money, then you will need to find models and resources to help guide you. For instance, one great model can be found in Ron Sider's book *Rich Christians in an Age of Hunger.* Sider advocates what he calls a "graduated tithe" that can help "break the materialistic stranglehold" in our lives. In a nutshell, this graduated tithe involves prayerfully deciding, with the help of trusted friends, how much money, realistically, we need to have to live. We then tithe 10 percent of that base, and for every $1,000 that we earn beyond that base we give an additional 5 percent. Although Sider sees this model as modest, he still believes it is "sufficiently radical that its implementation would revolutionize the ministry and life of the church."[1]

Your attitudes and actions toward money will not be the only things you become increasingly sensitized to as you live more like Jesus. You may be prompted by the Holy Spirit to spend more intentional time talking to coworkers or neighbors about God. You may feel called to make amends with others for lifelong anger issues you have been masking as justified but now realize block your love and work for Christ and others. Perhaps you have held certain beliefs or opinions on issues like abortion or capital punishment or homosexuality or the poor and are now seeing that you have been wrong. You may become sensitized to the fact that you are working for a company that exploits its workers or does harm to animals or to the environment, and you are now being called to challenge those practices or to leave the job in protest. Or maybe you sense that you are to leave the suburbs and move into intentional community in a city or on a mission field. Perhaps you have a certain talent or skill that you recognize could be used to provide services to those who cannot afford them. Perhaps you are working simply to have more *things* and find that this is not how Jesus wants you to live. Maybe your job is taking you away from being able to love your family and friends, and even Jesus, because of how busy you are, and you realize you need to look for other work.

If any of these ideas scare you because they seem right but too hard, please know that God will only awaken in you what has already been put there by grace and what the good in you is already attracted to. The only thing God really takes away from you is your desire for what is harmful, since God wants to give you the real desire of your heart—what is good, acceptable, loving, and just.

Whatever it might be for you, how do you discern when God is calling you to live differently? How can you know just how transformed you are supposed to be?

We believe that the spiritual practices we have outlined are necessary, but not sufficient, for this discernment. Even when making intentional intimacy with Jesus a regular part of our day, it will still be tempting to assume we can live certain ways of our own choosing—as long as we either disconnect certain choices from our faith or, after making a particular choice, we ask Jesus to bless it. Author and Quaker minister Bruce Bishop called these tendencies to compartmentalize how we live "sprinkling on a little bit of Jesus."[2] Even as we are striving to live more for Jesus, we often make daily life choices either by default *or* by what we think is reasonable *or* by how we feel, forgetting that following Jesus means engaging the totality of our being—heart, soul, mind, and strength.

I teach a college senior capstone course in which we discuss the integration of faith and learning in light of Christian worldview, calling, and vocation. Each time I teach this course, I find that several students view these issues through certain assumptions they have never questioned. Many of them assume they will get married, have children, and at least one, usually the man, will get a good job (translation: high paying). In addition, they plan to be good people (translation: nice and honest), raise good children (translation: nice and civil) in a good church (translation: music and preaching they both like). But when Paul says in Romans 12:1–2 that we are to offer our bodies as *living sacrifices* and that we are not to conform to the world, but instead be totally transformed, being good is most likely not good enough, and neither are our assumptions about how we plan to live.

> *Following Jesus means engaging the totality of our being—heart, soul, mind, and strength.*

To avoid "dis-integration" in how we live, we need to learn how to be led by the Spirit of God in *all* of life. Such whole-life discernment means developing the ability, in the context of Christian community, to make wise judgments about how to conduct our daily walk with God.

Seeking whole-life guidance does not, however, mean that we always have to do an intentional process of discernment for all of our actions. When we are living in intimacy with Jesus and in tune with the scriptures, oftentimes, in the words of my friend Ron, "you don't even need to pray about it." When we conform to the living word of God we have directives as to how to live. The Bible is full of verses on what the reign of God is like, on how to treat one another, and on helping make the world more just. But if we are so conditioned by our culture's status quo that we are blind to how radical these directives really are, then we need help. If we want to live for Jesus and his mission, we need to learn how not to avoid selecting out of our lives areas that are somewhat or even totally off-limits for God. We also need to learn how not to confuse God's will with motivations that arise from things that are not of God.

The writer of Proverbs helps us here by giving us a list of things to do:

- Accept God's words.
- Treasure God's commandments within you.
- Make your ear attentive to wisdom.
- Incline your heart to understanding.
- Cry out for insight.
- Raise your voice for understanding.
- Seek it like silver and search for it as for hidden treasures.

Then, we are told that we "will understand righteousness and justice and equity, every good path" (Proverbs 2:1–4, 9).

That's a tall order. How can we be daily committed to all of these things in a spirit of selfless love so that we will "understand righteousness, justice, equity, and every good path"?

Staying Committed

Tony and I believe that the following suggestions will help equip you for ongoing transformation in Christ. Some are specifically geared toward staying committed to intimacy with Jesus, some speak to intentionally and regularly living out Jesus' radical gospel, and others speak to both.

HELP 1.   *Pray.*

First and foremost, we must remember to ask the Holy Spirit for help in living our inward and outward lives in Christ-likeness. One way to do this is to ask for increased awareness of whatever you need to do or change in your life that results in the greater glory of God. Another way is to ask God for what we want. This might seem like an odd concept, since at first glance it looks quite selfish. But if we remember Saint Augustine's charge to "love God and do what you want," we know that if we put loving God first in our lives, we will want to do what God wants. For Ignatius, asking God for what we want assumed that if we are progressing spiritually, our first love *is* God; therefore when we ask God to give us what we want, we may not even know what we are asking for—we just know that God's response is our heart's true desire. Jesus knew this was an important question of faith and trust, as we see from an encounter he had one day when John the Baptist was with two of his own disciples (John 1:35–39). As the three men saw Jesus walking by, John said, "Look, the Lamb of God!" Immediately John's two disciples started following Jesus, which was more than OK with John since his heart's desire was to point people to Jesus. Jesus saw the disciplines following him and asked them, "What do you want?" It is a defining question for any of us who think we want to follow Jesus. The two men replied that what they wanted was to know where Jesus was going. Jesus then invited them along, and they went with him. If we want what God wants for us, we also will respond to Jesus' question by turning our wholes lives around and accepting the invitation to follow him. That is why Jesus said in Matthew 7:7, "Ask and it shall be given to you. . . . For everyone who asks receives."

Here's a way to ask for what we want: "Jesus, help me see what you want me to see about following you—then help me to do it. That is what I want. I ask that you make me aware of any new ways you want me to love you and others."

If you feel that you cannot honestly pray that prayer, then start with asking God to help you *to be willing to be willing* to be led toward that greater glory. You may even need to pray *to be willing to be willing to be willing*. . . . If you are not willing to even pray to be willing, then that means there are barriers in your life that are hindering intimacy and unity with God. You need to get to the point where you are willing to pray one of the willingness prayers before you can freely and more intentionally move forward in your journey with God. But no matter where you are in your walk with Jesus, pray as honestly and specifically as you can. Then sit with Jesus in silence, asking and trusting the Holy Spirit to work deep in your spirit to empower you to live more for Christ.

It may seem obvious to stress praying honest prayers, but in my life I have found that oftentimes I tell others my struggles without taking those very same struggles to God. I disclose to certain friends that I am frustrated with my failure to carve out consistent time alone for prayer. I complain that there always seems to be something that I let disrupt my time alone with Jesus. But if I only complain to my friends, I miss the obvious. I need to remember to pray like this:

> Jesus, I'm frustrated. I seem to have so much trouble carving out time alone with you. Even when I do, something comes up. The door, the dog, even the dirty dishes seem to be calling my name. *Please help me.* Help me get alone with you, for as little or long as you want for me today.

If you do not think that praying honest, forthright prayers like this is okay, remember the Psalms—such as David's prayer in Psalm 38:21–22: "Do not forsake me, O LORD; O my God, do not be far from me; Make haste to help me, O Lord, my salvation."

Or this one from Psalm 40:17b: "You are my help and my deliverer; do not delay, O my God."

Early Christian monks encouraged people to pray simple prayers like these. The one used the most was, *Deus in adjutorium meum intende*— ("O God, come to my aid"). And if that is not simple enough, here is another condensed prayer that my friend Jerry often prays: "Help!"

HELP 2. *Establish a specific quiet time and space for daily spiritual practices.*

If too often there is too much going on in your life, it can be hard to establish a regular time for engaging in holy habits—even though the three spiritual practices we have discussed can all be done in less than an hour a day total. But if you struggle with demands and distractions coming at you from all directions, you may be wondering how you could begin to have even an extra 10 minutes a day. You can find it if you reorder your time, even if you don't see how that is possible. You may even need some ruthless time management adjustments. Don't let what has been called "the tyranny of the urgent" crowd out what is important in your life. My friend Deb, who has a busy teenager and a busy husband, as well as a preschooler and a kindergartener in the house, was recently telling me how hard it is for her to have alone time with Jesus. She figured out that the only way she could do it was to get up 15 minutes earlier every day. I knew that was going to be a sacrifice, since Deb's days were so full that she was already not getting enough sleep. Like Deb, you may need to sacrifice something if you want to be more intentional in living for Christ.

If you are still thinking that you cannot possibly give up anything you are doing in your life, this is most likely not true. What *is* likely true is that you can eliminate things that are taking up too much of your time and energy, thereby distracting you from living a more holistic gospel. You may even need to get help from others in taking a serious inventory of your present priorities.

Even being busy with good things is not always good. As Christian artist Bryan Sirchio sings in one of his songs, "The greatest enemy of God's will for your life is all the good things everyone else wants you to do."[3] We can be so busy doing good deeds that we miss out on some great deeds God has for us to do. While watching the news a few years ago, I heard accolades for a "Mother of the Year." The mother had three children, was working full-time, and was volunteering for several organizations. I remember thinking that instead of applauding her, we should be helping her learn to say No. Thomas Merton, in his book *Faith and Violence: Christian Teaching and Christian Practice*, has suggested that a "life of frantic activity" while "invested with the noblest of qualities" may cause our souls to suffer.[4]

As the old saying goes, "If the devil can't make you bad, he'll make you busy." You may need to ask yourself if your busyness is an indication of something else going on, such as a fear you are consciously or unconsciously avoiding. You may need to slow down long enough to try to figure out what might be going on to keep you so busy. Like my friend Ron says, "You are not the fourth member of the Trinity." Actually, if I were, I *would* slow down, since even God took a day off after creating the world.

Sometimes we find ourselves in a season of life in which we are unusually busy, and even our friends agree that "for such a time as this" what we are doing is necessary. If this is the case for you, you can find inspiration from others who fought great challenges to make intentional time for God. Susanna Wesley, John and Charles Wesley's mother, who gave birth to nineteen children, used to sit on a chair in her kitchen and put her apron over her head when she wanted time to pray. Her children knew what this meant and gave her temporary relief for prayer time. Like Susanna, you may need to become creative in the ways you make time to be alone with Jesus, especially if you are in an unusual time of life.

> *We can be so busy doing good deeds that we miss out on some great deeds God has for us to do.*

Sometimes you can miss the obvious if you think you have nowhere to go to have quiet. Before a friend of mine went to the mission field, her car was her sanctuary. She was having trouble finding time alone in the midst of college dorm life, so she would drive somewhere quiet and sit with God in her car. The shower can also be a good place to pray. So can your living room—even if you are not alone. My friend Oreon gave me a green candle to light when I am having quiet time. The lit candle is a signal not to disturb me (unless someone is bleeding—I told my boys that is my one exception). And if you think you do not have anywhere in your home to go to have quiet, don't forget Susanna Wesley and her apron.

All of these are suggestions, not rules, for creating sacred space. I say that because it can be tempting to want to replicate the kind of space others have, thinking that doing so may help us have similar God-experiences.

Years ago, I was tempted to wait to have longer periods of quiet until I could figure out how to create the kind of cozy, noncluttered, private room a friend has for her times alone with God. If I had that kind of space, I thought, I, too, could have deep times of prayer like she has. I had to realize that the place I chose just needed to be quiet, with few to no distractions. I had been limiting when and where I could have good quiet time. In retrospect, I also believe I was stalling by telling myself that I was waiting until circumstances were just right.

HELP 3.   *Use music and the arts.*

Although we have emphasized silence, there is a time for music in cultivating space for God. Hymns and praise and worship music can help draw us into the kind of "spiritual mood" that will lead us into the stillness we need. When I used to be part of a centering prayer group, Russian choral music played in the background as we sat together in silence. But when I did centering prayer at home without the music, it was harder for me to get into silence. I bought the choral music, and I now enter more easily into the silence at home when I play that music.

Margaret Poloma, in her book *Main Street Mystics,* talks about music's special role in opening doors to contemplation. She contends from her research involving music's role in spiritual revivals that there are times "during which music facilitates a personal altered state of consciousness that brings many into a heightened sense of mystical unity with God."[5] Music and other rituals are potential "conduits through which the power flows" and as such are *a means* for the Holy Spirit to work in our lives, rather than an end in and of themselves.[6]

As you prepare for your quiet time with God, you may want to sing hymns or praise and worship songs all by yourself (whether or not you think you have a good voice, since no one will hear but God!). William Law, the Anglo-Catholic mystic and onetime mentor of John Wesley, gave directives on how to use singing as a help in personal devotions. In his classic book *A Serious Call to a Devout and Holy Life,* Law proposed that singing be used to create a state of awareness in which we are receptive to being filled with the Holy Spirit. He advised beginning daily prayer times with private singing or chanting of one of the Psalms, letting it flow in spontaneous creativity. Law believed that singing with chants and notes made up on the spot expressed what he called "the actions of the heart." He suggested that we could even imagine the heavens opening and that we are part of the angelic choir described in Revelation 7:9–12. This kind of singing, according to Law, raises up gladness in our hearts and awakens the good and holy in us, all the while dispersing the dullness of our souls.[7]

As Jesus said, "For out of the abundance of the heart the mouth speaks" (Matthew 12:34).

Paintings can also take us into sacred space with Christ. In his book *The Return of the Prodigal Son*,[8] Henri Nouwen told of how he was so taken by a poster of Rembrandt's *Return of the Prodigal Son* that on a trip to the Soviet Union he arranged to go to the Hermitage in Saint Petersburg and, for hours, sit and silently reflect upon the original painting. I have to admit that although I am a fan of Nouwen's writings, I was not very excited when I found I had to read about these reflections for a class assignment one year. I had heard so many sermons on the prodigal son that I could not imagine gaining any new insights from the book. But as I read, I was amazed by what the Holy Spirit showed Nouwen through his times of reflecting on the painting.

One time in particular that a painting helped lead me into deeper intimacy with Christ was during my first five-day silent retreat. Because I was struggling with some issues of faith and doubt, Father Bernie, my retreat director, gave me a copy of Italian painter Caravaggio's 1597 painting, *Doubting Thomas*. He told me to take several minutes, several times a day, to look at the painting and then put myself in it. So I did. I focused on being in Thomas's place, and on Jesus talking to me and allowing me to touch his wounds. The Holy Spirit used those times of imagining as powerful healers, freeing me from some of my preoccupations with fear and doubt, so I could focus more on Christ.

I now have copies of both Rembrandt's and Caravaggio's paintings hanging on a wall in my office. Just looking at them for a few moments helps me enter into a more quiet state with Christ.

Using paintings as part of our devotional life with God is not new. As Alister E. McGrath says in his book *Christian Spirituality*, "One of the most significant themes in Christian spirituality is that of *visualization*—the development of ways in which the divine may be represented visually, as something to be contemplated, without compromising the transcendence of God."[9] But many Protestants are concerned that visualization of the divine can be idolatrous, and that is a legitimate concern. Paintings can become idols on which we put too much importance (just as anything can) if we forget their proper place. We avoid moving into dangerous territory by always remembering that the images in paintings are a *means* to the end of knowing and loving God more deeply.

HELP 4.   *Cultivate other silence in your life.*

Cultivating other times of silence to be with Jesus can help you "sit down inside" so that what you do outside of those times flows more and more out of love for God and others. But to cultivate any silence in our lives is not easy to do when there is so much noise in and around us.

When I entered my spiritual direction program, the thought of the two five-day silent retreats that would be required during the next two years made me a wreck. I seriously wondered how I would be able to survive being in silence that long. My close friends provided no comfort, since they were amused by the thought of me being silent for *any* length of time. I realized that I could not think about the silent retreats too much, since just the thought was making me nervous. The day I was leaving for my first retreat, my friend Pam said sincerely to me, "I'm so jealous that you get to spend all this time alone with Jesus." I was also jealous—of her, because that's not how I felt. When I got to the retreat center, I started counting down to the exact time I was going to be allowed to leave. But then, during the next five days, what I hardly dared hope might happen *did* happen. The experiences I was already having in the program, specifically spending more time in silence with God through meditative reading and short times of silent prayer, were helping me become more comfortable with silence. I even loved eating in a room full of silent people! There were still many uncomfortable moments, but through all of the silence, the Holy Spirit was helping me learn so much more than I would have learned without the silence. I came away with a deeper dependence on Jesus and a clearer sense that working for a loving and just world is what God requires. I also came away with a strong desire to not talk as much (which I am sure greatly disappointed my husband). I felt like quoting the Saint Francis character in the movie *Brother Sun, Sister Moon,* when he said to his friend Bernardo, "Words, Bernardo, I used to believe in words."

I have since become increasingly comfortable with silence. I now often turn off the radio and CD player when I am driving alone. I fix meals or clean in silence instead of having music on. When I take walks alone I leave my headphones home. These might seem like simple things, but I don't think they are. I am discovering that the more I am in silence, the more I sense God speaking. My restless spirit is increasingly quieting down, as I am coming to understand in my heart Saint Augustine's famous quote: "You have made us for yourself, and our heart is restless until it rests in you."[10]

Although I recommend silent retreats, they are not a requirement for learning to cultivate more silence. You just need to recognize times when you can be in silence, and then make choices—to not, for instance, open that magazine in the waiting room or turn on the TV or music or computer or your own overly analytic brain or whatever it is that is distracting you from living more centered in Christ. Although the cover of *People* makes me want to open the magazine when I am in a waiting room (I wish I were kidding), more often than not I tell myself not to pick it up, and instead I sit in silence. Here is how my friend Janice described an experience with her own "waiting room silence":

> While I was waiting to see the oncologist I felt my anxiety level rising, so I began to think about the word *peace*. I wanted to feel God's peace, but I just couldn't even relax. I thought about the song "I've Got Peace Like a River" and decided to think about a river. I imagined myself sitting by a small babbling brook. As I sat there I suddenly imagined Jesus sitting next to me. He was wearing sandals and his feet were dark from the sun. I looked at him and he looked at me with compassion in his eyes. Then he reached over and put his hand on mine. Next he slowly stood up and placed his hand on my bald head and said, "It's going to be OK." I could feel the peace flood my spirit and tears began to trickle down my face. We just continued to sit and listen to the peace. When the nurse entered the room I realized I had tears on my cheeks, so I quickly wiped them away and went— in peace—to finish the appointment and then head into the chemotherapy treatment room.

If, unlike Janice, you are not quite sure what to do with the silence, simply ask Jesus to meet you in silence and then focus on Jesus' loving presence.

HELP 5.   *Get spiritual guidance from others.*

Henri Nouwen wrote, "Just as creative dialogue with other human beings cannot just be left to our natural responses, so too our intimate conversation with God needs formation and training. . . . It is therefore not so strange that people who search for a deep and persistent prayer life always ask for some help."[11]

We do need help from others, and not just *any* others. We cannot assume that other Christians are also committed to the kind of intimacy with Jesus that results in working for a more loving and just world. The spiritual companions we surround ourselves with should be people who help make us into evangelists and countercultural people whose values challenge the immoral values of the prevailing social order.

We need to be aware that other lovers of Jesus may not grasp how deep and wide Jesus' message really is. If that is the case, they can lead us astray by promoting their limited view of Jesus as enough, and also by confusing their own comforts or desires with God's or ours. Friends can, for example, discourage us from wanting to simplify our lives, even if we tell them that is what we believe we need to do to better serve God. If they see no need to give up things for Christ—or don't want to see it—they might think our desire to purify our lives more radical than necessary for living a Christian life.

We also need to be aware that spiritual helpers can confuse their own problems with the issues of those they try to help. Tony's pastor has humorously suggested, with due respect to Henri Nouwen, "Watch out for those 'wounded healers.' I find that wounded healers often go around wounding people."

What we need are Spirit-led lovers of Jesus to listen to us and help guide us, as well as motivate us, as we train to live radically in and for Christ. We need to be accountable to them to confirm that our experiences and learning, including our interpretations of Jesus' life and message, fit with Christian orthodoxy. In his book *Sacred Companions,* David Benner writes, "If you are making significant progress on the transformational journey of Christian spirituality, you have one or more friendships that support that journey. If you do not, you are not. It is that simple."[12]

There are four kinds of spiritual helpers who can greatly motivate us to stay on track with our quest for a holistic faith as long as they, too, are committed to this journey: a spiritual director or mentor, friends, an intentional small group, and an intentional church community.

SPIRITUAL DIRECTOR OR MENTOR. The reason I strongly recommend mentors or spiritual directors as a vital help is because they can assist us, through intentional guidance, in recognizing how the Holy Spirit is calling us to greater intimacy with God and service to others. I am using the word *mentor* to mean someone you and others see as spiritually growing and developing in ways that you believe can help you live a more holistic gospel. This someone could be a pastor, youth leader, teacher, businessperson, a mom, a dad, or anyone who is striving to be more like Christ.

What I want to talk about more specifically, however, are spiritual directors, since they are not as familiar to many of us. Spiritual directors are more formal mentors, since unlike some other spiritual helpers they have gone through specific training to help guide people into a greater intimacy with God.

To understand the role of spiritual directors, we must understand spiritual direction, or more specifically, Christian spiritual direction, since spiritual direction is not always Christian. Perhaps the most widely quoted definition comes from William A. Barry and William J. Connolly in *The*

Practice of Spiritual Direction. They write that Christian spiritual direction is "help given by one Christian to another which enables that person to pay attention to God's personal communication to him or her, to respond to this personally communicating God, to grow in intimacy with this God, and to live out the consequences of the relationship."[13]

Spiritual direction is about discerned intimacy with God and discerned action for the Kingdom of God. In fact, if a spiritual director does not eventually point us outside of ourselves, to focus on our intentional work for Christ in the world, we should seriously consider whether we are dealing with the right person. The goal for spiritual direction, unlike other kinds of counseling, is not to help gain a healthy adjustment to the world, since our present world is not what God envisioned for creation. Instead it is to learn how, as the ancient saying goes, to be "in the world but not of it." The Apostle Paul was talking about this very tension when he told the church in Rome, "Do not be conformed to this world, but be transformed by the renewing of your minds, so that you may discern what is the will of God—what is good and acceptable and perfect" (Romans 12:2).

If you decide to meet with a spiritual director, how often you get together depends—some people meet every 4–6 weeks with their director, and some, feeling the need to have more guidance and accountability in their lives, meet more often, such as once a week.

When looking for a spiritual director, I recommend the following criteria: (1) that the director is Christ-centered, (2) has an intimate relationship with Christ, (3) is the same gender as you, (4) has his or her own spiritual director, (5) is connected to a church community, and (6) is formally trained in spiritual direction.

You can start looking for a Christ-centered spiritual director simply by asking around. If you know of someone in spiritual direction, ask about his or her director. You could even call local churches to see if they have one or more directors on staff; or you can find "Spiritual Director" in some phone books. The problem, though, is that you might not know the spiritual orientation of the person. You want to make sure that he or she is in fact Christ-centered and believes in basic Christian doctrines. You might ask a potential director how he or she relates to what is said in the Apostle's Creed, since that is a good criterion for evaluating orthodoxy.

The second criterion, that the director has an intimate relationship with Christ, may seem redundant after having said that the person should be Christ-centered. But the fact that someone is Christ-centered theologically or philosophically does not mean that the person has an intimately transforming relationship with Jesus. You will want to meet with the director a few times to try to get a sense of his or her own spirituality before committing to spiritual direction. That won't be easy, because a good spiritual director will try to deal with your issues rather than providing any self-disclosure. So it is important that you pray for wisdom and discernment about the person.

Gender is the third consideration. As a general rule, I advise going to a spiritual director who is of the same sex. There may be things you want to talk about that are more appropriate to discuss male to male or female to female; in addition, you will avoid the possibility of attraction in the relationship. However, those attracted to people of the same sex may want to go to someone of the other sex. And since there could be additional reasons to make an exception to the gender rule, make it a matter of prayer and get advice from trusted spiritual companions.

> *The fact that someone is Christ-centered theologically or philosophically does not mean that the person has an intimately transforming relationship with Jesus.*

The fourth criterion is that the spiritual director have his or her own spiritual director. At the end of my two-year spiritual direction program, I was told I needed to continue to go to a spiritual director if I planned to *do* spiritual direction, since transformation is an ongoing process for us all. I caution anyone about going to a director who is not in direction.

The fifth criterion, that a spiritual director be connected to a church community, does not mean just any church. If your spiritual director is committed to a community devoted to a holistic gospel, there is a better likelihood that you will be guided to live in a more Christlike manner.

Last, I recommend looking for a spiritual director who was trained in a reputable program. There are, however, people who are deeply spiritual, with no formal training, who can be spiritual directors in the best sense of the term. The more formal programs available today, designed to help laypeople become spiritual directors, did not used to exist. People became spiritual directors as others sought them out because of their roles as priests, monks, or nuns, or because of their deep spirituality.

However, now that spiritual direction is becoming more popular, all kinds of people can call themselves spiritual directors, no matter what their level of spirituality or training. For instance, pastors are often viewed, by themselves and others, as spiritual directors because of their training in seminary, but that does not mean they make good spiritual directors. Spiritual directors are typically trained in listening, discerning, and using silence so that the Holy Spirit has room to bring insights to the directee of how to live daily for Christ and the Kingdom. Although a pastor can be gifted in preaching, that does not mean he or she is gifted in one-on-one spiritual direction. Again, I do not mean to suggest that a person who has not gone through a formal spiritual direction program cannot provide effective guidance for a person's spiritual development. But if what I described as spiritual direction is appealing, you may want to find someone who has been formally trained in guiding people into greater intimacy with Jesus and greater service to others. You can check out what program the person was in to see if it fits with the basic tenets of your faith. In addition, you may want to avoid a director whose training was heavy on techniques, such as role playing and listening skills, but light on crucial experiences that provide means to intentionally go deeper into Christ. I am thankful that my program provided both.

No matter who we seek to help guide us, we should make our choice a matter of prayer.

FRIENDS AS HELPERS. My friend Lisa and I have been walking together for years. I often whine to Lisa that I don't feel like walking, and then she reminds me that is why we commit to walking with each other—for accountability. She's right. As much as I love our talks when we walk, they are unfortunately not enough to motivate me when I tell myself that maybe we can walk and talk tomorrow instead. It is the accountability that keeps us regularly walking.

We really do need each other—in so many areas of our lives. As the writer of Ecclesiastes says, "Two are better than one, because they have a good reward for their toil. For if they fall, one will lift up the other; but woe to one who is alone and falls and does not have another to help" (Ecclesiastes 4:9–10). It is crucial for us to have friends who role-model love for Jesus, and who hold us accountable and help us discern how we are growing in our imitation of Christ.

My neighbor and friend Judy is a great role model of love for Jesus and others. You cannot talk to Judy for very long without sensing her deep care and compassion for bringing people into loving relationships with Jesus and then helping them grow in that love. And you couldn't follow her around for long without seeing her cook for, empathically listen to, or pray with someone.

My sister-in-law Barb is another role model. Whenever I am with Barb, it seems like she introduces me to yet another justice issue that was not on my radar. For instance, I did not know that buying coffee was one such issue, until Barb started giving me "Equal Exchange"[14] coffee. I didn't know that farmers, the environment, and our health were all treated in unfair and unhealthy ways—that is, until she told me about Equal Exchange's commitment to such things as paying farmers fair prices, trading directly with democratic cooperatives, supporting sustainable farming practices, and protecting the environment and our health through only producing shade-grown, organic coffee beans. Because I believe these are things Jesus calls us to care about to help create a more just world, I took Barb's message to my church to ask them to buy this type of coffee for our Sunday morning fellowship time.

My friend Oreon is one who helps hold me accountable and helps me discern how I am living for Christ. She introduced me to one of John Wesley's accountability questions that I now often use with others: "What is the state of your soul?" Whenever Oreon asks me this, I know what it means: No small talk—how am I *really* doing?

Our friends who love Jesus can help us discern God not only in our daily lives, but in major life decisions too. Shortly after Saint Francis's conversion, he was in "great anxiety and in great doubt" as to whether he should devote himself solely to a life of prayer or at times also to preaching. He sent a friend, Friar Masseo, to *tell*—not *ask*—two deeply spiritual friends, Sister Clare and Brother Silvester, to pray. Friar Masseo asked them each separately to seek God's will for Francis's decision. Friar Masseo was still with Brother Silvester when Brother Silvester received an answer in prayer. He then went back to Sister Clare, who had received the same answer: that Christ wanted Francis to "go through the world to preach, because He has not chosen you for yourself alone but also for the salvation of others."[15] And so that is what he did. Richard Foster, commenting on this incident, wrote in *Celebration of Discipline,* "That direction gave the early Franciscan movement an unusual combination of mystical contemplation and evangelistic fervor."[16]

A note of caution regarding friends and accountability: Be careful not to sabotage your accountability partner. Students I work with have admitted to sometimes avoiding their accountability partner because they did not do what they intended and did not want the person to know; or because they shared more than they intended to and now did not want to face the other person. If you say you want a friend with whom you can share and be accountable, you need to be aware of these temptations to sabotage accountability. When you are having trouble doing what you said you would do, be honest with your friend. Confession can be a great step to freeing ourselves to be even more accountable. This is not always easy, but Saint Paul tells us "to confess your sins to one another, and pray for one another" (James 5:16). In addition, by confessing, we are allowing our friend to "bear our burden"; something we are all called to do with one another (Galatians 6:2).

SMALL GROUPS AS HELPERS. Becoming involved in small groups for the purpose of training in spiritual practices will help us reach out to others more evangelistically and justly. If you cannot find a small group like this, you may want to form one.

John Wesley designed and organized "united societies" or "class meetings" whose purpose was to encourage devotional practice and social concern. Wesley's class meetings involved small groups of people with an appointed leader getting together weekly for discipline and instruction (which included getting a reading on the "state of their souls"). In addition, class members were to help meet the needs of each other by praying for and caring for one another, much like the early Christians did. Many small groups today use forms of the Wesley class meetings.

My husband and I have been involved in an ongoing small group of couples for years. Because we know each other well, but do not get to see each other on a daily basis, it can be too easy to spend our whole time together catching up on each other's lives. As much as that kind of sharing is important, when we did not have a formal plan for our time together we often did not get around to going deeper into each other's lives. A few years ago we discovered Richard Foster's Renovaré small-group accountability questions. We set a time to start taking turns answering one or more of the questions, and that helps us stay on track. Here is a small sampling of those questions.

- In what ways has God made his presence known to you since our last meeting? What experiences of prayer, meditation, and spiritual reading has God given you? What difficulties or frustrations have you encountered?

- Have you encountered any injustice to or oppression of others? Have you been able to work for justice and *shalom?*

- Has God provided an opportunity for you to share your faith
  with someone since our last meeting? How did you respond? [17]

The beauty of these questions is that not only can we talk about what we have been doing, we can take that sharing and examine how much we are in tune with loving God and others on a day-to-day basis.

CHURCH COMMUNITY. Some of us have grown up in environments in which we had to be in church whenever the doors were open, while others have never been committed to a church community, at best attending church sporadically. Most of us are probably somewhere in the middle. No matter how you personally might define *church,* if you read the Bible, you learn the importance of being committed to a community of Christians in order to worship Jesus and to carry out Jesus' mission to build the Kingdom of God. We cannot minimize in any way that commitment to church, in the sense of a community of believers, is a necessary component for intentional spiritual transformation in Christ. The church *is* the body of Christ. Saint Paul says in I Corinthians 12 that the church is made up of members each of whom has special contributions to make to the whole community of faith. The church is other than a mere social institution. It is a people who come together to have a shared mystical experience with the living Christ. As Christ himself said, "For where two or three are gathered in my name, I am there among them" (Matthew 18:20). Early Christians, as we have seen, devoted themselves to prayer, to each other, and to the needy. As a result "day by day the Lord added to their number those who were being saved" (Acts 2:47). I believe this is the kind of unity Jesus prayed for, regarding all believers (the church), in John 17.

This is church at its best. If your church isn't like this, you may need to ask for wisdom about doing something about it from within or consider finding another church. But before you do anything, get wise counsel from several others to see if your perception is fair, and to see if you may have been contributing to a lopsided community without even knowing it. Since this is a very serious issue, you will want to seek much grace-filled guidance in any decision you make.

Note that all of the kinds of people I have mentioned can guide you in living out your love for God and others. But if your friends or spiritual director or mentor or small group or church community are not helping you to live out a more holistic gospel, you need to seriously consider finding others who will. Discerning how to live every day in Christ-likeness will not be easy; having several sacred companions in your life who are also committed to living a holistic gospel will help you stay committed.

BEING A HELPER. Henri Nouwen, in *The Return of the Prodigal Son*,[18] wrote about how easy it was for him to identify with the wayward and even the eldest son in Jesus' parable of the prodigal son. He said it took him a long time, however, to see that he was being called to be the compassionate father. We too are called not only to *seek* sacred companions, but to *be* sacred companions. As we receive more guidance from others to live out a holistic gospel, we are, in addition, to give guidance to others, whether as a friend, mentor, spiritual director, or in our small group or church community. How we do this is a matter for prayer and discernment. We ask the Holy Spirit to help us notice when we can be helpers and we ask others to help us discern possible opportunities. As Jesus said, "It is more blessed to give than to receive" (Acts 20:35).

HELP 6.   *Discern choices and voices through the Wesleyan quadrilateral.*

I first heard of what is called the "Wesleyan quadrilateral"[19] many years ago on a church retreat. I remember writing down four crucial considerations for guiding our lives—*scripture, reason, church tradition, and experience*—and thinking they sounded like the best, most concise criteria I had ever heard for discerning God's will in a variety of circumstances. What I find so wise and useful about this model is how it helps us avoid making decisions based only on one Bible passage *or* what seems to make sense at the time *or* church tradition *or* our observations and perceptions of experience, to the exclusion of any of the other considerations. For instance, even though Wesley himself emphasized the primacy of scripture for how to live our lives, he was still aware that it is not the only source for discernment. Using the Bible alone for decision making, without any other considerations, can be dangerous, since it can be misused, misread, and taken out of context.

The following framework of the quadrilateral can greatly help you when your intimacy with Jesus challenges you to discern whether you should stay with your current life choices or move to a different place—physically, or in your current attitudes and actions. Whenever this happens, you ask yourself, as well as your trusted spiritual companions, forms of all of the following questions. Then, with their help, you weigh all four parts of this model as you try to, in the words of Saint Paul, "discern what is best" (Philippians 1:10 NIV).

1. Is what I am thinking about, or doing, or desiring to do in line with what scripture teaches?

2. Does it make sense in light of reason?

3. Is it consistent with church tradition—what Christians down through the ages have interpreted the scriptures to mean?

4. Does it resonate with the "testing of spirits" in my own experiences, as well as those of other Christians?

Let's say you have been considering whether or not to move into an intentional community committed to developing their intimacy with Jesus, evangelizing and working for justice for the poor and oppressed. That kind of community would certainly be in line with Wesley's first consideration, scripture, since it directly relates to Jesus' mission and the New Testament's description of early church behavior in Acts.

Regarding reason, one of the things you could do is study research done on the effectiveness of intentional communities working for the poor, along with paying attention to suggestions for being more effective.

Next, if you didn't already know, others would tell you that your idea is consistent with church tradition, since Christians down through the ages have lived in intentional community for Jesus' mission, beginning with the New Testament church.

I want to spend what could seem like a disproportionate time on the fourth consideration, experience. Your own and others' observations and perceptions of experiences with God and each other should not be taken lightly. These are to be viewed in light of the other three considerations, paying attention to how the Holy Spirit might be speaking to you. But this won't necessarily be easy, so there are many things to bear in mind *and* heart.

For starters, you want a realistic, not romantic, look at what this kind of living entails. Many people romanticize Jesus' call to live sacrificially for others, and then discover that in reality it is much harder than they thought it would be. That is why it can be helpful to talk to people who are already living that way. You might want to contact people like Shane Claiborne or Jonathan and Leah Wilson-Hartgrove, or those living with them, who are already experiencing the kind of community living or "new monasticism"[20] you are considering. Better yet, see whether you could visit a community like theirs, or perhaps even live in one for several months before making your decision to join or start one.

You also want to ask God to help you see and sort out any personal motives, issues, and desires that could be causing you to have trouble deciding what to do. Disclose doubts with a trusted mentor and with other spiritual companions, remembering that experiencing concerns, inadequacies, or roadblocks about the decision does not necessarily mean you should not do it. There are false voices out there, and even inside of us, and we need help in figuring out what is God's voice and what is not.

When trying to distinguish God's voice from others, it is also important to listen to repeated messages, whether from ourselves or others, to try to discern whether or not they mean anything and whether or not they are from the Holy Spirit. A former student of mine, Jacki, told me that while she was in college her dream had always been to get married and have children. She said that whenever someone mentioned the word *missions* she knew that was not for her; as a matter of fact, the thought scared her. But then she started hearing that word more and more, in chapel services and in other conversations. Eventually, as Jacki started to think about what she wanted to do after graduating from college, that word *missions* kept coming back, but without the fear that used to accompany it. During her junior year of college, a friend encouraged Jacki to apply for mission work with an organization called "Youth with a Mission" (YWAM). Shortly after her senior year, she was being trained to do missionary work with YWAM.

Jacki would tell you that, looking back, she does not know when her heart changed. What she does know is that she started to pay attention to a repeated word, and the word took root and grew in her, resulting in a life-altering decision. In fact, a friend's dad, who is a pastor, used to tease Jacki that she was running from her call to missions. She said they would both laugh, but that internally she would cringe. It was only after she had been at YWAM that he told her he had always believed in the truth of those words, but he did not know how much he should try to persuade her with his intuitions.

One of the best ways to discern whether or not you are listening to God's voice is to examine, through prayer and with trusted others, the beginning, middle, and end of possible life choices. You can do this by asking yourself, "What were my motivations and intentions at first, during, and finally at the end of the decision?" If you trusted God, prayed, and sought help from other lovers of Jesus throughout the process, then you have your answer—God was and is in it. You need to trust and remember that, because God is not a tricky God. You may be tricked and tempted by false or negative voices, but God will not trick you. God loves you. And even if misguided or sinful motivations led to certain experiences and decisions that were not of God, that does not mean the situation itself cannot be redeemed, as you again put your life back into God's hands. If, for instance, you lived in intentional community for what you now consider misguided or even wrong reasons, that does not mean the

Holy Spirit cannot rescue and redeem the situation and use it for God's glory. Or if you avoided the move for what you now know were selfish reasons, seriously consider whether or not it is still an option.

When using experience to discern, a good question to ask is based on I Corinthians 13:13: "Is there an increase in faith, hope, and love?" You can know the answer when you eventually grow in trust, praise, and gratitude to God; when you have more courage and determination to take risks for the Kingdom; and when you have more love, generosity, and compassion toward others, since all of these are attributes of Christ. You and others will notice the fruit of the Spirit being produced in your life: love, joy, peace, patience, kindness, generosity, faithfulness, gentleness, and self-control (Galatians 5:22). I say *eventually*, since you may not necessarily experience peace, joy, and increased freedom for a long time, possibly not until long after you have been living the decision. A decision to live a different way for God and others can lead you into increased risk taking and uncertainty, and a sense of loss for what will be missed. But if the work is of God, you will have an underlying sense that you are doing the right thing, even in the midst of these difficulties. As Dallas Willard said in *Renovation of the Heart,* "The person who wants the feeling of peacefulness will be unable to do the things that make for peace—especially, doing what is right and confronting evil."[21] Remember that it is the peace of Christ we are seeking, the kind that leads to working for peace.

If you do *lectio divina* focused on the last week of Jesus' human life on earth, you will experience many times when Jesus did not have *feelings* of peacefulness. He struggled with God in the Garden of Gethsemane to the point of sweating blood. He experienced severe emotional and physical pain. But he was determined to go through whatever he needed to, knowing that whatever happened would be of God, *because* he had put his complete faith, hope, love, and trust in God. So if you are going through an especially difficult time with decisions you need to make or have made regarding living more fully for Christ, it might be good for you to enter into parts or all of this week with Jesus through holy reading and reflecting.

In the midst of this process of discernment, keep praying and asking others to pray for God's will. As Wesley said in *A Plain Account of Christian Perfection,* "On every occasion of uneasiness, we should retire to prayer, that we may give place to the grace and light of God and then form our resolutions, without being in any pain about what success they may have."[22] You may even want to picture yourself standing before Jesus after your death, talking with him about the decision you are making or have made.

HELP 7. *Be healthy and rested.*

Loving and following Jesus means engaging the totality of your being—heart, soul, mind, and *strength* (Deuteronomy 6:5, emphasis mine). That's hard to do if you are not taking care of your body, which is "a sacred place, the place of the Holy Spirit" (I Corinthians 6:19 MSG). We know we are to take care of these sacred temples with what we eat and how we exercise. But we often don't think about how we are also to care for these dwellings of the Holy Spirit with the amount of sleep we get. According to the National Sleep Foundation, the average adult sleeps just under seven hours (6 hours, 58 minutes) a night during a workweek.[23] But sleep specialists say we need at least 8 hours a night. If you want to be alert enough to engage in spiritual practices, and have the strength to do the work Jesus wants you to do, you not only need to eat right and exercise, you also need to get enough sleep. Still, too many people believe that they will get more done if they sleep less, even though studies have found the opposite to be true. In reality, you get less done with less sleep, because you are not as productive as you would be with more rest. It is harder to stay focused and motivate yourself to engage in whatever you are doing, including your spiritual practices, when you are sleep deprived. Paul says in Ephesians to "pray in the Spirit on all occasions with all kinds of prayers and requests. With this in mind, be alert and always keep on praying for all the saints" (6:18). We can't be alert if we are not getting enough sleep.

Whenever you have trouble falling asleep or when you wake up in the night and can't get back to sleep, try repeating this verse from Psalm 4:8 until you fall asleep: "I will both lie down and sleep in peace; for you alone, O Lord, make me lie down in safety."

A Warning

All of these ideas can help you discover and commit to a holistic gospel. But for some of us, our tendency might be to use them for living one part of the message and mission of Jesus to the detriment of the others. If we only make use of them for growing in intimacy with Jesus *or* as a way to better love those in our circle of compassion *or* to be more committed to justice issues, then we miss out on all that Jesus has for us and for those we are to be serving.

PART THREE

TAKING INTIMACY WITH GOD INTO THE WORLD

Mary Albert Darling and Tony Campolo

AVOIDING
TWO TEMPTATIONS

Social action without prayer and
conversion to the Lord
lacks power and the ability to produce
long-lasting change
in the social-economic conditions of the people;
likewise, prayer and evangelization
without social action
leads to a pietistic withdrawal from the realities
of the human condition
and an escape from social problems
rather than a confrontation and challenge to change.

—Father John P. Bertolucci, *Viva Cristo Rey* (video)

AS A TEENAGER, Tony hated hearing the old hymn "In the Garden"[1] in church. Singing words like "He speaks, and the sound of His voice is so sweet, the birds hush their singing" did not fit the image of a tough street kid from West Philadelphia. But as Tony grew, so did his desire for what the song described. The idea of being alone "in the garden" with Jesus became an intimacy his soul deeply craved. He now loves to sing these words:

I come to the garden alone,
While the dew is still on the roses;
And the voice I hear, falling on my ear
The Son of God discloses.

Chorus:
And He walks with me and He talks with me;
and He tells me I am His own;
And the joy we share, as we tarry there,
None other has ever known.

He speaks, and the sound of His voice
Is so sweet, the birds hush their singing,
And the melody, That He gave to me,
Within my heart is ringing.

Tony is not alone in his love for what this song expresses. When you discover the wonders of being alone in the garden with Jesus, it can be tempting to want to stay there. But you can't. Jesus calls you out of the garden. Consider the words of the third verse of the hymn:

I'd stay in the garden with Him,
Though the night around me be falling,
But He bids me go; Through the voice of woe,
His voice to me is calling.

Loving Jesus means going out into the world. If you are spending time alone with Jesus and are not hearing "voices of woe," your spirituality has become self-centered, not Christ-centered. Loving Jesus means responding to Jesus' invitation to go in and come out of the garden daily. It means sharing the love of Christ with others, since the fruits of our relationship with Jesus are revealed by how we speak and how we act toward those Jesus called "the least of these" (Matthew 25:40).

We must be careful not to succumb to either one of two "garden" temptations—staying in the garden so much that we do not notice the needs outside, *or* not going into the garden at all because we are too busy responding to the "voices of woe."

The First Garden Temptation: Narcissistic Spirituality

"Narcissistic spirituality" is unfortunately not an oxymoron. If your spirituality becomes focused mainly on spending time communing with God in holy habits such as centering prayer or *lectio divina*, going to a Bible study group, hearing great preaching and teaching, looking for the next silent retreat, or attending a Christian conference, then you can easily become spiritually self-centered. This may sound strange—how could there be anything wrong with focusing on our personal relationship with

God? There is nothing wrong with that; in fact, it is what we all need to do, unless our spirituality—no matter how deep and intense we think it is—is not producing in us an urgency to bring Jesus' message of salvation and justice to others. If we fill up much of our time with activities that develop our personal relationship with Jesus and not with those individuals whom Jesus came to serve, then we miss the totality of Jesus' gospel. As the Christian psychologist Harold Darling wrote, "To continue to receive from God and fail to share of the abundance received leads to spiritual leanness."[2] We may think we are experiencing fullness in Christ when in reality we are only full of ourselves.

It is a common fallacy to see the term "mystical" in this one-sided way—as only a love relationship between ourselves and God. It is easy to equate mystics with people who love to spend time alone with God because sometimes what is written about them focuses only on one part of their lives—the inner part. Their intense love for Christ was so unusual that some of them, like Teresa of Avila, were asked to document their intimate experiences with Christ so that certain religious leaders could check for any possible heresy. (The good news is that no heresy was found in the writings of the saints we highlight in this book.) After these saints wrote about their intimacy with God, something unexpected happened: the writings became popular to degrees no one anticipated because they were so inspiring. However, while these saints had lives marked by private mystical communion with Christ, their spirituality flowed into sharing their deep love for Christ by "winning souls" and working for social reform.

If we read the lives of mystics and saints so that we can grasp something of their interior lives with Christ, we may be drawn into developing only that subjective relationship with God. If that is all we develop, then our desire becomes selfish and self-focused. It is the same desire and temptation that Peter had when he, James, and John were up on a mountain during Jesus' transfiguration, recorded in Matthew 17:1–3. We read that Jesus' "face shone like the sun, and his clothes became dazzling white. Suddenly there appeared to them Moses and Elijah, talking with him." Peter, James, and John found themselves in the middle of an intense mystical experience. What did Peter want to do because of this experience? He wanted all of them to stay there. But while Peter was laying out his plan, God came in a cloud and told them, "This is my Son, the Beloved; with him I am well pleased; Listen to him!" (Matthew 17:6). Listening to Jesus meant following Jesus down from the mountaintop experience because there were needs to be met in the world. Mystical encounters with God are not to be ends in themselves—they are to serve as motivators for action. When they came down the mountain, Jesus was immediately presented with the opportunity to heal a boy suffering from demon possession (Matthew 17:14–18).

Centuries later, a young Italian woman, now known as Saint Catherine of Siena, intensely struggled with the same mountaintop temptation, only hers lasted several years. Catherine's story clearly illustrates how a one-sided "just Jesus and me" spirituality can seem so right yet can greatly hinder us from engaging in Jesus' holistic gospel.

> *Mystical encounters with God are not to be ends in themselves—they are to serve as motivators for action.*

Saint Catherine of Siena

Catherine (1347–1380), born to Giacomo and Lapa Bienincasa of the Tuscany region of Italy, was the youngest of twenty-five children (no wonder she wanted to be alone with Jesus). From early on in her life, Catherine loved God with an intense devotion. Even at six years of age she desired nothing more than to be alone with Christ, her "Beloved." But this was difficult for Catherine to do, not only because of all the children in the house, but also because her mother, Lapa, fought hard to have her daughter live a "normal" life. In Lapa's mind, this normal life included the things young women of their time desired, namely marrying young and having children. But to Lapa's dismay, Catherine wanted only to be the bride of Christ.

At one point Lapa even banned her daughter from being alone in prayer by making her share a bedroom and spend most of her time working in the kitchen. Nevertheless, Catherine was so resolved that she created "in her mind a secret cell which she vowed she would never leave for anything in the world."[3] This internal cell worked well for Catherine, enabling her to be focused on Christ in the midst of the duties and trials of everyday life. She recommended the same to others. Once, when her confessor complained about his being too busy, she told him, "Make yourself a cell in your own mind from which you need never come out."[4]

It took Catherine's mother a long time to realize that God had a strong grip on her daughter, but she finally allowed Catherine "to live as the Almighty inspired her to."[5] At age eighteen, Catherine joined the Sisters of Penance of Saint Dominic, an order that allowed her to live at home. She was then able to spend most of her time alone in her own small room in prayer with Jesus.

At the age of twenty-three, Catherine felt God urging her to open the door of her room, come out of her seclusion, and "open the door . . . of other souls."[6] Saying that Catherine did not want to open that door and go out into the world is an understatement. Her desire for being alone with Christ was so intense that she believed seclusion and silence must be what God intended for her and for everyone who desired it. Like a child who thinks she knows what is best, Catherine pleaded with God: "I, as you know better than I do myself, have avoided all other company

> *A one-sided "just Jesus and me" spirituality can seem so right yet can greatly hinder us from engaging in Jesus' holistic gospel.*

so that I might find you, my Lord and my God; now that by your mercy I have found you . . . I surely cannot be obliged to forgo such an incomparable treasure and involve myself again in human affairs."[7]

Catherine reported that, to her surprise, God answered her in this way: "I have no intention of cutting you off from me; on the contrary, I wish to bind you more closely to myself, by means of love of the neighbour. You know that the precepts of love are two: love of me, and love of the neighbour. . . . I want you to fulfill these two commandments. You must walk, in fact, with both feet, not one, and with two wings fly to heaven!"[8]

God had spoken and Catherine obeyed, although it was literally painful for her to do so. She once claimed during confession that whenever she felt God calling her to leave her room and "go and talk to anyone, she felt such a sharp pain in her heart that it seemed as though it was about to break, and that no one except the Lord would have been able to make her do it."[9]

When Catherine became accustomed to leaving her room, her heart started to break for the less fortunate as she began working to help the poor and oppressed. After being convinced by Jesus that she was not to keep him all to herself, she left her room so often that she become known as the "social mystic" or, as Suzanne Noffke called her, the "mystic activist."[10] She passionately served, and fought against, injustices done to the poor and oppressed, which is no wonder since Catherine saw Christ in them. She believed that Jesus assured her that she was to care for the sick, the prisoner, and the poor by appearing to her as "the least of these." One such case is the miracle of the chapel of the *Mantellate*. One day as Catherine was leaving her time of prayer in the chapel and walking into the church, Jesus appeared to her as a poor traveler of about thirty years of age. This almost naked man asked Catherine to have pity and provide him some clothes "in the name of God." She gave him her sleeveless woolen tunic, but the man did not seem content with it. He asked for a linen tunic with sleeves. She then took him to her home, where he continued to ask for more and more clothes, including some for a friend in the hospital. When she was down to her last item of clothing, the tunic she was wearing, she profusely apologized to the beggar, telling him that she had given all she could and was now poorer than he. The man then left.

The next night, Jesus again appeared to Catherine as this poor traveler, holding in his hands her sleeveless tunic. He told Catherine that because of her generosity, he was going to give her an invisible garment that would protect her until the day when she would be clothed "with glory and honor before the angels and saints."[11]

Visions such as this provided the spiritual strength and courage Catherine needed to serve Jesus wholeheartedly through service to others. Catherine's ongoing times of contemplation with Christ were such that "all that she touched or was touched by in her activity was present in her prayer."[12] The girl who never wanted to leave her room so she could be alone with Christ became the woman who wrote, "A soul rises up, restless with tremendous desire for God's honor and the salvation of souls. She has for some time exercised herself in virtue and has become accustomed to dwelling in the cell of self-knowledge in order to know better God's goodness toward her, since upon knowledge follows love. And loving, she seeks to pursue truth and clothe herself in it."[13]

In the pursuit of truth, Catherine fought to "reverse every falsification she saw," which to some of her contemporaries made her seem like a "naïve fool."[14] They saw her getting involved in things that they said were way beyond her ability to change or understand. They were stunned when she complained to those in authority and had interviews with officials in Rome—including the Pope—concerning abuses of power. They thought her proclamations, such as how the poor have as much right to justice as the rich, were way beyond what any woman should be involved in, especially since women of her time were often seen as weak and ignorant. Even though some saw her activism as "neurotic and pathetic," Catherine herself called it "the madness of love."[15] Catherine believed God had told her that she, an illiterate woman, was being used to baffle the educated and wise who in their pride had moved far from God's truth.

Although Catherine's story is an inspiration to many, most of us probably cannot relate to the kind of intense desire to be continually alone with Jesus that she had for twenty-three years; still, many of us probably do have spiritual highs that we wish were more the norm in our lives, just as Peter did as a result of his mountaintop experience with Jesus. But if our lives were full of spiritual consolations, it would be hard to know what we really loved.

The Seduction of Spiritual Highs

One of the main reasons it can be tempting to want to stay in the garden with Jesus is that we can confuse the love of the *feelings* from our experiences of God with the love of God. Just as when people confuse loving the feeling of being in love with actually loving the other person, we can be so taken by the feelings associated with spiritual highs that we erroneously fall in love with those feelings instead of with Jesus.

We may then be tempted to do whatever will produce those feelings, forgetting that they are not the point of our intimacy with Jesus. Ignatius warned that the devil can even come as an "angel of light" through what he called "spiritual consolations."

Catherine of Genoa was very aware of the dangers of spiritual consolations. She was often overcome with such joyous feelings in her alone times with God that she was afraid she might unconsciously end up loving these joyous times instead of loving God. She did not want the consolations of God to distract her from God's love and from serving God. As we have seen earlier in this book, Catherine translated her mystical intimacy with Jesus into bringing others to Jesus with her words and actions. But this might not have been the case had she not understood the temptations involved in her intense times of intimacy with Jesus. After one particularly intense time, Catherine exclaimed, "O Lord, I do not desire to follow Thee for these consolations, but only for pure love."[16] She said, "I dread far more an attachment to a spiritual than to a natural delight" because "natural gratifications" (such as a good meal) were not as easily disguised as spiritual ones.[17] Catherine believed that spiritual highs could cause us to feel too good about our own spiritual states, which would then take our focus off of Christ. She warned that such a person "believing that he is well, sees not that he is hindered from a perfect good, that is, God Himself, pure, simple, separated from all things human."[18]

I do not go as far as Catherine of Genoa and ask God to take spiritual highs away. In spite of the dangers of spiritual highs, I do believe they are God-ordained; but as with anything, they can be abused and misused. Their true purpose is to express our love toward God, to receive the assurance of God's love, and to draw us into more love and service toward others. For instance, there are many times in my life when I need, and am thankful for, the "blessed assurance" that comes from not only knowing, but *experiencing*, that love through a spiritual consolation. Years ago while driving alone down I-94 toward Grand Rapids, Michigan, I found myself intensely wrestling with questions about God's existence. I remember feeling very fearful and asking God if God was real (as strange as that might sound). Very unexpectedly, these words came in my mind: "Yes. I'm real. It's true." Immediately, incredible and unexplainable assurance, peace, and joy washed over me. I felt God's presence in an intensely real way.

But I am still thankful for those who warn us not to let spiritual highs be the only motivation for spending time with Jesus and serving others. A friend told me that she had become addicted to spiritual highs produced by her prayer times so much that she said, "I'm afraid to pray because I'm afraid I'll just get drugged up." For other people this addiction to spiritual highs might come from intense times of praise and worship. We can get worked up emotionally and love the feeling, forgetting that the focus is to be on worshiping God, which then includes commitment to doing God's work in the world. Father Richard Rohr, founder of the Center for Action and Contemplation, once told Tony, "It is easier to worship Jesus than to follow him." It seems that we are especially susceptible to this unbalanced form of loving Jesus if the music we sing as part of our worship is mostly about our love relationship to God and rarely about our sharing that relationship with others in need.

We need to be aware that our love for the feelings produced by spiritual experiences can replace our love for Christ. If that happens, we become narcissistic, without the commitment to radically love God and others no matter how we are feeling spiritually.

A Word About Spiritual Desolations

When discussing spiritual highs, it is important to note that in addition to spiritual consolations, there are what Ignatius called "spiritual desolations." Ignatius believed that God may allow times of feeling spiritually dry or discouraged or even separated from God. Such times, he taught, could actually increase our faith, hope, and love toward God— as long as we resolve to keep on loving and seeking God through our spiritual practices as well as through serving others. We can grow spiritually during desolation as we learn to trust God more, and our feelings less, as our litmus test for the state of our soul. These times could help us to see that the assurance of being loved by God does not come only from how we feel.

The nineteenth-century French saint Thérèse of Lisieux was an exceptional example of this kind of assurance. The last eighteen months of her twenty-four years on Earth, Thérèse suffered with tuberculosis. It was a time of deep spiritual desolation for her, since along with her physical suffering, she did not feel God's presence. Thérèse resolved to love God in spite of this, as well as to trust that God loved her. She even decided to use her spiritual desolation to pray for others who did not feel God's love and presence. Thérèse is a moving example of what Ignatius taught: that we are to love the God of consolations, not the consolations of God.

When I feel dry or discouraged or distant from God, it is reassuring to know that others have times of spiritual desolation too. The good news is that unless you know of things in your life that are keeping you from intimacy with Christ, you do not have to worry that a time of spiritual desolation means something is wrong. If you do wonder, you can talk about what might be going on with trusted friends or a spiritual mentor or director. Most important, don't forget that Jesus is still connected to you even when you do not feel that connection. Persevere in patience, *believing* that Jesus is near and that God's grace *is* sufficient. Remember Saint Paul's words to the church in Rome that *nothing can separate you from God's love,* so that you know there is nowhere that God is not— God is even present in your darkness. Father Bernie Owens, the main teacher in my spiritual direction program, once had each of us in class put one of our hands in front of our face, so close that we could not see it; he then said *that* is where Jesus is when we are in desolation—so close we cannot even see him.

Whether we are in times of spiritual consolation or desolation, we are to be reaching out beyond ourselves to others, since we gauge our love for Jesus by our fruits more than our feelings. That is why we must not only be in the garden, but go out of it too. But, if we stay out too long, we succumb to the next temptation.

The Second Garden Temptation: Spiritless Service

When I was in junior high school, I found out that a fast-food restaurant was going to be built very close to our school building. I was convinced, for a variety of reasons, including environmental and health concerns, that this was a really bad thing. I became angry and militant in my attitude, and one day while I was ranting about that restaurant my mom said to me, "It's a good thing you didn't grow up in Nazi Germany or you'd be marching with the Nazis."

Yikes! That statement went straight to my heart—well, not immediately. At first I was militantly angry. Then I slowly realized that she was right. My sense of what I thought was justice was intertwined with intense anger. There was no love there. Even though I considered myself a Christian and assumed that my legitimate concerns with the fast-food restaurant were a result of my relationship with Christ, I had become angry, self-righteous, and intolerant toward those I believed to be wrong.

With her words, my mom planted a seed of awareness that something was wrong with the way I was handling the issue, but at the time it wasn't enough to stop me from reacting that way again. I had yet to read and learn from others about the dangers of a loveless sense of justice. Walter Wink, author of a trilogy on power and justice, writes, "Unprotected by prayer, our social activism runs the danger of becoming self-justifying good works. As our inner resources atrophy, the wells of love run dry, and we are slowly changed into the likeness of the beast."[19]

That is what was happening to me. What I thought was a mature sense of justice was really self-righteousness. I was not allowing Jesus to transform my angry heart with more Christlike attitudes and actions. I could use the excuse that Jesus was angry with the moneychangers in the Temple, but I would be giving myself much undeserved credit. I would like to chalk it up to being a junior high student, but I have sensed those feelings in myself too many times since. I didn't know then what I know now—that I was getting a buzz off of my anger and letting it, instead of love, fuel my actions and reactions. That can happen to anyone who sees injustices in the world through their own eyes instead of through the eyes of Christ.

When you are committed to evangelism and justice, it will not be long before you see how much needs to be done, how urgent those needs are, and how few are really doing anything. We can then easily fall into the temptation of working to compensate for others' lack of loving action so much that we do not take the time to strengthen our own inner lives in Christ. Worse yet, we may not even recognize the need for inner spiritual renewal. But if we do not take the time to nourish our lives in intimacy with Christ, our capacity for effectiveness will decline and our ability to long endure in our efforts will fade. As Thomas Merton explained in his book *Contemplation in a World of Action*: "He who attempts to act and do things for others or for the world without deepening his own self-understanding, freedom, integrity and capacity to love, will not have anything to give others. He will communicate to them nothing but the contagion of his own obsessions, his aggressiveness, his ego-centered ambitions, his delusions about ends and means, his doctrinaire prejudices and ideas."[20]

My friend Paul, who is heavily involved in justice issues, puts it simply: "If you want to work for justice, first get on your knees." Walter Wink expands on that idea, as well as on the dangers Thomas Merton points out, by emphasizing the importance of "getting on our knees" for *any* kind of action for God's reign. In his book *The Powers That Be,* he contends that

> prayer is never a private inner act disconnected from day-to-day realities. It is, rather, the interior battlefield where the decisive victory is won before any engagement in the outer world is even possible. If we have not undergone that inner liberation in which the individual strands of the nets in which we are caught are severed, one by one, our activism may merely reflect one or another counter-ideology of some counter-Power. We may simply be caught up in a new collective passion, and fail to discover the possibilities God is pressing for here and now.[21]

Another friend of mine, Bobbie, found out what can happen when we are so busy with justice work that we do not take the time to get on our knees and allow our intimacy with Jesus to fuel us. Unlike those who are tempted to stay too long in the garden with Jesus, Bobbie is driven to get out in the world and make a difference. Her story helps us see how spiritless service can seem so right, yet can prevent us from living Jesus' holistic gospel.

Bobbie's Story

Much of Bobbie's life has been spent traveling from one location to another, fostering one idea after the next, always with the goal of creating opportunities to implement change and solve the problems and needs of those around her. Her job the past four years required her to travel across the country working with volunteers to repair homes in poverty-stricken communities. In order to help them, Bobbie was allowed to come into their homes, see the damage that needed repairing, and figure out how she could be of service to them. Without fail, these circumstances typically provided a time when residents began to share their stories with her. Sometimes the story began with the misfortune of losing their jobs due to cutbacks; other times it started with the discovery of a chronic illness, relapse into substance abuse, or just living in the path of a tornado. No matter how their story began it always ended with vulnerability and hurting hearts.

When Bobbie started her job, she loved it. She enjoyed meeting the residents and being able to assist those who were suffering. Solving problems strategically was her gift, and with this job she could combine both her love for people and her talent. Bobbie believed that every person she met reflected the God she loved and worshiped. More than anything, she loved using her talents to help remove the suffering of those she encountered. Although she became better every year at understanding and solving the construction-related problems, it became harder to listen to stories that were rooted in more than just a leaky roof. The more Bobbie tried to listen, the less she felt she could do for the residents.

As Bobbie sat in a conference in the mountains of Colorado preparing for her fourth year on the job, she realized how weak and empty she felt. The awareness hit hard that she was incapable of ever solving all of the problems she encountered in her job, much less the world. For the first time, Bobbie saw herself as completely inadequate for the task, and she was angry with herself and with God.

In her anger, Bobbie prayed and searched for answers. Because she saw herself as someone who had been loving people, sacrificing time, using her talents, and working for the glory of God's reign, Bobbie thought she should be filled with feelings of joy, not feelings of anger and contempt. She knelt down and asked God one honest question: "What happened?" Bobbie told me that she should have known better than to ask God an honest question.

While in solitude with God, the Holy Spirit revealed to Bobbie a disturbing pattern—that she was only good with people who had problems she could fix. People's stories were opportunities for her to become a rescuer. Although most residents shared their story with her as the foundation for a relationship, she realized that she had begun to use their stories as quantitative data that would lead her to a solution. "I had become a machine," Bobbie wrote to me, "a machine whose batteries became recharged every time I solved a problem."

She was overwhelmed with grief because she realized that she had exploited the vulnerability of others. For two days Bobbie remained in solitude, and she slowly succumbed to the truth that she was in need of God's grace and guidance. During this time she read through the New Testament, and came across Luke 17:21, where Jesus said, "The kingdom of God does not come with your careful observation, nor will people say, Here it is, or There it is, because the kingdom of God is within you." After dwelling on this verse for a long period of time, Bobbie decided to reflect on what the Kingdom of God would be like. She saw it as a place filled with the glory of God, a place where our relationship with God will finally be restored and renewed.

As she reflected, Bobbie discovered one word that for her captured the essence of this Kingdom: joy. She saw the Kingdom of God as a time when we will exist in a permanent state of joy—in Bobbie's words, "a place where our souls will have departed from the mind that confuses, the heart that wanders, the body that breaks down, and the devil that deceives." She realized that the joy she had invented, only attainable through her own doing, was not real joy. Real joy was a manifestation of the Kingdom of God within us *now*—a fruit of the Holy Spirit in us, and available to us, every moment of every day.

Bobbie now finds this joy through setting aside time to sit in silence, consciously inviting God to come and be with her. Spiritual practices such as the prayer of examen, various liturgies, and prayers from the Book of Common Prayer create space in her life for the Holy Spirit to speak to her. She says that the more she spends time in solitude, the more she discovers God's presence in her daily living. In her words:

> Stories of residents I work with are transformed into prayers as I listen to them with the ears of Christ. Psalm 16:11 describes it perfectly: "You show me the path of life. In your presence there is fullness of joy." Experiencing the spirit of joy does not remove the pain in this world. Suffering becomes bearable because with God's grace I see opportunities for healing. This healing does not come from my ability to solve problems, but from Jesus. He has taught me how to share in people's lives and become part of their stories as we suffer together, so that at some point I may share my story of a restless woman who one day asked her Father, "What happened?" In His reply she found her freedom: "You left. But welcome back, my daughter."

Bobbie told me her story more than a year ago. She continues to regularly engage in spiritual practices, and recently shared that what had started out as a 20-minute contemplative prayer exercise has now become a weekly half-day routine. Bobbie said that she needs hours to sit and be still, where she used to think she needed none. She knows "it is a positive change," one that is "always an invitation to breathe and approach the preciousness of life with sincerity and intentionality."

Bobbie's story gives us a present-day account of how service that has become spiritless can once again be full of God and God's joy. It shows us how our intimacy with Christ *and* our action inform and impact each other as we daily come into and go out of the garden.

Learning to Come and Go

As much as I believe that the kind of holistic gospel Tony and I have been describing in this book is how Jesus wants us to live, I also realize that living this way day in and day out is difficult. But it is necessary. We need to be in the garden to be renewed, and we need to go out and help to bring

God's reign through evangelizing and working for justice for the whole Earth. At times we will be energized through our intimacy and our work in the world. Other times the garden will be dry and the world will be messy, disillusioning, and discouraging. But we need them both—Jesus intended that they work together, informing and impacting each other. To better grasp this necessary interplay between the two, it is important to understand what is called "praxis," a concept Tony discusses in our final chapter.

CONNECTING
INTIMACY AND ACTION

A FEW YEARS AGO, Eric (not his real name), a young white middle-class college student, was working with a group of African American teenagers from a poor city neighborhood. Following a music program the group presented at a wealthy suburban church, Eric gained a new consciousness of what goes on in America as he watched how the police demonstrated racial oppression. It all started when the group of teenagers got back on the old church bus, and Gooter, a fourteen-year-old, shouted out, "We better get outta here quick! Who knows what they'll do with a bus full of niggas in this neighborhood." The bus, packed with teenagers, instantly erupted into a roar of laughter.

Little did Gooter realize that his joke would be prophetic. Already Eric had sensed the urgency to get the bus, filled with black city kids, out of the affluent white suburb. But before he knew what was happening, three police cars circled the bus. An officer approached the bus and yelled, "We've already had ten complaints from the neighborhood! You've got 15 minutes to get the bus and all these kids out of here; otherwise I'm taking the whole bunch down to the station." Eric realized that it was probably best not to cause trouble, so he decided to bite his tongue and comply. But the teens did not bite their tongues, and one angrily yelled from the back of the bus, "This wouldn't happen if we were white." That comment carried over all the yelling and discontent that was surfacing quickly and pierced Eric's heart; he knew that the young man was right.

Eric, like so many other youth workers in urban America, had to reevaluate what he thought about the American ruling establishment in the context of his interaction with the police that evening.

This kind of reflection and reevaluation in the context of action is what sociologists call "praxis." It means that what we think and what we do should not be separated. We learn best when we rethink our beliefs and convictions at the same time we are living them out.

Robert Merton, the onetime dean of American sociology, referred to praxis as the "serendipity method of investigation." Merton argued that we all start with certain presuppositions and then we act upon them. But as we try to live out what we believe will result from our actions, we are likely to find that things just do not work out as our presuppositions had led us to expect. So we reflect on our presuppositions and recast them into a new set of expectations that more closely match our new experiences. Then we experiment again, this time with new theories of what to expect from our actions. Again we are surprised by unanticipated results, and again are forced to recast our thinking. The process is ongoing, and we make a serious mistake if after several learning experiences we think we have arrived at a final and true understanding of reality.

I utilize praxis in ministry. Every year I recruit college students to come and work with programs for inner-city children and teenagers under the auspices of our missionary organization called the Evangelical Association for the Promotion of Education.[1] Almost every one of these volunteers comes with preconceptions of what they will encounter in the "at-risk" neighborhoods where they will work. Not surprisingly, in just about every case their preconceptions are shattered by their actual experiences, and they are forced to rethink and recast their beliefs. In addition, each new framework for ministry that they thoughtfully create in reaction to their encounter in the real world is eventually challenged. Life experiences continually require reflection and recasting. And so the process continues. Learning about urban environments in the context of action is far different from learning in a classroom, detached from what is happening out there on the streets of the city.

The same thing is true when it comes to becoming spiritual. There are many who believe that we should first become spiritual before we go out into the world and only then try to convert people to Christ or work for justice for all of creation. However, we believe that our intimacy with Christ is best developed *in the context* of carrying out our responsibilities, as Christians, together in community. By working together, we find ourselves bound together in a common cause. The unity that comes out of such a bond is not only human, but also spiritual. In this unity or "oneness" with one another, we feel the presence of Christ. Once again we are reminded that Jesus told us that when people gather together in Jesus' name, to do Jesus' will, God is in the midst of them.

Three years ago I was a guest speaker at the University of Manchester in England, describing to students of a sociology class the work that our mission organization, Urban Promise, is carrying out in several cities of America. Afterward, two young men lingered. They asked me if they could come and work as missionaries in our inner-city ministries. They wanted to take a year off and serve in an American city to get a feel for the social problems that exist in our urban communities. I was thrilled with their offer until they said, "We want to be missionaries to the inner city, but we have to tell you that neither of us believes in God. Can we come and serve with you anyway?"

It took me just a moment to reflect upon their offer, and then I answered, "Of course you can, but there are certain rules you have to follow. The whole time you are with us, you have to *pretend* that you are Christian. You are not to let on to anybody that you have no religious faith. You will attend the Bible studies when they are held. You will teach the boys and girls about Jesus and you must be ready to tell them Bible stories each and every day. When the staff meets for prayer meetings you must attend. If you are willing to do such things, you are welcome to be among us."

> *Our intimacy with Christ is best developed in the context of carrying out our responsibilities . . . together in community.*

By the end of that summer, both of them had become Christians. Today, both are Anglican priests in the United Kingdom. What they *did* influenced their beliefs.

This approach follows the methodology for training disciples that Jesus himself employed. Consider the fact that in scripture Jesus did not spend three years training his disciples before sending them out to preach, to teach, and to heal. Quite the contrary. Not long after recruiting his disciples, Jesus sent them out two by two, instructing them to "go nowhere among the Gentiles, and enter no town of the Samaritans, but go rather to the lost sheep of the house of Israel. As you go, proclaim the good news, 'The kingdom of heaven has come near.' Cure the sick, raise the dead, cleanse the lepers, cast out demons. You received without payment; give without payment" (Matthew 10:5–8).

The disciples were intimidated by the charge they received from Jesus. Even though they had spent some time with him, still they did not believe they were prepared for the tasks that they had been given. But Jesus said, "And you will be dragged before governors and kings because of me, as a testimony to them and the Gentiles. When they hand you over, do not worry about how you are to speak or what you are to say; for what you are to say will be given to you at that time; for it is not you who speak, but the Spirit of your Father speaking through you" (Matthew 10:18–20).

The disciples were soon to discover that spiritual empowerment would come to them not only from spending time with Jesus, but also in the context of ministry. When they returned they told Jesus "all that they had done and taught" (Mark 6:30). Then, because there were so many people "coming and going" around them, Jesus told his disciples to "come away to a deserted place by yourselves and rest a while" (Mark 6:31).

In accord with what we find in the lives of those early disciples, we believe that spirituality mystically expands within us as we carry out the works of evangelism and justice. And we must never forget that praxis includes taking time to reflect on our experiences with Jesus and to rest. Thus, praxis is not only a way of learning, but also a way of growing spiritually.

We have already discussed how mystical Christianity can create within us a passionate concern for those who are alienated from God, and for whoever or whatever suffers from oppression. But what we have not, up until this point, much explored is how spirituality can intensify in the context of evangelistic work, and how our engagement in meeting the needs of the world can nourish our own souls. The dynamic interplay of our spirituality and of our evangelistic and justice work is how we believe God will make us into the actualized human beings that we were predestined to be when we became Christians (Romans 8:29–30). If we have regular alone times with Christ *while* we are engaged in doing evangelism, and if we can pray and meditate on scripture even *while* we are struggling to change the world, we may find that the closeness to God sought by Christians down through the ages can be realized in our own lives. If we live out Christ's calling to share the gospel with others, to work for justice in society, and to preserve and protect God's creation, there is a good likelihood that Christ will become increasingly real to us and an assurance of salvation will intensify in our hearts and minds. The Holy Spirit's presence becomes dramatically real to us as we do what we are commanded to do in ministering to the needs of others. In the context of our labors and struggles, we come to see something of the reign of God realized in us and through us as we progress toward spiritual maturity. This is Christian praxis, and it is to be carried out in the context of Christian communities, since being lone rangers for Christ is a surefire recipe for burnout and disillusionment.

The Spirituality of Martin Luther King Jr.

Few people in modern history have understood praxis better than Martin Luther King Jr. He, more than most others, saw the interactive relationship between spirituality and working for social justice. Any who wanted to join him in his marches for freedom and justice were required to go through a process of spiritual preparation, just like the disciples did when they spent time with Jesus. But again, like the disciples, they were not to stay indefinitely in preparation, even if they did not feel totally equipped. When they moved into action, King recognized that overcoming the demonic spirits inherent in racism and poverty would require a more powerful countervailing spirit, which he called "soul force." Before each and every civil rights march or demonstration, the participants were asked to spend time in silence, calling upon God to empty them of hostility toward their oppressors and to give them the courage to face the ordeals that lay ahead. King saw the need for a transcendent power to flow into his followers if they were to be able to love their enemies and return good for the evil they would confront as they marched for freedom. There was the realization in the heart and mind of King that without God those who would be persecuted for righteousness' sake would turn bitter and, in their hatred, would lose their souls regardless of what political battles might be won.

Many of those who participated with Martin Luther King and went through those hours of spiritual preparation will testify to the awareness of the presence of God's Spirit. But as noticeable as that holy presence might have been, there are those who report that it was not to be compared to the awesome experience of the Holy Spirit that was felt *during* the civil rights demonstrations. As they sang and marched arm in arm, something supernatural happened. Over and over again, I have heard testimonies by those who experienced a special sense of the Holy Spirit as they joined with others and marched against racism and sang the songs of freedom. Together they sensed a spiritual oneness. When they were taunted, and sometimes physically abused, by those who came against them, they sensed a special empowerment from God and an unusual assurance that they were doing God's will. Without a doubt, something mystical happened that gave them incredible joy. Undoubtedly, they were experiencing what Jesus had promised his followers when he said,

"Blessed are you when people revile you and persecute you and utter all kinds of evil against you falsely on my account. Rejoice and be glad, for your reward is great in heaven, for in the same way they persecuted the prophets who were before you" (Matthew 5:11–12).

Praxis in Preaching

In evangelistic work there is further evidence of spirituality in praxis. During my own preaching there are times when I feel that I am experiencing a special anointing by the Holy Spirit. In the action and context of interacting with a group of people through preaching, truths come to me of which I was unaware during my times of preparation. I wish I could say this happens to me every time I preach, but on those occasions when it does, I am mystically seized with a sense of expectation for life-transforming responses from my listeners. I cannot make these times happen, and I do not know when they are going to happen, since they occur *while* I am preaching. During these times when the Spirit is upon me, I sense that what I am saying has a special relevance to the congregation that does not emerge from my study and preparation. When I finish such "anointed" messages and call upon people to make decisions to commit their lives to Christ, I know what many of them will do. That is because in the midst of my preaching I am conscious that God is at work, not only in me, but in those who are listening.

Because of what I have realized about praxis in preaching, now while I am preaching I am simultaneously praying. Call it a form of multitasking if you want, but over the years my experiences during preaching have taught me to plead with God during my messages to help me to say what those in the congregation most need to hear. There are even times when I can pick out a particular person in the audience, and I ask the Holy Spirit to flow through me toward them. While still preaching, I gain an awareness that I am speaking directly to that individual's need.

It is in praxis that we find our final argument for why mystical spirituality should never be separated from evangelism and the struggle for justice. What we do and how we pray so interact and feed each other that there is no way to adequately maintain either without the other. That is why we read in scripture that faith without works is dead (James 2:17). But the Bible also says that good works alone are inadequate. The Holy Spirit, an undeserved gift that we receive from God, must empower what we do. Without that spiritual dynamic we can do nothing that will have any lasting significance for the Kingdom of God. Thus scripture says, "For by grace you have been saved through faith, and this is not your own doing; it is the gift of God—not the result of works, so that no one may boast" (Ephesians 2:8–9).

Grace and works do not contradict each other. They complement and support each other. In the midst of all the Kingdom work that we do, we should be sensitive to the Spirit's empowering presence. If we do that, we will sense ourselves growing closer to Christ and in the certainty that Christ is with us.

The Spirituality of Iona

The Iona colony in Scotland is a place to visit if you want to witness praxis in action. The people who make up this colony are living examples of how the Holy Spirit can provide the impetus and the energy for progressive world reform. This religious community, started by Saint Columba in the sixth century, has been revitalized over the past few decades to become a spiritual retreat for peace activists. But that is not the whole story.

To visit the Iona colony, located on a small island just a few hundred yards off the western coast of Scotland, is to step onto holy ground. From the moment I set foot on the island, I was aware that there was something mysteriously wonderful about the place. People around me seemed to speak in hushed voices as though by instinct. To step into the ancient stone chapel that is the worship center of Iona was to step back in time, and I had the sensation that I was hearing the chanting of medieval monks echoing within its walls.

But Iona is not a place of escape from the world. Quite the contrary, it is a place to go to get spiritually equipped to change the world. This community of believers is committed to what they call a "spirituality of connectedness" that is "rooted in an engagement and encounter with God in the midst of the world."[2] This spirituality of connectedness includes a deep relatedness to nature. The island of Iona is often called a "thin place" with transparent windows between the material world and the spiritual world. The *Iona Community Worship Book* documents the community's affirmation that "God's glory [permeates] all of creation."[3] One well-loved prayer that the Iona community has shared with many others across the globe expresses this intimacy with nature:

Deep peace of the Running Wave to you.
Deep peace of the Flowing Air to you.

Deep peace of the Quiet Earth to you.
Deep peace of the Shining Stars to you.
Deep peace of the Son of Peace to you.[4]

According to Norman Shanks, author of *Iona: God's Energy*, "Nothing is to be excluded from the workings of the Spirit: not only prayer, but also politics, social justice, personal relationships."[5] One of the members of the community said to me, "People come here for peace *of* mind, but they go from here with peace *on* their minds."

A survey of what goes on at Iona will provide ample evidence of what this person was talking about. Along with a commitment to daily personal devotional practices, there are seminars for members of the colony, as well as for visitors, that cover a variety of justice issues. During times of worship, commitments are made to work for peace in troubled places such as Northern Ireland and the Middle East. The activists who are nurtured through the ministries of Iona are continually forming task units and committees to develop and carry out peace actions, which include public demonstrations, lobbying governments, and speaking out on behalf of ecological and other justice issues at the stockholders' meetings of multinational corporations.

This community is governed by "The Rule":

1. Engage in daily devotional disciplines.
2. Share and be accountable in the use of money.
3. Use time for work, family, leisure, worship, rest, volunteering, and developing skills.
4. Work for justice and peace in society.
5. Meet with each other for support and accountability (which includes committee work).[6]

Responding to Jesus' mandate for evangelism, this community stated that "the call to witness in context challenges the witnessing church to create an inclusive community, critically engaged in action, questioning the inequality of access to resources, and recognizing the positive nature of diversity in a community which is united but not uniform, and in which individuals receive from one another as well as give."[7]

It is important to know that most of the members of the Iona community do not live on the island. Instead, after being inspired and challenged there, they are scattered across the British Isles, and even around the world. The members, however, sign a covenant to return to the island at stated times for spiritual renewal and for rituals of recommitment. They maintain regular contact with the network of other covenanters so that efforts for a rediscovery of spirituality and for creating peace and justice can be coordinated around the world. Taking their places in schools, churches, offices, markets, and workplaces, these dispersed members permeate all spheres of society with their spiritual commitments for a transformed world.

Wherever there are gatherings of people taking stands for the poor and exploited, it is likely that members of the Iona community are there. Whenever there is a need for voices to speak for those who have no voice, you just might hear words spoken by those who have been spiritually inspired on that small Scottish island. And whatever needs to be done to break down the walls that imprison people because of race, religion, or sexual identity will be attempted by those who have prayed and sung together at Iona. This little community has had far-reaching effects in its efforts for unity, peace, justice, and the integrity of creation. It stands today as a living testimony of how spirituality and action are linked in such a way as to nurture each other.

Hopeful Signs in the Emergent Church

Over the past couple of decades, hundreds of churches have grown up that defy easy categorization. They are composed of Christians who have tired of the superficial forms of worship that often characterize both mainline and evangelical churches. These Christians find many of the concerns that preoccupy church councils and denominational gatherings to be meaningless, and they view many issues that are so divisive throughout Christendom these days as irrelevant. The Christians who identify with this movement are often called "the emergent church." There are hundreds of their congregations across the country and, while they form a loose confederation, they steer clear of any talk of becoming a denomination.

These emergent churches generally hold an evangelical stance, in that they take the Bible seriously and are committed to leading people into personal and transforming relationships with a resurrected and living Christ. On the other hand, they shy away from those issues, such as homosexual marriage, that have been used of late to define evangelicalism. Accentuating individual choice, those who are part of the emergent church movement, for the most part, consider it tyranny for an ecclesiastical body to impose its views on anyone.

In many cases, the members of this movement grew up in evangelical churches, but have become skeptical, and sometimes even cynical, about their past religious experiences. They look back with some degree of anger on what they consider the manipulations by evangelists who play psychological tricks on congregants—especially on vulnerable young people—to get them to come down church aisles at the end of sermons to the singing of a sentimental salvation song. Regularly you can hear them tell how earnest they were when they said yes to such invitations "to get to know Jesus personally and intimately," only to discover that nothing spiritual happened to them as they knelt in prayer at the altar. Many of them, disillusioned by such all-too-typical evangelistic techniques, have come close to despairing of ever having a mystical encounter with the living Christ.

We mention these people here to highlight the ways that they seek spiritual experiences, and how these experiences relate to evangelism and justice work. In these respects we find that the emergent churches certainly break the molds of what we usually expect from traditional evangelicalism.

A friend of mine, who pastors an emergent church, gave me a taste of their worship when he invited me to preach for his congregation. When I arrived for the service, which was held in a converted barn, I was in for several surprises.

I expected to hear a hubbub of voices as I entered. Since there were several hundred cars in the parking lot, I assumed that there would be hundreds of young adults chattering away. Instead, and to my surprise, what awaited me was a room that stunned me with its silence. Around the sides of the auditorium there were small clusters of worshipers in deep, prayerful meditation. Upon further investigation, I found that they were meditating in front of pictures depicting the Stations of the Cross. For me, praying at the Stations of the Cross had always been a Roman Catholic thing to do. Prayerfully endeavoring to enter through sanctified imagining into the sufferings of Jesus at each of the places where he stopped while stumbling toward his death on Mount Calvary has long been a hallmark of Catholic worship, but to see non-Catholics doing so was unexpected, to say the least. Equally surprising was the realization that the rest of those who had come to worship were silently praying—some of them on their knees.

The room was darkened and in front was an altar with lit candles on each side of a crucifix. The crucifix, which I also associated with Catholicism, also surprised me.

I was hearing music, but the kind of music I heard was unexpected. Instead of an organ prelude, a CD of Gregorian chants was being played. The setting was definitely solemn.

When the worship service got under way, there were more surprises waiting for me. The congregation sang some old hymns—but to the accompaniment of a band made up of a drummer, a keyboard player, and a couple of guitarists.

Later, during the prayer time, these young adults were invited into the kind of centering and contemplative praying that was prescribed in ancient church tradition.

The mood created by all I saw and heard conditioned the manner in which I preached. Instead of my usual bombastic style, I instinctively resorted to a quiet, almost meditative, style.

After the service, I asked the pastor a lot of "whys." I wanted to know why the service was constructed as it was; why the Stations of the Cross; why the centering and contemplative praying; why the Gregorian chant music; and most important—why did this kind of church service appeal so much to such a sizable congregation of young people?

"These are mostly young adults who are tired of the kinds of concerns that seem to preoccupy most evangelical Christians," he said. He went on to explain that he, along with most of these young people, found it absurd that some Christians were disturbed over such things as the president of the United States putting "Happy Holidays" instead of "Merry Christmas" on greeting cards. He thought that instead, Christians ought to be irate over the president's announcement during Advent that there would be federal budget cuts in after-school programs for poor children and in Medicaid.

"People come here," he said, "because they want to be with other people who are committed to doing more for the twenty-five thousand women who become pregnant each year because of rape than just yelling, 'No abortions!' These are people who believe that our national character is more evident in the fact that less than two-tenths of 1 percent of our national budget is designated for the poor of Third World countries than it is in our worrying over whether or not intelligent design is taught in our classrooms."

I was very sympathetic to the issues that he and his church members were raising, and I understood why they wanted to be part of a congregation that shifted the discussion to ethical issues that so many of us in the evangelical community ignore. But their social concerns did not explain the Catholic character of their worship service nor the emphasis that was placed on prayer forms that had more in common with mystical Christianity than on the kind of "praise worship" that increasingly typifies the contemporary worship services in many growing evangelical churches.

"So many of us just got tired of the stuff that goes on in contemporary worship," he said. "A lot of it is bad music, and the singing, while focused on God, does little in the way of deepening our spirituality or making us conscious of the needs of others."

As I listened to this pastor, I realized that these emergent church members had found that when it came to deepening them spiritually, most of what was offered in evangelical churches had left them wanting something more. Some of them had come from those mega-churches that are now so common across America. They spoke with great gratitude about the blessings that they had received in those user-friendly churches. They readily admitted that such churches were the primary reason that after years of indifference they were giving Christianity another chance. Over and over again I heard testimonies of how they had been "saved" in evangelical churches. But then they complained that after being "saved" they pretty much heard the same salvation story over and over again.

When it came to critiquing mainline churches, these emergent Christians were even more disparaging. They simply said that they found them to be boring, frozen in worship forms that seemed tired and based on routine. They explained that going to traditional denominational churches was an emotionally deadening experience.

Where the Spirit is, there is also a passion for living out love and justice in the world.

I should not have been surprised by what I learned that Sunday. I should have expected that time-tested prayer methods of centuries-past saints and mystics were providing avenues to deeper spiritual experiences. After all, it was not as though such mystical spirituality was beyond my own experiences. I had already discovered it myself, after so much of praying in my own Protestant tradition had proved to be little more than a listing of requests *to* God, providing little in the way of real communion *with* God.

Given my own experiences, I should not have been surprised that so many younger people in these emergent churches had gone the same route. They too were finding a wealth of blessings in the mystical spirituality of Catholic saints. Once I began to realize what these emergent Christians found so attractive in their newfound spirituality, everything else fell into place: lit candles, a crucifix, the Stations of the Cross, the Gregorian chanting, and the silent meditation. While I could not explain or legitimate all of it in rational theological terms, nevertheless it made sense to me. Furthermore, the social concerns of that church did not surprise me. That was because I had already come to see that where the Spirit is, there is also a passion for living out love and justice in the world.

Some Help from Richard Foster and Renovaré

Someone who would smile benevolently on what I have been discovering about mystical spirituality is Mary's and my friend, Richard Foster. For several years, this Christian leader, coming out of the Evangelical Friends International (EFI) tradition of the Quakers (officially, the Society of Friends), has been encouraging church people like me to give serious attention to intentional spiritual formation resulting in love and service for God and others. His seminars and small groups on spirituality, called Renovaré, offered around the world, have attracted thousands of spiritually thirsty Christians who are seeking ways to deepen their relationships with God. Those who participate in these gatherings often are Christians from mainline churches who have had a profound awareness that unless something more meaningful broke loose in their lives, their souls were apt to shrivel up and die.

Many clergy of mainline denominations show up for Foster's seminars hoping to learn things that will help them to bring spiritual renewal to their dying churches. They are aware of spiritual cravings among their congregants, and they know that these congregants are turned off what they see propagated by some charismatic preachers and healers on television. They come hoping to see if there are ways to connect with the charisma of God without such sensationalist tactics.

It is not surprising that Richard Foster is a Quaker, because spirituality was, from the beginnings of Quakerism, an essential part of the movement. George Fox, the founder of the Society of Friends, taught, in accord with what is written in John 1:9, that the Spirit of God is a sacred presence in every person who is born into the world. It was Fox's belief that if we would sit in stillness and "wait patiently for the Lord," eventually God's Spirit within us would stir and we would feel the Spirit quaking within us. A Sunday gathering of Quakers at one of their meetinghouses provides ample evidence that this tradition of settling and waiting for the Holy Spirit to move in people, as taught by Fox, is still alive and well in today's world.

Foster, continuing Fox's emphasis of "yielding to the Spirit within," has also gleaned from this movement a deep concern for justice. Recognizing that Christ is a living presence in every man and woman encountered, it is easy to understand why Quakers will in no way support such social evils as capital punishment and war. If we accept literally Jesus' words, "Just as you did it to one of the least of these who are members of my family, you did it to me" (Matthew 25:40), then to do harm to another human being is to do harm to Jesus himself.

How can any Christian pull the switch on someone strapped to an electric chair if, in looking into that person's eyes, there is a conviction that Jesus is staring back through that criminal's eyes? And how is it possible to kill on the battlefield if, instead of seeing an enemy, the Christian recognizes that Christ is sacramentally present in the person caught in the crosshairs of his or her rifle? The kind of Christianity espoused by Quakers embraces a spirituality that leads to a commitment to end any and all kinds of oppression and injustice wherever they may be found. Their Quaker spirituality makes them aware of the holiness of others, whether they are Christians or not.

Given such beliefs, it is not surprising that Quakers can be found at the forefront of many justice movements, including the struggles to end slavery, to fight against poverty, to reform prisons, to champion environmental responsibility, and to promote peace—for which they are most famous. Nor is it surprising that Richard Foster, following in the Quaker tradition, should embrace these same causes.

If you should attend one of the Renovaré seminars, you will be introduced to forms of the spiritual practices that Mary has discussed, as well as to other "holy habits." Foster has put together books that are compilations of the writings of Catholic and Protestant saints and mystics, making them readily available to those of us who might not have easy access to them. During his seminars, he explains how these saints developed their spiritual disciplines, and how he himself has employed these disciplines in his own spiritual journey. But you should be careful about attending one of these seminars if you are not ready to become an activist for justice and an evangelical witness to those who are spiritually lost. The spirituality that emerges from the disciplines and exercises that are taught in these seminars generates a powerful and compelling compassion for those who are oppressed, whether that oppression is spiritual or social.

Over the years I have recruited several thousand young people from colleges and universities across the country to join in ministries for needy children, both in Third World countries and in urban America. On two different occasions, groups of our young workers have attended Renovaré seminars, and on both occasions they were powerfully impacted.

One of the directives for their daily devotions that they picked up from Foster's teachings was practiced by Benedictine monks, namely praying through the Psalms. It had never occurred to our young evangelical mission workers to use the Psalms as a prayer book, but they decided to give it a try.

It was not as though the Psalms provide a systematic theology. But they did give expression to the unspoken emotions these young Christians were feeling toward the injustices they were encountering. As they prayed through the Psalms, they found their own questioning, frustration, and anger articulated as the Psalmists complained about injustices perpetuated by the political-economic systems. These Psalms, however, also gave expression to hopes and assurances that justice would prevail on the day that God triumphed in history. As they prayed through the Psalms, these young committed Christians gained inspiration and conviction that the seeming present prevalence of evil was not the final page of history and that God's will would be done in the end. The Psalms, used as a prayer book, did not provide answers to the troubling situations that plagued the oppressive world in which they daily tried to minister. They did, however, generate confidence and hope, as well as energy and motivation for these young people to stand against oppressors, giving voice to those who have no voice.

Our young workers soon realized that Christian charity is good but not enough, and that justice is required. Coming from privileged backgrounds, they knew that they should be contributing to the health and well-being of others. The Psalms had made them aware that to whom much is given, from them will much be expected. However, something quite mystical happened to them as they prayed through the Psalms, and that was the realization that charity was only the beginning of the responsibilities. They were learning that there are evil forces at work in political and economic institutions of society that must be confronted and overcome.

It is one thing to directly help victims of socioeconomic oppression, but something more is needed. The structural evils built into the socioeconomic system must be challenged and changed. That awareness which calls for justice was generated in praying the Psalms. As surprising as this might seem to some, the Psalmists' emotions created a revolutionary disposition in our young missionaries. George Fox would have applauded what was happening to them under the influence of the teaching of Richard Foster, one of his twenty-first-century disciples. They learned that the kind of spirituality taught in Quakerism does not create passive monks. Instead it produces committed social activists.

The Spirituality of Underground Movements

What I have been describing as the dynamic relationship between spirituality and ministry is presently being vividly demonstrated by two specific groups of young people with whom I have had some association over the years. One is in England and calls itself SPEAK. The other is based in the Kensington section of Philadelphia and calls itself "the Simple Way."

SPEAK

SPEAK is a network of groups of young people, mostly university students in England, who have organized themselves in order to change government policies that they believe are creating and sustaining poverty in Third World countries. Specifically, they concentrate on canceling the debts of poor countries and bringing an end to trade policies that they believe are impoverishing farmers in the Third World. SPEAK has worked hard to influence the British Parliament and the prime minister. Its members have held prayer vigils at Westminster and forums at venues throughout their country to discuss their concerns; they have mobilized churches to lobby for debt cancellation; and they have organized student chapters of their organization in many British universities.

When I visited with the leaders of SPEAK in the basement of an Anglican church in London, I asked them what they were reading to keep them informed and inspired. I was surprised when they told me that they were into the writings of Thomas Merton. I was well aware that this Trappist monk had made some strong and serious remarks on social issues ranging from poverty to war, but as I pointed out to them, he was primarily a modern Catholic mystic and his writings were, for the most part, aimed at helping people find their way to God. They readily agreed with my assessment of Merton, but then went on to point out that the mystical spirituality that he advocated is such that it drives people into intense commitment to witnessing for Christ by working for justice. They referred me to a specific passage in Merton's book *Contemplative Prayer* as evidence of this point. It read, "The most important need in the Christian world today is this inner truth nourished by this Spirit of contemplation: the praise and love of God, the longing for the coming of Christ, the thirst for the manifestation of God's glory, his truth, his justice, his kingdom in the world."[8]

SPEAK members spend significant time each day in the kinds of meditation that Merton prescribed as a way of entering into communion with God. They find these times of spiritual meditation a major source of inspiration and guidance for their justice activities. With great conviction they remark, "We don't know what keeps those agnostic social activists going. Without God we'd burn out in a very short time."

It must also be noted that not only do meditations guided by the likes of Merton, Foster, and Dallas Willard inform and inspire their social action, but the reverse is also true. Members of SPEAK report that as they confront the principalities and powers in unjust social institutions, they sense the Holy Spirit empowering them. The members of SPEAK say that in their struggles for justice they are up against more than just humanly created structural evil in economically motivated institutions. They also recognize that they are engaged in spiritual warfare. They believe that there are demonic spirits standing behind that structural evil. Belief in satanic forces is part of their worldview, and they often remind those they talk to of what Paul wrote in Ephesians 6:12: "For our struggle is not against enemies of blood and flesh, but against the rulers, against the authorities, against the cosmic powers of this present darkness, against the spiritual forces of evil in the heavenly places."

Given their theology of spiritual warfare, it is easy to understand why they are convinced that the power of the Holy Spirit is so important. In confronting such principalities and powers, they believe that Christians need more than human resources. They say that if they are to stand and win victories for the coming Kingdom of God, they must be spiritually equipped to do battle. Again, they point to Paul's writings:

> Therefore take up the whole armor of God, so that you may be able to withstand on that evil day, and having done everything, to stand firm. Stand therefore, and fasten the belt of truth around your waist, and put on the breastplate of righteousness. As shoes for your feet put on whatever will make you ready to proclaim the gospel of peace. With all of these, take the shield of faith, with which you will be able to quench all the flaming arrows of the evil one. Take the helmet of salvation, and the sword of the Spirit, which is the word of God. Pray in the Spirit at all times in every prayer and supplication. To that end keep alert and always persevere in supplication for all the saints. (Ephesians 6:13–18)

In the context of struggles for social justice, SPEAK members seek an infilling of the Holy Spirit, and in these struggles they testify as to how the Holy Spirit's presence and work become an empowering reality. Furthermore, they say that experiencing the Holy Spirit while engaged in working for social justice nurtures their souls and gives them a deeper relationship with God. Again and again, SPEAK members tell how they come to an increasing intimacy with Jesus and assurance of salvation in the midst of action.

This interplay between spiritual meditation and social action is exactly the kind of relationship this book has promoted. Our intimacy with Christ should drive us out into the world to tell the salvation story and to work for a more just society; and such work in the world should drive us to our knees in prayer and help us into closer friendship with Jesus as each informs and impacts the other.

The Simple Way's Way

Still another example of the praxis of spirituality on the one hand and evangelism and justice on the other is found in a small group of young people who call themselves the Simple Way. This movement got started in response to a confrontation between some homeless people and the civil authorities of the city of Philadelphia.

A few years ago a group of homeless people decided to escape the winter cold by breaking into a deserted and boarded-up Catholic church in the Kensington section of the city. They attracted the attention of the media when the Catholic diocese decided to take steps to have the police evict these destitute people from the church. A group of students at Eastern University, in a Philadelphia suburb, watched this confrontation and decided to do something to express their solidarity with the homeless people. Taking some bedding, the students spent their nights sleeping with the homeless in the church and then commuted back and forth to the university each day to attend classes.

The students did what they did in the hope of showing their desire to obey the teachings of Jesus by being at one with the poor, the outcast, and the oppressed. What took them by surprise was the spiritual impact that these homeless people would have on them. In the face of conflict with the police, the students joined together with the poor in prayer. The images of church leaders who claimed to be followers of Jesus tossing these desperate people out of the place where they had found shelter from winter storms would not make for good public relations.

Joining these troublesome squatters at the church was a young countercultural Catholic priest who dared to conduct worship services with them, and even offered them the Eucharist. Between the leadership of that priest and the prayer fellowship created by the evangelical students from Eastern University, the whole setting took on deep spiritual meaning and significance. There were long conversations about what the Bible had to say about the poor and about the social justice required by God. There were times of prayer in which these evangelical students learned some of the ancient prayer styles that Mary discussed in Part Two of this book.

The spiritual consciousness of the students was raised in dramatic and unexpected ways, most notably about what it means to be a Christian. These students became aware that the middle-class Christianity of their home congregations was a watered-down version of what Jesus required of his disciples. As they read scripture and entered into ancient prayer practices—all in the context of struggling for justice on behalf of the homeless—they were led to adopt the lifestyle of radical Christians, and especially the lifestyle of Francis of Assisi. These brothers and sisters in Christ purchased an inexpensive row house in the Kensington section of the city and decided to live together in a shared spiritual community called the Simple Way.

Kensington, one of the most rundown sections of the city, became for them a place to do ministry. They set up a food pantry and tutored neighborhood children. They connected with an activist nun and worked along with her to find some alternatives for housing the homeless. While all of that was happening, they were also able to get some tradesmen to install showers, cooking facilities, and a safe heating system in the old abandoned church so that it could temporarily serve the housing needs until other arrangements could be made.

All of these young people who came to live in community in Kensington went through life-changing transitions. The stories of a few of them might provide some idea of how radical these life changes proved to be.

Shane Claiborne, the informal leader and spokesperson for the group, has become a nationally known speaker, addressing young people at conferences, colleges, and universities. He calls them to live out the radical and simple lifestyles spelled out by Jesus in the Gospels and lived out centuries later by Saint Francis. The money he earns in honoraria is given away to the poor. Like Francis, he lives a life of poverty in obedience to what he believes are Christ's teachings. And just as with saints before him, Shane's simple lifestyle greatly reduces his use of the Earth's limited resources. Everywhere he goes he is inspiring other young people to imitate what he is doing. Consequently, communities like the Simple Way are cropping up all across the country. You can read about such "local revolutions and ordinary radicals" in Shane's book *The Irresistible Revolution.*[9]

A friend of mine, Josh (not his real name), was profoundly changed by the Simple Way community and lifestyle. One day a family member confronted Josh: "You are wasting your life. Don't get me wrong. I believe in being Christian up to a point . . ." He then stopped in the middle of his sentence, realizing the implications of what he had just said; before he could continue, Josh asked, "Could that point be the cross?"

In case you are wondering how much Shane and some of his friends, like Josh, imitate Saint Francis, consider what they did on the eve of the

Second Gulf War. Just before the bombing of Baghdad began, Shane, along with a handful of like-minded young people, flew to Jordan, hired a couple of vans, and drove across the desert into Iraq. They wanted to be with the people of Iraq when the invasion by the American-led army began. The adventures they had as they made themselves one with the Iraqi people is a story worth reading. One member of this group, Jonathan Wilson-Hartgrove, has written up this story, published under the title *To Baghdad and Beyond.*[10]

Going into the camp of your nation's enemy is what Francis did hundreds of years ago in Egypt. The reports from Shane and his friends provide ample evidence that in living out the demands of the gospel there can be what they call "a second conversion." Those who prayerfully and literally live out the commands of Christ are likely to find that, like these special young people, they are transformed from believers in Christ into radically committed disciples. To know them is to be aware that the Spirit of the Lord truly is upon them.

One other story about a member of the Simple Way concerns a young woman who was referred to me by the Dean of Students at Eastern University for some counseling. This student had become extremely depressed and was seriously considering leaving school. The Dean thought that I might be able to help her.

During the weeks in which I was counseling her, she somehow became significantly involved in the efforts that the Simple Way members were making on behalf of the homeless people in the Catholic church in Kensington. It was not long before I was able to discern a noticeable change in her demeanor and attitudes. She was no longer depressed and making plans to drop out of school. It was obvious that her life had taken a dramatic turn. When I asked her what had changed, she told me that for the first time Christ had become real to her. In glowing terms she described feeling Christ's presence and being aware of being loved by him. She went on to say that her spiritual transformation began during one of the Masses conducted by the priest who had joined up with the group in the closed-up church. "It was as though the radiance of Christ's presence was everywhere in the place that morning," she said.

Although this young woman is no longer living with the other Simple Way members, she is still in the same neighborhood and stays very connected with them. Living in a nearby house, she takes care of some needy children who require a great deal of special loving attention. Her spiritual life continues to deepen as she spends time alone with Christ, but she also testifies to the powerful influences of the Holy Spirit that come while loving and ministering to the needy children in her care.

What all of these stories are meant to demonstrate is how mystical spirituality at its best is interwoven with evangelism and commitments to justice. Without ministry to others, we believe, spirituality is so heavenly founded that it does little earthly good.

What we have said should not be seen in any way as disparaging of those nuns who are cloistered or those monks who go into monasteries. But we are saying that their spirituality is valid only insofar as their prayers in their secluded lives connect with those on the outside. In medieval times, townsfolk wanted monasteries and convents nearby because they were convinced that those who served God in such places would send out spiritual vibrations, so to speak, that would bless and bring unity to their communities. The prayers of those faithful brothers and sisters set loose a radiance of the Holy Spirit that they believed would be for good.

> *Mystical spirituality at its best is interwoven with evangelism and commitments to justice.*

God-ordained spirituality, in one way or another, must involve a commitment to intimacy with Christ that results in evangelism and justice work—that is, if we want to strive for what Jesus lived, died, and rose again for: unity or oneness (John 17:20–23). Otherwise our spirituality becomes a form of arrested spiritual development that verges on narcissism. Kenneth Leach, in his book *The Eye of the Storm,* wrote, "Spirituality can be a dangerous diversion from the living God, from the demands of justice, from engagement with reality. It can be a form of illusion."[11]

The movements and the people we have been describing do not suffer from any such illusions—they are certainly people whose intimacy with Christ is, in the words of Dietrich Bonhoeffer, "for the sake of others." This kind of connectedness is the holistic gospel that seeks unity in God— and that should be the goal of all spirituality.

POSTSCRIPT

ALL OF THE SPIRITUAL practices and stories you have just read are meant to be more than simply illustrations of the thesis of this book. They are meant to be signs of the kind of Christianity that we believe is breaking loose in the twenty-first century. It is a Christianity that moves beyond many of the concerns that have preoccupied the church in the modern era. From the time of the Renaissance until the end of the twentieth century, theologians were working continuously to make our faith fit in with a worldview prescribed by science and governed by reason. That is why the church during this era put such a strong emphasis on apologetics. We so appreciate the work of C. S. Lewis, who in his book *A Case for Christianity*[1] made much of Christianity plausible to the modern thinking person.

Apologetics still have their place, and even today we are pleased with the works of the likes of John Polkinghorne and Hugh Ross, who have made Christianity a viable ideology in the context of the latest cosmologies being developed by astronomers. But the postmodern era through which we are moving is an age in which there is a growing awareness of the limitations of confining religion to rational and scientific categories. While not negating the importance of creating a synthesis between faith and reason, we are now realizing that there is truth that cannot be apprehended through the methodologies prescribed by Western rationalism and empiricism. What is more, there is a growing realization among us religionists that even as we developed theologies that were supposed to answer all of the questions posed by modernity, we sensed in the depths of our being an array of questions and longings that we could not put into words. As we journey through this era with its new paradigms, we will not let these "groans that words cannot express" (Romans 8:26) be silenced, and consequently, we are making room in our lives for the truth that can be encountered through spiritual mysticism.

In our limited exploration of mystical Christianity, we have sought to make clear that its purpose is not simply and only to provide spiritual and emotional "highs" for spiritually dry Christians. The ultimate purpose for mystically intimate experiences with Christ is to make us into persons through whom God can transform the world that is into the world that God intends it to be. We believe that the Holy Spirit saves us from the deadness of our souls, not just so that we can have the joy of Jesus in our hearts, but so that others might also experience that joy. We have been saved not by good works, but to do good works.

We are convinced that God desires to create a spiritual people so that the Kingdom prayed for in the Lord's Prayer might be realized "on earth as it is in heaven." God incarnated in Jesus of Nazareth seeks to be incarnated in us, and that is what being Christian mystics is all about. The God who "so loved the world that he gave his only Son, so that everyone who believes in him may not perish but may have eternal life" (John 3:16) endeavors to fill us with the same Spirit that was in Jesus (Romans 8:11), so that we might be instruments through whom all of creation might be rescued from its travail (Romans 8:19–23).

The end of history is the triumph of God wherein "the kingdom of the world has become the kingdom of our Lord" (Revelation 11:15). It is to that end that we should seek to become increasingly alive in Christ and filled with the Holy Spirit. As Spirit-filled people, we become the church through which all principalities and powers, and the structures that they control and represent, are brought under the dominion of Christ (Ephesians 1:21–23). Christian mysticism is not an end in itself, but rather is the means to creating a kingdom of people who will not rest until we see "justice roll down like waters and righteousness like an ever-flowing stream" (Amos 5:24).

NOTES

All scripture references are from the New Revised Standard Version, unless otherwise noted.

CHAPTER ONE

1 James, W. *The Varieties of Religious Experience*. New York: Modern Library, 1902, pp. 370–372.

2 Buber, M. *I and Thou*. New York: Scribner, 1958.

3 Wilder, T. "Our Town." *Three Plays: Our Town, The Skin of Our Teeth, The Matchmaker*. New York: HarperCollins, 1957, p. 100.

4 Buechner, F. *Listening to Your Life: Daily Meditations with Frederick Buechner*. San Francisco: HarperSanFrancisco, 1992, p. 2.

5 Brother Lawrence. *The Practice of the Presence of God with Spiritual Maxims*. Grand Rapids, Mich.: Spire Books, 1967, p. 11.

6 Ibid., p. 30.

7 Ibid., p. 34.

8 Ibid., p. 30.

9 James, *Varieties of Religious Experience*, p. 244.

10 Ibid., p. 186.

11 Otto, R. *The Idea of the Holy: An Inquiry into the Non-Rational Factor in the Idea of the Divine and Its Relation to the Rational*. Oxford: Oxford University Press, 1957, p. 12.

12 Augustine, "The Infinite Light." *The Confessions of St. Augustine*. (Edward B. Pusey, trans.). New York: Collier, 1909, pp. 109, 110.

13 Bunyan, J. *Grace Abounding to the Chief of Sinners and the Life and Death of Mr. Badman*. London: Dent, 1956, pp. 37, 53, 73, 82.

14   Griffin, E. *Wonderful and Dark Is This Road: Discovering the Mystic Path.* Brewster, Mass.: Paraclete Press, 2004, p. 11.

15   Pascal, B. *Pensées and the Provincial Letters.* New York: Modern Library, 1941, p. 95.

16   Griffin, *Wonderful and Dark,* p. 89.

17   Kierkegaard, S. *Attack upon Christendom.* (W. Lowrie, trans.). Princeton, N.J.: Princeton University Press, 1968, pp. 166–167.

18   Dorr, D. *Spirituality and Justice.* Dublin: Gill & Macmillan, 1984, p. 15.

CHAPTER TWO

1   American Baptist Churches USA's working definition of *evangelism.* [http://www.evangelismconnections.org/partnerdefinitions.htm]. Sept. 2006.
      Here is their more extended theological definition of *evangelism,* also found on this Web site: "Evangelism is the joyous witness of the people of God to God's redeeming love, which urges repentance and reconciliation to God and each other through faith in Jesus Christ—who lived, died, and was raised from the dead.
      "Through renewal with Jesus, believers are empowered by the Holy Spirit and incorporated into the church for worship, fellowship, nurture, and engagement as disciples in God's mission of evangelization and liberation within society and creation, signifying the Kingdom that is present and yet to come" (Official definition of *evangelism,* adopted by American Baptist Churches USA in 1984).

2   Pascal, B. "The Memorial." *Pascal Selections.* (R. Popkin, ed.). Old Tappan, N.J.: Macmillan, 1989, pp. 69–70.

3   Foster, R. J. "Focusing on Spiritual Disciplines." *Heart-to-Heart: The Renovaré Newsletter,* May 2003, p. 4.

4   Bright, B. *Four Spiritual Laws.* Orlando, Fla.: NewLife, 1995.
      They are as follows: (1) God loves you and offers a wonderful plan for your life. (2) Man is sinful and separated from God. Therefore, he cannot know and experience God's love and plan for his life. (3) Jesus Christ is God's only provision for man's sin. Through Him you can know and experience God's love and plan for your life. (4) We must individually receive Jesus Christ as Savior and Lord; then we can know and experience God's love and plan for our lives.

5   Laubach, F. *Prayer: The Mightiest Force in the World.* New York: Revell, 1946.

CHAPTER THREE

1 "St. Francis, Rabbits, and Fish," first recorded by Thomas of Celano (13th century), retold by J. Feister in *Stories About St. Francis and the Animals,* p. 2. [www.americancatholic.org]. Nov. 2006.

2 Ibid., p. 1.

3 Ibid., p. 3.

4 White, L. "The Historical Roots of Our Ecological Crisis." In R. Gottlieb, ed., *This Sacred Earth: Religion, Nature, Environment.* (2nd ed.). New York: Routledge, 2004, p. 200.

5 Saint Francis's complete "Canticle of the Sun," in T. Campolo, *How to Rescue the Earth Without Worshiping Nature.* Nashville, Tenn.: Nelson, 1992, pp. 79, 80.

O most high, almighty, good Lord God, to thee belong praise, glory, honor, and all blessing.

Praised be my Lord God with all creatures and especially our brother sun, who brings us the day and who brings us the light;

Fair is he and shines with a very great splendor: O Lord, he signifies to us Thee.

Praised be my Lord for our sister the moon, and for the stars, which he hath set clear and lovely in the heavens.

Praised be my Lord for our brother the wind, and for the air and cloud, calms and all weather by the which Thou upholdest life in all creatures.

Praised be my Lord for our sister water, who is very serviceable unto us and humble and precious and clean.

Praised be my Lord for our brother fire, through which Thou givest us light in the darkness; and he is bright and pleasant and very mighty and strong.

Praised be my Lord for our mother the earth, the which doth sustain us and keep us, and bringeth forth divers fruits and flowers of many colors, and grass.

Praised be my Lord for all those who pardon one another for His love's sake, and who endure weakness and tribulation; blessed are they who peaceably shall endure, for Thou, or most Highest, shalt give them a crown.

Praise ye and bless the Lord and give thanks unto Him and serve Him with great humility.

6 Pope John Paul II. "The Ecological Crisis: A Common Responsibility." In Gottlieb, *Sacred Earth*, pp. 208–209.

7 Saint Francis, "Canticle of the Sun."

8 Brueggemann, W. *The Prophetic Imagination*. Philadelphia: Fortress Press, 1978, p. 13.

9 Thurman, H. *Jesus and the Disinherited*. Nashville, Tenn.: Abingdon-Cokesbury Press, 1949.

10 Thurman, H. "Suffering." In W. E. Fluker and C. Tumber (eds.), *A Strange Freedom: The Best of Howard Thurman on Religious Experience and Public Life*. Boston: Beacon Press, 1993, p. 53.

11 Ibid., p. 47.

12 Walker, T. "African-American Resources for a More Inclusive Liberation Theology." In Gottlieb, *Sacred Earth*, p. 282, n. 8. Walker's note reports that "Howard Thurman narrated this story on the occasion of his visit to Livingstone College in Salisbury, North Carolina, during the spring of 1978."

13 Wesley, J. *The Journal of the Rev. John Wesley*. (N. Curnock, ed.). London: Epworth Press, 1938, vol. 1, pp. 475–476.

14 Wesley, J. *The Letters of the Rev. John Wesley*. (J. Telford, ed.). London: Epworth Press, 1960, vol. 1, p. 207.

15 Quoted in Hyland, J. *God's Covenant with Animals: A Biblical Basis for the Humane Treatment of All Creatures*. New York: Lantern Books, 2000, p. xii.

16 Wesley, J. "The General Deliverance." (Sermon 60). *The Works of John Wesley*, Vol. 2: *Sermons II, 34–70*. (A. Outler, ed.). Nashville, Tenn.: Abingdon Press, 1985.

17 Ibid., pp. 445 and 449.

CHAPTER FOUR

1 Russell, A. J. *God Calling*. Grand Rapids, Mich.: Spire Books, 2001.

2 Hurnard, H. *Hinds' Feet on High Places*. Wheaton, Ill.: Tyndale House, 1975.

3 Sider, R. *Rich Christians in an Age of Hunger*. (20th anniv. rev.). Dallas, Tex.: Word, 1997.

4 Warren, R. "Purpose Driven in Rwanda." *Christianity Today*, Oct. 2005, p. 34.

5 Willard, D. "The Making of the Christian." *Christianity Today,* Oct. 2005, p. 43.

6 Hazard, D. *Rekindling the Inner Fire Devotional Series.* 10 vols. Minneapolis: Bethany House, 1990s.

7 We recommend Thomas à Kempis. *Imitation of Christ: A Timeless Classic for Contemporary Readers.* (W. Creasy, ed.). Notre Dame, Ind.: Ave Maria Press, 1989.

8 Fleming, D. *Draw Me into Your Friendship: The Spiritual Exercises: A Literal Translation and a Contemporary Reading.* Saint Louis, Mo.: Institute of Jesuit Sources, 1996, p. 176.

9 Serrick, J. "A 'Note' from the Director." *Manresa Matters.* Summer 2005, p. 4.

CHAPTER FIVE

1 Keating, T. *The Mystery of Christ.* New York: Continuum, 2000, p. 39.

2 Nouwen, H. *Making All Things New: An Invitation to the Spiritual Life.* San Francisco: HarperSanFrancisco, 1981, p. 68.

3 Campolo, T. Adapted from *Let Me Tell You a Story.* Nashville, Tenn.: Word, 2000, pp. 81–82.

4 Foster, R. J. *Streams of Living Water.* San Francisco: HarperSanFrancisco, 1998, p. 20.

5 Thomas à Kempis, *Imitation of Christ,* p. 52.

6 Wesley, J. *The Works of John Wesley,* Vol. 1. (A. Outler, ed.). Nashville, Tenn.: Abingdon Press, 1984, p. 107.

7 Capalbo, B. (ed.). *Praying with St. Theresa.* (P. Clifford, trans.). Grand Rapids, Mich.: Eerdmans, 1997, p. 56.

8 Howe, F. R. *The Saint of Genoa: Lessons from the Life of St. Catherine.* Chicago: Union Catholic Publishing Company, 1883, p. 160.

9 Wesley, J. *An Extract of the Life of Monsieur de Renty.* (3rd ed.). Salem, Ohio: Schmul, 2002.

10 Ibid., p. 5.

11 Ibid.

12 Ibid., p. 32.

13 Ibid., p. 45.

14 Ibid., p. 47.

15 This would be in accord with the scripture that says, "Whoever, therefore,

2

eats the bread or drinks the cup of the Lord in an unworthy manner will be answerable for the body and blood of the Lord" (I Corinthians 11:27).

16 Wesley, *Extract,* p. 48.

17 Ibid., p. 41.

18 Ibid.

19 Howe, *Saint of Genoa,* p. 62.

20 Ibid., p. 72.

21 Ibid., p. 131.

22 Ibid., p. 63.

23 Saint John of the Cross. *The Dark Night of the Soul and the Living Flame of Love.* (B. Zimmerman, trans.). London: Fount, 1995, p. 123.

CHAPTER SIX

1 Foster, R. J. *Prayer: Finding the Heart's True Home.* San Francisco: HarperSanFrancisco, 1992, p. 32.

2 Wesley, *Extract,* p. 6.

3 Tetlow, J. A. *Choosing Christ in the World.* Saint Louis, Mo.: Institute of Jesuit Sources, 1999, p. 43.

4 In his book *Spirituality of the Beatitudes,* Michael Crosby discusses the problems associated with desiring power, prestige, and possessions over what is to be valued if we want to be a part of God's reign. See Crosby, M. H. *Spirituality of the Beatitudes: Matthew's Challenge for First World Christians.* Maryknoll, N.Y.: Orbis, 1981.

5 A description from the exhibit "Petra: Lost City of Stone." Grand Rapids, Mich.: Calvin College, Prince Center, June 2005.

6 Pennington, M. B. *Lectio Divina.* New York: Crossroad, 1998, p. 52.

7 Dupré, L. *The Deeper Life: An Introduction to Christian Mysticism.* New York: Crossroad, 1981, pp. 54, 56.

CHAPTER SEVEN

1 Capalbo, *Praying with St. Theresa,* p. xvi.

2 Merton, T. *Faith and Violence: Christian Teaching and Christian Practice.* Notre Dame, Ind.: University of Notre Dame Press, 1968, p. 222.

3 Ibid.

4 Pennington, *Lectio Divina,* p. 27.

5 Willard, D. *The Divine Conspiracy.* San Francisco: HarperSanFrancisco, 1997, p. 106. For further discussion and clarification of this crucial understanding of Jesus' Sermon on the Mount, see ch. 5 in *The Divine Conspiracy.*

6 Ortberg, J. *If You Want to Walk on Water, You Have to Get Out of the Boat.* Grand Rapids, Mich.: Zondervan, 2001.

7 Hazard, D. *Majestic Is Your Name.* Minneapolis: Bethany House, 1993, p. 32.

8 Ernesto Cardenal. *The Gospel in Solentiname.* (D. D. Walsh, trans.). Maryknoll, N.Y.: Orbis, 1978, vol. 2, p. vii.

CHAPTER EIGHT

1 Merton, *Faith and Violence,* p. 216.

2 Keating, T. *Open Mind, Open Heart.* New York: Continuum, 1997, p. 30.

3 Ibid., p. 33.

4 Nouwen, H. "Moving from Solitude to Community to Ministry." *Leadership,* Spring 1995, p. 83.

5 Foster, R. J. *Prayers from the Heart.* San Francisco: HarperSanFrancisco, 1994, p. xv.

6 Shanks, N. *Iona: God's Energy: The Spirituality and Vision of the Iona Community.* London: Hodder & Stoughton, 1999, p. 84.

7 Quoted in Moll, R. "The New Monasticism." *Christianity Today,* Sept. 2005, p. 45.

CHAPTER NINE

1 Sider, *Rich Christians,* p. 196.

2 Bishop, B. "Sprinkling on a Little Bit of Jesus." *Quaker Life,* Mar. 2000, p. 26.

3 "The Greatest Enemy," words and music by Bryan C. Sirchio. From *Justice and Love.* Crosswind Music Ministries, 1999. Used by permission of Bryan C. Sirchio.

4 Merton, *Faith and Violence,* p. 216.

5 Poloma, M. *Main Street Mystics.* New York: AltaMira Press, 2003, p. 38.

6 Ibid., p. 40.

7 Law, W. *A Serious Call to a Devout and Holy Life*. (P. G. Standwood, ed.). New York: Paulist Press, 1978, pp. 209–224.

8 Nouwen, H. J. *The Return of the Prodigal Son*. New York: Image Books, 1992.

9 McGrath, A. E. *Christian Spirituality*. Malden, Mass.: Blackwell, 1999, p. 110.

10 *The Confessions of St. Augustine*. (J. Ryan, trans.). Garden City, N.Y.: Image Books, 1960, p. 43.

11 Nouwen, H. J. *Spiritual Direction*. Cincinnati, Ohio: Forward Movement, 2002.

12 Benner, D. *Sacred Companions*. Downers Grove, Ill.: InterVarsity Press, 2002, p. 16.

13 Barry, W. A., and Connolly, W. J. *The Practice of Spiritual Direction*. San Francisco: HarperSanFrancisco, 1986, p. 8.

14 Equal Exchange, 50 United Drive, West Bridgewater, MA 02379. [www.equalexchange.com]. Sept. 2006. Another socially and ecologically just company is Pura Vida Coffee in Seattle, (877) 469-1431. [www.puravidacoffee.com]. Nov. 2006.

15 Heywood, W. (ed.). *The Little Flowers of St. Francis of Assisi*. New York: Vintage Spiritual Classics, 1998, pp. 34–35.

16 Foster, R. J. *Celebration of Discipline*. San Francisco: HarperSanFrancisco, 1978, p. 155.

17 *Renovaré: Bringing the Church to the Churches*. Englewood, Colo.: Renovaré, p. 6.

18 Nouwen, *Prodigal Son*.

19 Thorson, D. *The Wesleyan Quadrilateral: Scripture, Tradition, Reason, and Experience as a Model of Evangelical Theology*. Grand Rapids, Mich.: Zondervan, 1990, p. 21. The Wesleyan quadrilateral was developed in the 1960s by Albert Outler, a United Methodist theologian and the preeminent Wesley scholar of the twentieth century, as a way of summarizing Wesley's theology. Donald A. D. Thorson further explains the origin of the model in his book *The Wesleyan Quadrilateral*: "The 'Wesleyan quadrilateral' is a paradigm, or model, of how Wesley conceived of the task of theology. Wesley neither coined the term nor used it; it represents a modern attempt to summarize the fourfold set of guidelines Wesley used in reflecting on theology. Outler first referred to the Wesleyan quadrilateral in the late 1960s while serving on the commission on doctrine and doctrinal standards of the

United Methodist Church. Outler thought the term would serve as a helpful way to refer to the complex interaction among the four sources of Wesley's theology."

20 Moll, R. "The New Monasticism." *Christianity Today*, Sept. 2005.

21 Willard, D. *Renovation of the Heart*. Colorado Springs: NavPress, 2002, p. 123.

22 Wesley, J. *A Plain Account of Christian Perfection*. Kansas City, Mo.: Beacon Hill Press, 1966, p. 80.

23 Winner, L. "Sleep Therapy." *Books and Culture*, Jan.-Feb. 2006, p. 7.

CHAPTER TEN

1 Miles, C. A. "In the Garden." *Hymns for the Living Church*. Carol Stream, Ill.: Hope, 1974, p. 398. Originally published 1912.

2 Darling, H. *Man in Triumph: An Integration of Psychology and Biblical Faith*. Grand Rapids, Mich.: Zondervan, 1969, p. 92.

3 Blessed Raymond of Capua. *The Life of St. Catherine of Siena*. (G. Lamb, trans.). London: Harvill Press, 1960, p. 43. Originally published 1934.

4 Ibid.

5 Ibid., p. 59.

6 Ibid., p. 105.

7 Ibid., p. 107.

8 Ibid., p. 108.

9 Ibid., p. 106.

10 Catherine of Siena. *The Dialogue*. (S. Noffke, trans.). New York: Paulist Press, 1980, p. 9.

11 Gillet, M. S. *The Mission of St. Catherine*. (M. T. Lopez, trans.). London: Herder, 1955.

12 Catherine of Siena, *Dialogue*, p. 8.

13 Ibid., pp. 8–9.

14 Ibid., p. 9.

15 Ibid.

16 *The Spiritual Doctrine of St. Catherine of Genoa*. Compiled by her confessor, Don Cattaneo Marabotto. Rockford, Ill.: Tan Books, 1989, p. 11.

17 Ibid., p. 202.

18 Ibid., p. 203.

19 Wink, W. *The Powers That Be*. Minneapolis: Augsburg Fortress, 1998, p. 181.

20 Merton, T. *Contemplation in a World of Action*. Garden City, N.Y.: Image Books, 1973, pp. 178–179.

21 Wink, *Powers That Be*, p. 181.

CHAPTER ELEVEN

1   The Evangelical Association for Education (EAPE) was started by Tony Campolo in 1978 to provide literacy programs to children in inner-city America as well as in several other countries.

2   Shanks, *Iona: God's Energy*, p. 109.

3   *The Iona Community Worship Book*. Glasgow, Scotland: Wild Goose, 1991. [http://www.ogdoad.force9.co.uk/celt/iona.htm]. Nov. 2006.

4   The Iona Community, found on cards and other publications. [http://www.ogdoad.force9.co.uk/celt/iona.htm]. Nov. 2006.

5   Shanks, *Iona: God's Energy*, p. 16.

6   Ibid., pp. 66–70.

7   Ibid., p. 214.

8   Merton, T. *Contemplative Prayer*. New York: Image Books, 1996, p. 115.

9   Claiborne, S. *The Irresistible Revolution: Living Life as an Ordinary Radical*. Grand Rapids, Mich.: Zondervan, 2006.

10 Wilson-Hartgrove, J. *To Baghdad and Beyond*. Eugene, Ore.: Cascade Books, 2005.

11 Leach, K. *The Eye of the Storm*. Quoted in Shanks, *Iona: God's Energy*, p. 36.

POSTSCRIPT

1   Lewis, C. S. *The Case for Christianity*. Old Tappan, N.J.: Macmillan, 1958.

THE AUTHORS

TONY CAMPOLO is professor emeritus of sociology at Eastern University in Saint Davids, Pennsylvania. A graduate of Eastern College, Tony earned his doctorate from Temple University and previously served for ten years on the faculty of the University of Pennsylvania.

As founder and president of the Evangelical Association for the Promotion of Education (EAPE), Tony has worked to create, nurture, and support programs for at-risk children in cities across North America and has helped establish schools and universities in several developing countries.

Tony is the author of thirty-four books and is also a media commentator on religious, social, and political matters. He has been a guest on television programs including *The Colbert Report, Nightline, Crossfire, Politically Incorrect, The Charlie Rose Show, Larry King Live, CNN Dayside, CNN News,* and *MSNBC News.* He presently hosts *Across the Pond,* a weekly program on the Premier Christian Radio Network in England, and is frequently a guest on radio stations throughout the United States, Canada, the United Kingdom, Australia, and New Zealand.

An ordained minister, Tony has served American Baptist churches in New Jersey and Pennsylvania and is presently an associate pastor of the Mount Carmel Baptist Church in West Philadelphia.

Tony and his wife, Peggy, live in the Philadelphia area and have two grown children and four grandchildren.

MARY ALBERT DARLING is associate professor of communication at Spring Arbor University in Spring Arbor, Michigan, and teaches at the undergraduate and graduate levels. She is a graduate of Spring Arbor, with a double major in philosophy and religion and in psychology. She received her master of arts degree in communication arts and sciences from Western Michigan University. In November 2002 she completed a two-year program in spiritual direction offered by the Manresa Jesuit House in Birmingham, Michigan. She designed and teaches a class on spiritual direction in Spring Arbor University's master's program in spiritual formation and leadership. In addition to teaching, for which she received Spring Arbor University's Teaching Excellence Award, Mary regularly does spiritual direction, primarily with university students. She also speaks on such topics as the connections among faith, learning, and living in interpersonal and public communication. Mary especially loves talking about spiritual transformation and the spiritual disciplines.

Mary is married to Terry Darling, professor of psychology at Spring Arbor University. They have two teenaged boys, David and Michael; a yellow Lab, Amelie; and two cats, Cocoa and Cappuccino.

Besides her family and friends, teaching, and working with college students, Mary's other interests include traveling, books, good quotes, and good coffee.

INDEX

Other Books of Interest

A New Kind of Christian
A Tale of Two Friends on a Spiritual Journey
Cloth
ISBN: 978-0-7879-5599-1
Winner of the *Christianity Today* Award of Merit for Best Christian Living title, 2002

"This is a book that heightens the depths and deepens the peaks. Like all the best things in life, it is not to be entered into lightly, but reverently and in the fear of a God who is waiting for the church to stop asking WWJD, 'What would Jesus do?' and start asking WIJD, 'What is Jesus doing?'"

—Dr. Leonard Sweet, E. Stanley Jones Chair of Evangelism at Drew University, founder and president of SpiritVenture Ministries, and bestselling author

The Story We Find Ourselves In
Further Adventures of a New Kind of Christian
Cloth
ISBN: 978-0-7879-6387-3

"As with *A New Kind of Christian*, once I started reading this book I could not possibly put it down. Be prepared once again to go on the adventure of having your heart and mind feeling both comforted and uncomfortable, stimulated and stirred, challenged and changed, agreeing and disagreeing. . ."

—Dan Kimball, author, *The Emerging Church: Vintage Christianity for New Generations*, and pastor, Graceland/Santa Cruz Bible Church

The Last Word and the Word After That
A Tale of Faith, Doubt, and a New Kind of Christianity
Cloth
ISBN: 978-0-7879-7592-0

"Brian McLaren has written a remarkable book on hell and the grace of God. And it is one hell of a book! . . . It evidences yet again why McLaren is an emerging voice to be taken seriously concerning new modes of church and new practices of faith."

—Walter Brueggemann, minister, United Church of Christ; professor, Old Testament, Columbia Theological Seminary, Decatur, Georgia

Brian D. McLaren is an author and activist. To learn more about him, visit brianmclaren.net.

So Much More
An Invitation to Christian Spirituality
Debra Rienstra
Hardcover
ISBN: 978-0-7879-6887-8

"*So Much More* is a radiant manifesto for the fully realized Christian life. Rienstra speaks to the heart without mawkishness, speaks to the mind without logic-chopping, and speaks to the doubtful without patronizing. With good humor, and with erudition worn lightly, Rienstra provides a compelling Christian account of sin and grace, reason and revelation, the longing for God, the mystery of suffering, and the pathways of love and service."
— Carol Zaleski, professor of religion, Smith College

"*So Much More* is indeed so much more—more than your typical book on apologetics or theology or spirituality. Debra Rienstra is a gifted writer who imparts much wisdom in all of these areas-and more. This is a fine book for a person who is beginning a Christian pilgrimage. But it also gives much guidance and encouragement to those of us who are well along in the journey."
— Richard J. Mouw, president and professor of Christian philosophy, Fuller Theological Seminary

What does it truly mean to live as a Christian? This intimate, engaging, and beautifully written book speaks to the heart of Christian faith and experience rather than to any one branch or theological position. Debra Rienstra weaves her own experiences as a Christian into chapters on central topics such as transcendence, prayer, churchgoing, the Bible, sin and salvation, and suffering. This is a book for people who don't have all the answers, those who are still thoughtfully considering the depth and breadth of their faith and would like an evocative and sympathetic companion to accompany them on their journey.

Debra Rienstra is a professor of English at Calvin College and the author of *Great with Child: Reflections on Faith, Fullness, and Becoming a Mother.* She lives in Grand Rapids, Michigan.

Soul Graffiti:
Making a Life in the Way of Jesus
Mark Scandrette
Hardcover
ISBN: 978-0-7879-8437-3

"*Soul Graffiti* is not so much a book as it is an encounter—a deadly serious encounter-with a Christianity that is urban, American, un-institutionalized, and now. If you truly like your own Christian walk just the way it is, you definitely should not read this book."
—Phyllis Tickle, religion analyst and compiler, *The Divine Hours*

"Mark Scandrette guides us in this beautifully written and brilliantly illustrated book along a path towards actualized spirituality in a postmodern world. The book provides new avenues to ancient truths."
—Tony Campolo, professor of sociology, Eastern University

"Through Mark's rich insights and reflections, and especially through his stories about Jack, Richard, Gary, Caroline, Emperor Arcadia (you'll never forget him!), Michelle, Beryl, and many others, you'll get an honest and inspiring view of what 'the emergent conversation' is really about, and what it's for."
—Brian McLaren, author/activist (brianmclaren.net)

With a profoundly postmodern sensibility, *Soul Graffiti* is a heartfelt and personal book that makes a meaningful and practical connection between the message proclaimed by Jesus and the daily life of those who seek to follow his path. Using graffiti as a metaphor for the paradoxical grittiness of modern life and our transcendent yearning to be seen and known, Mark Scandrette—a prominent leader in the emergent church movement—offers readers inspiration, motivation, and direction, along with fresh new resources that help them transcend the messiness of their all-too-human lives and show them how to connect more fully and intimately with Jesus, his life, and his teachings.

Mark Scandrette (San Francisco, CA) is a senior fellow with Emergent and is president and cofounder of the San Francisco-based organization ReIMAGINE! He has an extensive background providing leadership in church and community-based organizations. To learn more about Mark Scandrette, visit www.markscandrette.com or www.soulgraffitibook.com.

What We Were Made For:
Christian Reflections on Love
Sondra Wheeler
Hardcover
ISBN: 978-0-7879-7738-2

"With unflinching and lucid honesty, this meditation on the nature of varied forms of love wrestles with a central enigma of the Christian faith: how can flawed and sinful humans find the wherewithal to love others as God does? While human love is not sufficient to meet the challenges of human relationships, Wheeler argues that if it is disciplined by Christian practice, informed by God's grace, and modeled on God's love revealed in Jesus Christ, it can be a powerful instrument for healing."

—*Publishers Weekly,* starred review

"Shelves are full of shallow self-help books that promise to unravel the secrets of love. That's why we can give thanks to God that Sondra Wheeler has produced this volume that goes deep and true to the divine sources of the love we need in our lives. Her book will inspire each student, parent, child, and spouse who is looking for love in all the right places."

—Mike McCurry, former White House Press Secretary

Not a devotional or inspirational book, *What We Were Made For* is a wide-ranging and wise exploration of love in Christian life that will give readers greater depth and understanding of one of Jesus' most challenging teachings. Sondra Wheeler draws on a wealth of historic and contemporary sources to pose provocative questions, drawing readers into new insights and considerations of what love means as a central part of Christian faith. She addresses the nature of the distortions and corruptions of love, and provides needed resources for living daily life—from romances and marriages to friendships and relationships with coworkers to love as applied to strangers and enemies.

Sondra Wheeler is Martha Ashby Carr Professor of Christian Ethics and teaches bioethics, the history of theological ethics, and the virtue tradition as well as biblical ethics at Wesley Theological Seminary. She is a respected scholar and speaker.

DISCUSSION/REFLECTION GUIDE

By Mary Albert Darling and Tony Campolo

*with much appreciated help from Spring Arbor
University students and the Golden Gate Community
Church in San Francisco*

This guide has been designed for use during individual times of reflection with
God as well as for discussion in small groups and classes. Each chapter's guide
includes supporting scriptures, authors' notes, questions for reflection and/or discussion, and reflection activities. Any or all parts of each chapter guide can be
drawn upon to further understand, explore, and experience a deeper intimacy with
God that inspires and fuels us to evangelize and work for justice.

Preface and Chapter 1:
What Mystical Christianity Is All About

Supporting Scriptures

Ephesians 3:16–19; Romans 8:11; I Corinthians 13:1 and 12; I Corinthians
2:12–14; John 10:10; II Corinthians 12:2–4; Micah 6:8; Matthew 28:18–20; Luke
4:18–19; John 14:12–21; John 15:26–27; John 17:20–23; Colossians 1:27

Authors' Notes

In Chapter One, Tony lays the groundwork for understanding what is at stake if
we do not experience our relationship with God as more than following a set of
biblical guidelines. It might seem strange that we intentionally choose the words
mystic and *mysticism* to describe this relationship, since these words have lots of
meanings, including many negative connotations. We use them to distinguish a
depth and breadth of our relationship with God, through the power of the Holy
Spirit, that reason and "right living" alone cannot attain. We believe that all of
us have experiences that can be called mystical. We hope this chapter will help

you understand and discern those experiences that can help you live in the trans-forming power involved in having "Christ in you, the hope of glory" (Colossians 1:27)—a power that not only changes you, but energizes you to change the world.

Reflection and Discussion Questions

1. What comes to mind when you hear the phrase "mystical Christianity"? (If the use of the phrase is particularly troublesome to you, you may want to read ahead to the last part of Chapter Three, specifically where Tony warns of some dangers in certain views of mysticism.)

2. What is the difference between seeing a personal relationship with God as fol-lowing a set of biblical guidelines and seeing that relationship as mystical? Why might we need both?

3. Tony gives examples of different types of mystical experiences to show how the Holy Spirit reveals God's love to us in a variety of ways. Can you identify any of these types of experiences in your own life, even though you may not have called them "mystical"? If so, how did or could they deepen your intimacy with God?

4. Can you think of instances when you have been aware of God in your every-day life? What are some ways you could become more aware of God's pres-ence in your daily life?

5. Tony writes about a "holistic gospel" involving three components of conver-sion: personal, interpersonal, and societal or political.

   Which component are you most comfortable with?

   Which one(s) make you less comfortable and why?

   What are some possible steps you could take to explore living out any com-ponent(s) you are less comfortable with?

6. Tony closes the chapter with an explanation of what it means for us to be the "now body" of Christ, based on Romans 8:11—that the same Spirit that was in Jesus can live in us. Have there been times when you have tried to live like Christ out of your own strength? Have there been times when you've yielded to the Holy Spirit to empower you to live like Christ? What have been the dif-ferences between the two?

SUMMARY QUESTION How can intimacy with Jesus empower us to evange-lize and work for justice?

Reflection Activities

1. Watch the film *Brother Sun, Sister Moon* (a 1970s Franco Zeffirelli rendition of the life of Saint Francis of Assisi) and reflect on or discuss how Saint Fran-cis chose and lived out a holistic gospel.

2. Reflect on any mystical experiences you might have had and how those could or do energize you to evangelize or work for justice. Consider sharing your experiences or reflections with a trusted friend or mentor. If you have any ques-

tions or concerns about your experience(s), ask a group of mature Christian friends and/or a pastor to help you "test the spirits" (I John 4:1) and discern the experience(s).

Chapter 2: Christian Mysticism and Personal Evangelism

Supporting Scriptures

Matthew 28:18–20; Matthew 4:18–21; Matthew 10:1 and 5–10; Matthew 10:11–23; Luke 19:10; Acts 1:8; Acts 4:1–20

Authors' Notes

Although a good part of Chapter Two focuses on a more traditional view of evangelism—calling a person to a specific moment of decision to believe in and follow Christ—we hope it's also clear that some individuals have a more gradual conversion experience; either way, Jesus calls his followers to share the "good news," which includes sharing with others the meaning of Jesus' life, death, and resurrection. But not everyone finds that easy to do, and even those who initially are excited to share Jesus with others find that the excitement can wear off. What we hope to do in this chapter is show how an ongoing intimacy with Jesus Christ creates in us a desire to keep sharing the message and mission of Christ with others.

Reflection and Discussion Questions

1. The chapter starts with Tony's own story of being evangelized. In what ways was this kind of evangelism familiar or unfamiliar to you? What comes to mind when you hear the words *evangelize* or *evangelism*? If you have had experiences with evangelizing or being told you *had* to evangelize, how have they affected the way you see evangelism?

2. How might those who are not Christians respond to the words *evangelize* or *evangelism*? If their responses are negative, how could a Christian's intimacy with God help change those perceptions?

3. Why do you think Tony suggests spiritual practices and learning from other saints as ways to renew our "first love" and empower us to evangelize? How does this "first love" intimacy with God relate to the verses in Matthew 10:19–20 that say that the Holy Spirit will give us the words?

4. One of the most paraphrased lines of Saint Francis is that we are to preach the gospel and, if necessary, use words. What does this look like in the day-to-day lives of Christians? What might this have to do with evangelism?

5. Tony writes that "mystical spirituality provides an incredible impetus to evangelize. The Holy Spirit makes us sensitive to the right time and place to witness, as well as giving us the right words and actions."

   What are possible dangers of *not* being sensitive to the time, place, words, or actions when evangelizing?

   Can you remember a time when the Holy Spirit made you sensitive to the right time, place, words, or actions involving evangelizing?

6. The chapter closes with the purpose of evangelizing, based on Jesus' words in Matthew 28:18–20—to make disciples and teach them to observe all that Jesus has commanded. How might these verses help us better understand and do evangelism?

SUMMARY QUESTION How does intimacy with Christ help us to share the message and mission of Christ with others?

Reflection Activities

1. Spend time alone with Jesus and reflect on a time you committed or recommitted to following him. Picture yourself there. How were you experiencing God's love? Stay with those thoughts or feelings for a while. Consider writing down and/or sharing your reflections with someone.

2. Reflect on barriers you might encounter when you engage in evangelism. If you have fears or concerns about evangelism, picture yourself sitting and talking with Jesus about them. Take several moments *to listen* for what Jesus might say to you. Then ask the Holy Spirit to give you the strength and desire to do what Jesus wants you to do, along with when and where he wants you to do it.

Chapter 3: Christian Mysticism and Working for Justice

Supporting Scriptures

Exodus 22:21–27; Deuteronomy 15:11; Isaiah 1; Isaiah 58; Isaiah 62; Ezekiel 16:49; Amos 5:21–24; Micah 6:8; Matthew 25:31–46; Luke 4:14–30; Luke 6:20–26; Luke 10:25–37; Luke 11:42 and 46; John 15:1–17; I Corinthians 13; Philippians 3:10–16; I John 3:11–24

Authors' Notes

In Chapter Three, our purpose is to give readers a new or deeper sense of how intimacy with Christ fills us with passion to "do justice." Our hope is that you will discover or rediscover what the Bible says about justice and that you will further explore what it means for us as followers of Jesus to live out those passages in our everyday lives.

Reflection and Discussion Questions

1. This chapter opens with a story of Saint Francis encountering Jesus as a leper in disguise. How would some of your encounters with oppressed and ostracized people change if you viewed them as Jesus in disguise?

2. Tony writes, "When the Spirit of God moves you to unfathomable depths of love and the suffering of others becomes yours in a mystical way, you will have an irresistibly urgent compulsion to speak on behalf of those who suffer and to fight for a world that is more just." Can you give an example of how this has happened in either your life or the life of someone you know?

3. With verses like Micah 6:8 saying that God requires us to "do justice," why do you think justice is often seen as something only certain people are called to "do"? Why is the word *justice* sometimes divisive among Christians? What can we do to bridge these gaps and be more unified in our justice work?

4. In Luke 4:18–19, Jesus reads from Isaiah that "the Spirit of the Lord is on me, because he has anointed me to preach good news to the poor . . . to release the oppressed, to proclaim the year of the Lord's favor." In Matthew 25:35–40, Jesus says that whatever we do to "one of the least of these," we do it to Christ. How can we have "the Spirit of the Lord" on us to live out these verses?

5. Tony suggests that the Bible be read "through the eyes of the poor and the oppressed." How might reading the Bible this way change the way we see justice issues?

6. John Wesley believed that although ministering to the poor and oppressed was necessary, still it wasn't enough, because the system itself must also be changed. Why are many Christians today hesitant about changing social and economic systems, even after discovering injustices in those systems?

7. Tony writes that "the beatitudes are the manifesto for a revolutionary lifestyle" and that if we follow them, "they will turn society as we know it upside down."

Since we can't be involved in all of the issues he mentions, and we may not even agree with all of them, how can intimacy with Christ help us discern not only what issues to be involved in but also the extent of our involvement?

What do you think of Saint Francis's and Wesley's belief that our relationship with God includes caring for all oppressed aspects of God's creation, including animals and the environment?

SUMMARY QUESTION If we take this chapter to heart, how can we and our churches combine intimacy and action to practically convey the gospel message of justice?

Reflection Activities

1. Watch the *Amazing Grace* film about William Wilberforce and the abolition of slavery. Reflect on and/or discuss what you can learn about intimacy with God and working for justice.

2. Commit to spending 5 minutes a day for a week reflecting on Luke 4:18–19 or another short passage listed in this chapter's supporting scriptures; or read one of the longer scripture passages every day for a month to absorb it into your spirit. You might want to try reading one of these passages through the eyes of the poor and oppressed.

3. Engage in a service project in which you are in direct contact with people who are poor or oppressed. Before and after the project, reflect on I Corinthians 13:3 and Philippians 3:10–11 and ask the Holy Spirit to fill you with the love of God and to help you enter into the sufferings of others.

Chapter 4: Awakening to Mysticism and a Holistic Gospel (Even If You're Not a Monk)

Supporting Scriptures

Isaiah 55:6–9; Ephesians 3:16–19; II Corinthians 3:17; John 10:10; Psalm 42:1; Matthew 4:19; John 21:15–19; Acts 10 and 11:1–18; Romans 12:1–2 and 11; Matthew 9:36 and 14:14; Mark 8:2; Philippians 1:9–11

Authors' Notes

We all have our own stories of what was or was not emphasized in our homes spiritually. In Chapter Four, Mary shares how she grew up with a partial gospel, how the Holy Spirit moved her out of her comfort zone, and how three "new" prayers changed her relationship with Christ and others. We hope that as you read this chapter, it will stir in you a desire to revisit and reflect on your own spiritual journey, including possible "gospel gaps"—ways in which you may have settled or gotten "stuck" in your relationship with God and others due to a partial view of the gospel.

Reflection and Discussion Questions

1. What people or books have inspired you to want to live in deeper intimacy with Christ and/or more actively for Christ in the world? If so, in what ways have they changed how you live your life?

2. Mary writes, "I now realize that I cannot really be a Christian without being a mystic." What do you think she means by this? Do you agree with her? Why or why not?

3. Many of us have grown up with a partial view of the gospel. What parts of the gospel, if any, were emphasized to you when you were growing up? What, if anything, was left out? What were your initial images of Jesus? How have these views affected how you see living for Christ?

4. Mary describes her and Bev's spiritual reawakening. If you have ever had an intense and/or extended time of spiritual awakening or reawakening, what was it like, and what were the results? If it didn't result in long-term intimacy with God or action for God in the world, why do you think that was?

5. Mary writes that "we can have misguided loyalties to comfortable patterns because what is new to us does not always feel right."

   Has there ever been a time when you have been challenged in your Christian life to do or believe something different that made you uncomfortable? What happened?

   Are you sensing any new way(s) the Holy Spirit is nudging or urging you out of your comfort zone and into deeper intimacy with God or action in the world?

SUMMARY QUESTION   What can we and our churches do to close "gospel gaps" that are in our lives?

Reflection Activities

1. Spend some time alone with God, reflecting on your own spiritual journey: your first impressions of Jesus and your own "gospel gaps." Ask God to help you see areas where you need to close some gaps. If you feel led, share your reflections with a small group or another trusted lover of Jesus.

2. During the next week, read one of the following passages a day and then reflect each day on (a) how Jesus kept pushing Peter into new ways of following him, even though Peter was often slow in "getting it" and many times failed; and (b) how the Holy Spirit might be speaking to you through these verses: (Day 1) Matthew 4:18–20; (Day 2) Matthew 14:22–33; (Day 3) Matthew 16:22–23 and 17:4–9; (Day 4) Matthew 26:31–35; (Day 5) Matthew 26:69–75; (Day 6) John 21:15–19; (Day 7) Acts 10 and 11.

Chapter 5: Cultivating Holy Habits

Supporting Scriptures

II Peter 3:18; Jeremiah 6:16; Ephesians 3:7; I Timothy 4:7; I Peter 3:15; Luke 2:52; Matthew 26:36; Mark 1:35; Luke 5:16; Colossians 2:6–7; II Corinthians 5:14; Matthew 7:7; Ephesians 5:1–2; II Corinthians 3:18; Matthew 6:1; Matthew 23:3–5; Matthew 15:7–9; Matthew 19:25–26; II Timothy 3:5; Galatians 5:22; James 2:14–18

Authors' Notes

The Bible is clear that we are to grow in our love for God and others. But too often we claim to be living as Christians without making radical change in our lives. We begin Chapter Five with this quote from G. K. Chesterton: "The Christian ideal has not been tried and found wanting; it has been found difficult; and left untried." How do we not leave Christianity "untried"? We believe the answer is through "holy habits"—those practices that help us grow in love and intimacy with Christ and fuel us for action in the world. In this chapter, we discuss the how's and why's of cultivating holy habits, along with the temptations and dangers of making them ends instead of means.

Reflection and Discussion Questions

1. Do you think spiritual training is necessary in order to live an abundant Christian life? If not, why not? Why do Mary and Tony say that spiritual practices are so important?

2. What do you suppose Thomas Keating meant when he wrote that our "false self" (the self outside God) adjusts "to the circumstances of the spiritual journey as long as it does not have to change itself"?

3. How can you cultivate holy habits in your daily life? How could you schedule your day or week to intentionally and regularly include some of these practices?

4. How could you encourage someone who is discouraged, distracted, or "stuck" in their spiritual practices?

5. Mary writes that the goal of engaging in spiritual practices is being formed into Christ-likeness, and that if we forget that goal we may be in dangerous territory. What dangers can you think of in this regard? How can we help each other avoid the temptation to have spiritual practices become ends in and of themselves, instead of means to the end of loving God and others?

6. Mary tells the story of trying to have her two sons pick a fruit of the spirit to practice each day and how that spiritual exercise went "sour." Can you think of a time when you tried to change an attitude or action in your life and couldn't, but then found that through a spiritual practice the Holy Spirit had changed you?

SUMMARY QUESTION   How do spiritual practices fuel us to evangelize and work for justice?

Reflection Activities

1. Read a biography of Susanna Wesley, John Wesley's little book from his Christian Library on the life of Monsieur DeRenty, or more on Catherine of Genoa (discussed along with DeRenty in the last part of this chapter) for further inspiration about what fruits come from a life of holy habits.

2. Ask and wait for the Holy Spirit to reveal to you a specific spiritual practice that God wants in your life; then commit to practicing it every day for a month. At the end of the month, pray for guidance about continuing it and/or starting another one.

Chapter 6: Moving from Self-Awareness to God-Awareness: The Prayer of Examen

Supporting Scriptures

Psalm 139:23–24; Psalm 4:4; Psalm 26:2; Lamentations 3:40; Jeremiah 17:10; Matthew 6:31–34; Matthew 5:8; Luke 9:23; John 16:13; Romans 8:26–27; I Corinthians 2:9–10; II Corinthians 13:5; Philippians 4:8

Authors' Notes

Although the Bible has many verses that ask God to examine us, we may not think to actually pray that way. Yet doing so is life changing. Our hope is that you will trust the process of the prayer of examen and commit to praying it regularly. You may even consider praying it before getting into the following Reflection and Discussion Questions to help provide context for your reflections.

Reflection and Discussion Questions

1. Ignatius of Loyola told his followers that if they were to abandon any prayer in a day, never to abandon the prayer of examen, not even for a day. Why might this be such an important prayer?

2. When praying the prayer of examen, why is it so important to remember that it

is the Holy Spirit who is to search us? How can this prayer help us move from self-awareness to awareness of who we are in God?

3. When and where could you do this prayer during your day? If you had an especially busy day, when and where might you creatively fit it in?

4. Why is it so important to pray this prayer in a spirit of thankfulness?

5. The main focus of this prayer is Step 2: reviewing our day. As crucial as it is in this prayer to remember the good, why might it be easier to focus on when we did *not* live out of love and freedom for Christ? Why is this dangerous, and how can we avoid this temptation?

6. Mary suggests praying this prayer as a gateway to purification with awareness of what distracts us from "purity of heart" (Matt 5:8). What are some distractions or "disordered desires" that can hinder you from fully loving and serving God?

7. "Asceticism" and "detachment" can have negative connotations and results, yet Ignatius and countless others have found these as paths to a deeper and purer love for God and others. How can asceticism and detachment draw us into deeper intimacy with Christ that helps us to do God's work in the world?

SUMMARY QUESTIONS How can engaging in the prayer of examen help you develop a life of deeper intimacy with God and further action in the world? How can you make this prayer a regular part of your life?

Reflection Activities

1. Commit to praying the prayer of examen each day for the next week, and meet with a trusted spiritual friend or mentor to talk about what the Holy Spirit is revealing as well as any struggles you may be having with the prayer. Then consider establishing a specific plan for incorporating this prayer into your life as a holy habit (see Chapter Nine for help).

2. Spend time in prayer asking God to reveal to you a "disordered desire" in your life; then every day for a week, pray the adapted steps of the prayer of examen found at the end of the chapter. Talk to a spiritual mentor or friend about what the Holy Spirit is revealing to you.

Chapter 7: Becoming God's Friend: *Lectio Divina*

Supporting Scriptures

John 15:14–15; John 10:2–5; John 1:14; Psalm 1:2; Psalm 119:11, 15, 48, 97, 105; Colossians 3:16; John 5:39–40; also see the chapter for ideas on specific passages of scripture for shorter and longer periods of *lectio divina*.

Authors' Notes

It is amazing that Jesus calls us not only to follow him but to be his *friend*! To be someone's friend, we need to get to know that person and what he or she is about.

One of the best ways to get to know Jesus is through the reflective reading and responding to scripture called *lectio divina* that is the focus of this chapter.' Before starting the Reflection and Discussion Questions, you may want to meditatively pray a passage of scripture in this way, since it might be helpful to draw on an actual experience of *lectio divina* while responding to the questions.

Reflection and Discussion Questions

1. Can you remember a time when the Holy Spirit spoke to you while reflecting on a passage of Scripture? What happened?

2. Why is it important to meditate or reflect on scripture in addition to studying scripture? What are some possible dangers of *not* engaging in this kind of scripture reading?

3. Why is it important to consider a variety of passages for *lectio divina* instead of only certain ones you might be used to or attracted to?

4. Mary mentioned two temptations she has during lectio: analyzing instead of reflecting on a passage, and putting too much importance on getting an insight. How can you avoid these temptations?

5. When discussing the fruits of lectio, Mary writes, "If praying the scriptures does not lead to . . . sharing Jesus through evangelism or justice, it is not true lectio. . . ." Do you agree? If so, how can we avoid making lectio too much about us and not enough about others? If you don't agree, why not?

6. Responding (or taking a "word" with you) is an important part of *lectio divina*. Can you give an example of how developing the habit of taking a thought or image with you could help you live a more holistic gospel?

7. The chapter closes with an example of how *lectio divina* has made a revolutionary difference in Latin American communities. Do you know of other instances in which praying the scriptures has made a difference? How might group lectio make a difference in your community or the world?

SUMMARY QUESTIONS How can engaging in *lectio divina* help you develop a life of friendship with Jesus that empowers you to do what Jesus commands? How can you make this kind of praying a regular part of your life?

Reflection Activities

1. Commit to the reflective praying of scripture each day for the next week, and meet with a trusted spiritual friend or mentor to talk about what the Holy Spirit is revealing as well as any struggles you may be having with the prayer. Then establish a specific plan for incorporating this prayer into your life as a holy habit (see Chapter Nine for help).

2. Pray and talk to others about starting a *lectio divina* group to regularly gather for a time of scripture reading, silent reflection, and sharing.

Chapter 8: Deepening Our Intimacy with God: Centering Prayer

Supporting Scriptures

Exodus 14:14; I King 19:11–13; Psalm 37:7; Psalm 46:10; Psalm 62:5; Habakkuk 2:20; Isaiah 30:15; Isaiah 40:31 (KJV)

Authors' Notes

Prayer for many of us involves *talking to* more than *listening to* God. Yet God also calls us to "be still" (Psalm 46:10) and "wait upon the Lord" (Isaiah 40:31 KJV). Centering prayer is a "stillness" prayer in which we are with God in intentional silence. It is a prayer of faith, since we are not expecting to "hear" anything—the goal is to be with God in silence. So many have claimed that this prayer changed them more than any other holy habit, even though they did "nothing." But that is the beauty of this prayer—it reminds us that it is always God who initiates change in us. It is our belief that the Holy Spirit will transform you more and more into Christ-likeness through this prayer too, as you yield to God's Spirit mystically at work deep in your spirit.

Reflection and Discussion Questions

1. In the opening of the chapter, Mary tells how she used to always want to "fill silence with *something* because too much of it seemed either uncomfortable or unproductive." How comfortable are you with silence? Have you ever practiced centering prayer? Is the idea of being still before God something that is difficult to comprehend? Why?

2. How do you think something as seemingly *passive* as centering prayer could change you?

3. Why does Mary recommend choosing a word for centering prayer? What are other ways you could deal with internal or external distractions during centering?

4. Since it's not always easy to find quiet places and spaces in our lives, what are some creative ways to have times of uninterrupted silence for this prayer?

5. Why might there be resistance to adopting centering prayer as a spiritual practice? What was said in this chapter that might help alleviate those concerns or fears?

6. Mary writes that it isn't easy for her to regularly sit in silence, and that when she does sit it is sometimes hard to "sit still." Why is it be important to "just keep showing up," even if you struggle with centering prayer?

SUMMARY QUESTIONS How can you make centering prayer a regular practice to help you develop a life of intimacy with God that empowers you to do God's work in the world?

Reflection Activities

1. Commit to centering prayer for 10 to 20 minutes each day for the next week, and then meet with a trusted spiritual friend or mentor, preferably someone who does this prayer, to discuss any reactions or struggles you may be having with this kind of praying. Then seriously consider incorporating this prayer into your life as a holy habit.

2. Pray about joining or starting a centering prayer group in your community or church. If there is a centering prayer group in your area, but you are not familiar with it, first check to see if you are okay with the group's theology.

Chapter 9: Committing to a Holistic Gospel

Supporting Scriptures

Matthew 16:24–26; Romans 12:1–2; Colossians 3:1–3; II Corinthians 5:14–20; Proverbs 2:1–4, 9; Philippians 1:9–11; Matthew 7:7; Psalm 38:21–22; Psalm 40:17b; Luke 16:13; Ecclesiastes 4:9–10; James 5:16; Galatians 6:2; Matthew 18:20; Acts 2:47; Acts 20:35; I Corinthians 13:13; Galatians 5:22; Deuteronomy 6:5; Romans 8:28; I Corinthians 6:19; Ephesians 6:18

Authors' Notes

We know that walking with God, loving others, and working for change in the world are what God requires (Micah 6:8). Jesus calls us to radical transformation, yet even though we know we have the power of the Holy Spirit in our lives and that Jesus' "yoke is easy" and his "burden is light" (Matthew 11:30), we often do not do what is required to follow him. Our hope is that in Chapter Nine you will find tools for discerning and living out what it means to commit to the holistic gospel in your daily life.

Reflection and Discussion Questions

1. Mary starts the chapter telling how she came to realize that she loved to read about the spiritual lives of others more than to engage in that depth of relationship with God herself. Have you ever found yourself inspired (or perhaps convicted) by the spiritual lives of others? Were you able to translate that inspiration into your own life with God? If not, why not?

2. Have you gone through any times of spiritual awakening or renewal that have resulted in new ways of believing, thinking, feeling, or acting? What did those ways look like, and were you able to continue them?

3. Have you ever had a fear of what God may ask you to do or to give up? What did you do with that fear? What do you think Psalm 37:4 means when it says that if you trust in God, God will give you the desires of your heart?

4. Mary writes that we often make daily life choices by default, by how we feel, or by what we think is reasonable according to our culture's standards. When trying to live a holistic gospel, how should our decision-making processes be different from those of the rest of the world? Do you see the Wesleyan Quadri-

lateral helping here? Are there other criteria that might be helpful or even necessary?

5. What do you think about the idea of possibly being too busy, even with good things? Have you ever purposely distracted yourself from God with your busyness? How could you avoid these temptations?

6. Susanna Wesley, who gave birth to nineteen children, used to sit in a chair in her kitchen and put her apron over her head to signal her prayer time. When it comes to spending time alone with God, what could be a feasible time and place for you? What can you do to get yourself to "show up" to that daily time and place?

7. Why is it so important to get help from as well as help others in our life with God? Why is it unhealthy and dangerous to be a "lone ranger" for Christ? Are there any exceptions?

SUMMARY QUESTIONS What specific suggestions in this chapter can you incorporate into your life to equip you to discern and commit to living out a holistic gospel? What are other ways to stay committed to intimacy with Jesus and action in the world?

Reflection Activities

1. List what you think are your top three to five values, then list the top three to five ways you spend your time and money in a typical week or month. Look at the two lists: Are the ways in which you spend your time and money consistent with your values? If not, reflect on why that is and on what you need to do to live more in harmony with your values.

2. Reflect on specific barriers in your life that hinder intimacy with, and action for, God. Share those barriers with a trusted friend or spiritual mentor who is committed to a holistic gospel. Together come up with a specific plan to deal with those barriers, as well as ways you can be accountable to your plan.

Chapter 10: Avoiding Two Temptations

Supporting Scriptures

Psalm 42:1–2; Psalm 40:6–11; Galatians 5:22; James 1:22–25; James 2:14–18; Matthew 25:31–46; Matthew 17:1–9 and 14–20; Luke 4:18–19 and 6:12–31; Luke 10:38–42; Luke 17:21

Authors' Notes

Although we may believe that a holistic gospel calls us to intimacy with God and action in the world, that does not mean we will equally desire both. There are those of us who are drawn more to one than the other. But both intimacy and action are needed, in the context of Christian community, if we are to live like Jesus. Jesus spent time alone with God, time with other believers, and time evangelizing and doing justice (see Luke 6:12–31 and 4:18–19). It is our hope that Chapter Ten will make you even more aware of what can happen when we have too much intimacy with God without action, or too much action without the intimacy.

Reflection and Discussion Questions

1. Having favorite verses in the Bible that we tend to go to more than others can be a good clue as to whether we are drawn more to intimacy with God, action for God, both, or neither. Do you have verses or passages you tend to favor more than others? If so, what might that tell you?

2. How can personal times of spiritual nourishment lead to "narcissistic" spirituality? Have you ever been tempted toward this kind of spirituality? How can we know if we are experiencing fullness in Christ or are just full of ourselves?

3. Catherine of Siena fought with God when God called her out into the world, but God eventually won. Have you ever fought with God calling you to the world? Who won?

4. Mary writes that one of the reasons it can be tempting to stay in intimacy with God is that we are so taken by the feelings associated with spiritual highs that we erroneously fall in love with those feelings instead of with Jesus. How can we be more aware of the differences between the two?

5. Sometimes people go through spiritually dry times even when there is no known sin or wrongdoing in their lives. How can these times of spiritual dryness actually be good? What advice would you give someone going through a spiritually dry time?

6. Mary gives an example of a time in junior high when her justice work was "spiritless." What does it mean to be "spiritless" in our service? What are the dangers of this kind of service? How can you determine if you have become self-righteous or militant in your action for God?

7. How could you encourage intimacy with God in those who feel such an urgency to evangelize or work for justice that they do not take the time to be spiritually filled?

SUMMARY QUESTION How can we, as the body of Christ and as individuals, avoid having intimacy without action or action without intimacy?

Reflection Activities

1. Take some time each day in the next week to reflect on whether your life has intimacy with God without enough action or action for God without enough intimacy—or neither. Ask the Holy Spirit to examine you in these areas and show you how you can live more holistically for Jesus.

2. Reflect on how you feel and react when you hear about or witness an injustice. Notice your feelings of anger or sadness as well as how you feel toward those who committed the injustice(s). Ask God to help you respond to all involved with the kind of love that is God honoring.

Chapter 11: Connecting Intimacy and Action

Supporting Scriptures

Isaiah 55:8–9; Philippians 2:12–13; Matthew 10:5–8, 18–20; Mark 6:30–31; Luke 4:14–21; Luke 5:36–39; Ephesians 2:8–9; Acts 10; James 2:17; John 17:20–26

Authors' Notes

Paul told us in Philippians 2:12–13 to "work out your salvation with fear and trembling, for it is God who works in you to will and to act according to his purposes." That is a good verse for what we are trying to communicate in this final chapter: that our intimacy with God and our action in the world for God are to inform and impact each other. With the Holy Spirit as our guide, we are to reflect on and evaluate our beliefs and convictions as we are living them out. We believe that if we are willing to live out the holistic gospel in this dynamically practical way, we will move closer and closer to that day when Jesus' prayer is answered and we are all "brought to complete unity" (John 17:23).

Reflection and Discussion Questions

1. Tony opens the chapter with a story of a college student whose experience with a group of inner-city kids caused him to reevaluate how he saw the ruling establishment. Have you had an experience that changed or challenged your beliefs or feelings?

2. Why might the idea of praxis make some people nervous? What might be the dangers of *not* allowing our experiences to influence our beliefs about, and intimacy with, God?

3. How can evangelism and justice work *intensify* our intimacy with Christ? Can you give an example of this in your own life or in the life of someone you know?

4. How should our intimacy with God inform and impact how we respond to contemporary concerns such as these: poverty, abortion, the AIDS crisis, human trafficking, civil rights for minority groups, immigration, war, the environment, and treatment of animals?

5. Tony used Martin Luther King Jr. and those who participated in his work as examples of the interactive relationship between spirituality and justice. How did their times of prayer and silence impact their civil rights work? What might have been different had they not had those times of prayer?

6. Of the models of community presented in this chapter, was there one that stuck out to you as one you'd like to be involved with? If so, what made it appealing? If not, do you have a model you would recommend, from your own or others' experiences?

7. Tony tells the story of a friend who was told by a family member, "You are wasting your life. Don't get me wrong. I believe in being Christian up to a point . . ." and Tony's friend responded, "Could that point be the cross?" How can we encourage each other to deny ourselves, take up our crosses daily, and follow Christ (Luke 9:23)?

SUMMARY QUESTION What are some specific steps you can take to integrate the following facets of Jesus' teachings into your life so that they inform and impact each other: relationship with God, commitment to community, evangelism, and justice?

BOOK SUMMARY QUESTIONS How has this book caused you to reevaluate how you see intimacy with God, evangelism, and justice work? Why is it important to live out intimacy with Christ and action in the world in the context of community?

Reflection Activities

1. Read Acts 10 and reflect on how Peter had to reevaluate his beliefs and convictions in the context of his vision and his encounter with Cornelius. Pay specific attention to Acts 10:34, where Peter says, "I now realize how true it is that God does not show favoritism but accepts men from every nation who fear him and do what is right." Ask the Holy Spirit to reveal any way(s) in your life that God might be calling you to "realize" something that could change the way you see a belief or conviction. If something is revealed, have a spiritual mentor, director, or group of other lovers of Jesus help you "test the spirits."

2. Reflect on the community of believers you are a part of, or would like to be a part of, in the context of what you are discovering about living a more holistic gospel. Ask the Holy Spirit to guide you in further ways to be involved in your own body of believers or to guide you in finding a community committed to intimacy with God, evangelism, and justice.